KIWICAP

An Introduction to
New Zealand Capital Markets

Financial Health Warning

This book represents a snapshot of the New Zealand financial markets over the period 1995–1996 and a survey of their economic history up to that point in time. Financial markets are in a constant process of change and you should not assume that the states of the world described herein are necessarily those applicable at the time you read this book. Likewise, the snapshot is a personal view. While the author has done his best to ensure that all information was correct at the time of writing, errors and misinterpretations can arise and the responsibility of taking any particular course of action based on the information and views in this book must rest with the reader alone.

KIWICAP

An Introduction to
New Zealand Capital Markets

Roger J. Bowden

The Dunmore Press

©1996 Roger J. Bowden
©1996 The Dunmore Press Ltd

First Published in 1996
by
The Dunmore Press Ltd
P.O. Box 5115
Palmerston North
New Zealand

Australian Supplier:
Federation Press
P.O. Box 45
Annandale 2038 NSW
Australia
Ph: (02) 552-2200
Fax: (02) 552-1681

ISBN 0 86469 276 5

Text:	Times New Roman 9.5/11.5
Printer:	The Dunmore Printing Company Ltd, Palmerston North
Cover design:	Vanessa Halley
Cover Photograph:	The National Bank of New Zealand

CONTENTS

Preface

This book is about the New Zealand financial environment, with special reference to the financial markets. Although a case could be made for widening the scope to include real capital – things like office blocks, farms and fine art, all of which have markets of sorts, the primary intention is to provide institutional ambience for studies in treasury, investments and general financial management. Of course, merely describing what is out there would be a sterile and boring exercise. So what this book sets out to do is to interpret as simply as possible the institutional details and market practices in the light of (reasonably) up-to-date finance theory.

The Kiwicap project also has other agendas and one of these is the public interest. A large chunk of Chapter 1 describes what a best-practice financial system might look like. After reading the rest of the book the reader might be able to form an opinion of how far the contents measure up to this sort of benchmark. Readers will certainly be able to appreciate the radical reshaping of the financial landscape that took place in the early to mid-eighties. However, many problems remain, some of which (such as securities regulation) are probably solvable and others of which (such as market liquidity) may remain endemic to a small capital market. The book also contains a bit of economics here and there, especially on the interest rate/exchange rate nexus. There is probably scope for a more comprehensive treatise on the economics of New Zealand financial markets, so perhaps the incomplete efforts herein will stimulate somebody to come up with the goods. I should not say that there is breathtaking insight on any or all of the economics and finance – it is not that kind of book. But hopefully what is there will better inform public discussion on interest rates, security prices, exchange rates and the institutional practices and rules that influence these things and are in turn influenced by them.

So much for the hype, now for the help. As the project progressed, more and more people from the financial community became involved. I am grateful to everybody who responded to requests for information, not all of whom can be named. Thank you for your contribution. Several people, however, were so helpful that they simply must be named and I do so without implicating them in any remaining errors of fact or judgement. Starting with the University of Waikato, Peter Fitzsimons of the Law School (he of the incredible course outline for his securities law paper), very kindly brought me up-to-date on legal developments. And Dawn Bowden, a former market player turned lifestyler, pitched in with help on market practices and jargon. The truly moving descriptions of swaps dealing owe much to her. Ross Tucker helped with final preparation of the manuscript. Moving north, thanks go to Greg Boland and the education and research staff at the

New Zealand Futures and Options Exchange, for all their information and help, and to Dianne Kidd of FPG Research, for information on funds. In Wellington, Brendan O'Donovan and colleagues at the National Bank of New Zealand, were immensely helpful on the fixed interest front, as will be obvious from the provenance of many of the tables and figures. David Mayes at the Reserve Bank, set me straight on aspects of monetary policy and its operations. Some of the above also contributed detailed comments on the manuscript draft (so thanks again!) and here I must also record a special debt to Jim McCulloch of Frater Williams, stockbrokers and to Mark Tume and Mark Hurley of the Bank of New Zealand Treasury. Neil Bradley of ECNZ kindly supplied material on cross-currency interest rate swaps, incorporated as a case study in Chapter 7. Helen Walshaw, administrator of the New Zealand Society of Corporate Treasurers, kept me supplied with Treasury Notes (the journal, alas, not the real thing). And I enjoyed the production collaboration with Sharmian Firth and staff at Dunmore Press. Finally, a very special vote of thanks to the erstwhile real boss of the Finance Department at the University of Waikato, the truly amazing Tania Robinson, who did all the typing and organisation. While I am grateful to all who contributed in any and every way, their help does not implicate them in the opinions, interpretations and data contained in the book.

Books like this just happen, they're not made. *Kiwicap* is the laboured outcome of a foolish rush of blood to the head just before I returned to New Zealand in early 1994, when I volunteered to teach a course in New Zealand capital markets without bothering to check whether sufficient unto the day were the references thereof. However, your correspondent is a disgraceful old hand at remedying didactic ignorance. The solution was to get the graduate students, as they were then, each to research a topic and to present a seminar on their findings. It is from these seminars that the present book evolved. Some of the students will still be able to recognise their own work. Subsequent development has unfortunately superseded the contribution of others. Nonetheless, I am grateful to all of them. They have now become utterly famous as the Kiwicap Class of 1994:

David Croy	Kiwi-based FX derivatives
Robert Croy	financial liberalisation
Cayne Dunnett	international borrowing, Kiwi eurodollar
Carl Grant	FX spot
Darryl Groufsky	equity derivatives
Glenn Hawkins	stockmarket efficiency
Kemika Huntrakul	interest rates, historical
Sophea In	equity performance, historical and comparative
Kanitha Lamlert	NZFOE, operations
Hayley New	other financial institutions
Kerry Nitz	liberalisation – the economic background
Warren Potter	interest rate swaps, domestic
Marius Pratiknjo	interest rate options
Kevin Roche	CAPM, performance
Bruce Russell	NZFOE, trading
Lincoln Snell	equity market internationalisation
Stu Wilson	privatisation, equity capital changes
Penny Winter	patterns of share ownership.

Roger Bowden
December 1996

Chapter 1

Overview

1.1 History is Bunk,[1] but Here Goes Anyway

It was not always thus with the New Zealand economy. To understand things as they are you have to know a little about how they came to be and you have to appreciate how past economic events have given rise to political fallouts that in turn may influence future economic policies. Old Karl Marx's most lasting contribution may well turn out to be his social dialectic theory, whereby reactions follow actions, leading to a progressive synthesis of views of the world and political institutions; he just got the end point wrong. There are those who would say that the command economy of New Zealand during a large part of the post-war period had Socialist features; others who would say that because of dominance and control by the triumvirate of government, the trade unions and big business, New Zealand was run more along classic National Socialist lines (aka Fascism). Whatever the labels, the watershed of 1984 led virtually to another economic universe via the black hole into which the economy had fallen by the early eighties. So, from the command economy to deregulation; action and reaction, with the synthesis perhaps still to emerge. In this history, the financial aspects that are our primary concern cannot be recounted without an understanding of the broader economic events and policies that shaped them.

We will start the story about 1960, by which time the post-war – and post-Korean War – New Zealand economy had pretty well settled down into a more or less stationary state. New Zealand does have a most interesting economic history prior to this, but that is another story for another author. We can usefully divide the period 1960 to the present into three major periods, with a short transitional period in between the first two:

I.	1960–1970	The starship *Local Enterprise*
	1970–1974	Holy economy! The asteroid field
II.	1975–1983	Drawn into a stagflationary black hole
III.	1984+	Through the deregulatory worm-hole into a 'brave new world'.

Period I

Many oldies recall this period as the lost comfort zone of New Zealand economic history. It was characterised by full employment (a minuscule unemployment rate); moderate rates of growth in Gross Domestic Product (GDP) averaging an unexciting 2.5 per cent per annum; high levels of physical investment; low levels of external debt; low rates of inflation and interest rates. The trick was turned by a policy regime that favoured the development of import substitution industries, most particularly through an extensive and draconian regime of import quotas. In line with other countries at the time, the exchange rate was 'fixed', or adjusted very infrequently. All foreign exchange (FX) transactions had to go through the Reserve Bank which maintained extensive foreign currency reserves to support the currency. The very existence of import quotas and other restrictive devices was a good indication that the New Zealand dollar (hereafter NZD) was overvalued. Farmers, as the major export sector, were not particularly happy – nor were purchasers of new motor cars, who had a long wait unless they could produce 'overseas funds'. On the other hand, the strength of local industry was such that at times there were shortages of labour, leading to an inflow of migrant workers from the Pacific Islands and elsewhere to service the manufacturing shops of Auckland.

The 1970–1974 period saw the first real stresses develop. Inflation took a sharp jump in 1971; economic historians will argue about whether this was caused by, or merely validated by, large wage rises for industrial awards granted by the then Arbitration Court. At the same time there was a world commodity markets boom, leading to a favourable current account in the balance of payments (recall that these are our accounts with the rest of the world). The government of the time followed an expansionary fiscal policy, with small to moderate budget deficits. It embarked on a vigorous borrowing programme, using internal borrowings to buy foreign currency from the Reserve Bank to pay for its external currency transactions, in particular to retire foreign debt. Indeed New Zealand's official debt actually declined over this period. However, the inflationary bubble had started to expand and 1973, with the first oil price shock, was an ominous year.

Period II   1975–1983

About this time, New Zealand was on the receiving end of a double whammy: the oil price shocks of 1973 and 1979 and a fall in world commodity prices. From the widening current account chasm it became even more apparent that the NZD was overvalued, even though the Reserve Bank did step in and make one or two adjustments to its par value. There was nonetheless the feeling that with wages so closely following or even leading inflation, there was little point in monkeying around with the nominal exchange rate as a way of fixing the current account: a depreciating exchange rate would result in further inflation and internal costs would immediately adjust upwards, negating any real adjustment.

So things went from bad to worse. The public debt rose from insignificant levels in 1974 to 48 per cent of GDP 10 years later [expressing debt as a per cent of GDP is pretty meaningless,[2] but everybody does it]. Though still low by OECD standards there were nonetheless significant increases in unemployment. Real gross investment expenditure increased by an average of only 1.1 per cent between 1975 and 1984. Moreover, New Zealand's competitive position was being eroded not only by commodity price pressures but by the rise of the South East Asian economies, against which the local industry could in many cases be protected only by ever more rigorous import controls. Reflecting the hard economic times, the government itself started to run large fiscal deficits, averaging 6.4 per cent of GDP over the period. Policy action was limited to ever more rigorous controls (some of which we will discuss for the financial sector below) and an ever more complex system of export subsidies to try and stem the balance of payments haemorrhage.

And government planning reached a nadir with the 'think big' projects in energy and steel at the beginning of the eighties, financed by a massive external borrowing programme. Clearly, cosmetic patch-ups would not work – there had to be fundamental change, as a matter of historical necessity.

Period III 1984

The historical necessity took the unlikely form of a newly elected Labour government in July 1984. Its hand was forced by a pre-election run on the currency which emptied the Reserve Bank's foreign exchange reserves and in fact resulted in a suspension of FX sales. The new government devalued the currency on 18 July. It also removed all interest rate controls and exchange controls on capital movements. The New Zealand dollar was set free and floated in March 1985. It had to be; the Reserve Bank had already lost $746 million attempting to defend the New Zealand dollar in the forward markets.

These events were the watershed for other major changes, which in some instances became inevitable given the changes in the financial regime: reform[3] in the industrial sector, with the abolition of wage and price controls and a considerable diminution in the bargaining power of the general work force; a dismantling of export subsidies and tax breaks; a phased in reduction of import quotas and tariff levels; widening of the tax base, in particular a much greater reliance on indirect taxes via the introduction of Goods and Services Tax (GST) in 1986 (foreshadowed in the 1984 Budget); and structural changes in the public sector, initially with corporatisation and later with sell-offs of government trading enterprises.

The adjustments were painful. The next few years saw soaring unemployment, declining (further) growth and high interest rates, especially at the short end (an inverted term structure, as we will see in Chapter 2). On the other hand, the current account deficit decreased, one of the few bright spots. However, net overseas debt continued to grow, though much of the immediate impetus was a simple valuation effect resulting directly from the earlier devaluation of the currency.

By the late eighties, however, things had started to lift a little. Following improvements in commodity markets, the New Zealand terms of trade (the price of exports in ratio to the price of imports) was up. The current account continued to improve, while net overseas debt peaked at around 65 per cent. By the early nineties it was apparent that things were settling down to a new operational equilibrium that would work. It was a vastly different economic landscape from that which preceded it.

Financial Regulation

It is hard for us nowadays to comprehend the scale of government direction of the capital markets as it existed by the early eighties. Here is a short checklist:

1. Interest rate controls
   * no interest on cheque accounts
   * three per cent diktat on ordinary savings accounts
   * minimum 30-day maturity for interest-bearing deposits at trading banks
   * ceilings on loan rates both of banks and other financial institutions.

2. The captive government and semi-government bond market. Regulations required a wide variety of financial institutions to purchase government securities at yield rates set by the government. As of 11 February 1985, for Trustee Savings Banks, 38 per cent of assets; for

Life Offices 31 per cent; for private super funds, 41 per cent; for finance companies, 30 per cent; for building societies, 19 per cent; and for Trading Banks, reserve asset ratios held largely in the form of government stock. With these sorts of asset requirements, deficit financing was a piece of cake.

3. Credit guidelines issued to all institutions, as to both the growth of credit and its allocation as between industrial sectors.

4. Entry barriers to the financial services industry, especially in banking.

5. FX constraints such as restrictions on:
    *   private overseas borrowing
    *   access to New Zealand financial markets for foreign-owned companies
    *   New Zealand financial institutions borrowing overseas
    *   New Zealand residents buying foreign exchange for investment purposes.

Over the stagflation period, real interest rates (the nominal rate minus the rate of inflation) were generally negative, no matter what the instrument. This had several undesirable implications:

(a) It was not much of an incentive to save in the form of anything but real assets (houses, etc.). This added to recorded inflation. In addition, deficient saving has adverse macroeconomic fallouts, often leading to lower growth and higher balance of payments deficits.
(b) Credit rationing resulted. As the interest rates were too low, only the best borrowers obtained bank and other credit. As banks naturally went for low-risk propositions, the supply of funds for high-risk investment projects, necessary for growth, dried up.
(c) There were pressures on the exchange rate. As we will see in the FX chapter, you can run a large current account deficit quite happily if foreigners are content to hold your securities, or land or other assets. If NZD interest rates are too low to compensate for the risk of a devaluation, or if there are investment restrictions on foreigners, then they will not be happy about retaining New Zealand dollars and the exchange rate remains vulnerable.

Financial Deregulation

Such controls could not and did not survive the 1984 watershed. Interest rate controls were removed in July 1984 and exchange controls in December 1984. Reserve ratio requirements were given the push in February 1985, as were compulsory investment requirements on many of the financial institutions. The Reserve Bank Act 1986 established a new regulatory system for banks, with an emphasis on removing anticipated segmentation between banks and other deposit takers, as well as allowing the entry of overseas banks and the creation of new local banks from building societies, trustee savings banks and the like. The reserve ratio system for banks was replaced by the Basel capital adequacy system. All these changes are reviewed in Chapters 3 and 4. And inward and outward controls on foreign exchange dealings were abolished in December 1984, prior to the floating of the New Zealand dollar in 1985. Later developments, which we will survey in due course, concerned the conduct of working policy, especially in relationship to exchange rates and interest rates. They embodied a general policy shift away from fiscal action to monetary action with the primary objective being the control of inflation.

We do not discuss the sharemarket crash of October 1987. Nor do we cover the margin trading,[4] flotations and frenzied speculation that preceded it and the corporate crashes that followed it: DFC, Chase, Landmark, Equiticorp and so on. The episode is a part of New Zealand's financial history that has left its mark on operating procedures for banks and other financial institutions, as well as an enduring heap of problem loans. Surprisingly, however, it left little mark on New Zealand securities law. Initiatives by the Securities Commission on aspects such as takeover provisions ran into opposition from the Stock Exchange and other quarters (see Chapter 5) and the furore has quietly receded into the background. At any rate, it must have been fun (for those who won), but it is not part of our story. Probably it will all happen again some day.

Much argument subsequent to deregulation centred around the 'sequencing issue'. Various economists had argued that before the capital account is freed up, the government should put its own house in order by bringing fiscal deficits to heel. In addition, the government of the day should act to control inflation and remove distortions in domestic capital markets, labour markets and goods markets. Only then should the New Zealand dollar be allowed to float freely, with no restrictions on FX capital markets transactions. But with the advantage of hindsight it is rather hard to see that the Labour government could have acted other than it did, faced as it was with impending disaster in the FX markets. And perhaps only the discipline created by the freeing of financial markets, including the unemployment that inevitably developed, could do the trick of breaking up the wage-price nexus and allowing the real exchange rate (Chapter 7) to do its equilibrating trick for our external accounts.

1.2   The Good, the Bad and the Ugly

What sort of things do we look for in a financial system anyway, and how far short of the ideals are we now in New Zealand? Such considerations should be at the back of your mind as you read this book. If nothing else, it will provide entertainment.

First, remember what a financial system basically does. It is simultaneously a payments system and a device for circulating funds from deficit users to surplus users. The payments aspect will be to the fore in Chapter 3 on the banking system and we shall say little more about it here except to point out special aspects such as efficiency in transfer. This in turn means not only speed, but the absence of credit or other risk while the funds promised are still in the clearing pipeline. Payment systems can exhibit considerable *systemic risk* from this source. Thus as you go through, note the various general and specific clearing and settlement systems: the cheque system, eftpos; on the wholesale side, austraclear; and the settlement systems used by the stock and futures exchanges. Generally speaking, clearing of private transactions via cheques, etc. is still rather slow. Transfer or transactions taxes such as stamp duty are another sign of economic inefficiency.

The funds recycling bit is a lot bigger in scope. A good financial system should (a) enable savers to solve their intertemporal allocation decisions as between consuming now and consuming later; and (b) enable firms to allocate funds between production now and production in the future, by means of additional physical investment. A very basic requirement is the physical transfer of monies between saving and spending units. As a borrower, where can I go to get my hands on the funds I need? Apart from this, however, a financial system should allow saver/spenders and maximising firms to plan their decisions quite separately from each other, but nevertheless in harmony. The interest rate (in the present instance) is a market price that ensures both the anonymity and the consistency. Savers decide how much to save when they know what the interest rate is, just as firms decide how much physical investment to make on the basis of the interest rate. So the interest rate becomes a market sufficient statistic for both classes of user. If firms want to invest more than savers want to supply, then this interest rate will rise to clear the market. In an ugly financial system this will not happen; we saw earlier the sorts of inefficiency that resulted from credit rationing, where a free market for funds and free-market clearing rate of interest did not apply.

In the above example, both surplus units (savers) and deficit units can carry out their separate decisions by maximising the value of their wealth, once the latter was determined by discounting saving or funding plans by the market equilibrium interest rate. An incidental but nonetheless very important function of the markets is therefore to correctly establish wealth and to enable the user to ascertain how his or her wealth will be determined by various alternative decisions. It is a short step from this to claim that a good market should enable the correct (and public) realisations of wealth. This sort of principle crops up all over the place. For instance, the market should be able to identify whether a company stock is correctly priced; it may not be if management is lazy and could easily be replaced – indeed the market is the ultimate source of discipline on such managers. Such realisations often occur during takeover battles, as we shall see in Chapter 5. Sometimes wealth can be maximised by an unbundling process. An example is the common practice where shares in a mutual dairy company can be transferred to another purchaser only with the sale of a farm. An efficient capital market should enable unbundling of the constituent activities: farming and share ownership.

Included in value is the correct pricing of risk and by implication making correct decisions in risky situations. Here, too, there are several dimensions. In the first place, people are very often on different sides of the transaction, so far as risk is concerned. A commodity user is concerned at the possibility that future prices might rise, while a producer is worried that they might fall. And other sorts of people might have quite different attitudes to risk than either of these people. A good financial system should be able to take advantage of these different circumstances or preferences, with the operation of derivatives market such as futures or options. In the jargon, there should be markets for risk. Such markets have indeed been a feature of the deregulated New Zealand economy. It might be claimed that the previous regulated economy had fixed exchange rates, interest rates or prices; and therefore no occasion for risk protection needed to arise. But this is simply not true: devaluations of the NZD, for instance, did occur and when they occurred they tended to be humdingers. The market should act to reduce risk by offering means of protection against it. You will find discussions of derivatives scattered throughout the book, especially in Chapters 2, 6 and 7. However, the 'hedging' medium need not be anything as fancy as derivatives – you can reduce risk by constructing portfolios of freely traded and correctly priced securities on the New Zealand Stock Exchange or other capital markets.

Typically, though, not all risk is completely reducible to zero. Where this occurs, the market should ensure that the irreducible risk is correctly priced into the security. If exchange rate risk to an overseas investor on New Zealand bills or bonds cannot be diversified away, or can be vaccinated against only at a cost, then the market should price a risk premium into NZD interest rates. If nothing else, this should then be a sign to policy-makers that the market is unhappy with the *volatility* caused by its macroeconomic policies, or with the country or political risk that might be entailed. In general the market should price risk correctly – there is some evidence that share prices have in the past carried an 'equity premium' relative to bond yields that is too high. If so, this would signal an economic efficiency working against the issuers of equity capital and the physical investment in plant and equipment that it finances.

Reduction of risk by pooling assets is characteristic of *financial intermediaries*, such as banks, building societies and other deposit-taking institutions. So, too, is *maturity transformation*: banks take in lots of small demand deposits, but because not all are repayable at any one time, can use them to fund longer-term assets such as bonds or home mortgages. We need to understand precisely what is meant by 'maturity' – in this context, not nearly as easy as it sounds. More recently, a form of unbundling has arisen whereby issuers of mortgages can detach them from their balance sheets by selling them after origination, in a parcel of mortgages. Closer examination, however, casts doubt on whether this is really *disintermediation*, because the parcel has to be massaged ('enhanced') by a generating institution into a form offering regular repayments of interest to the intending purchases; and this sort of massaging is intermediation. However, disintermediation has indeed occurred in the Euromarkets (q.v.). Where once upon a time Euroloans from banks were a popular source of fundraising for companies, now those companies access the markets directly by issuing securities in their own name. The intermediation/disintermediation dimension therefore has some points of interest.

While we're on the intermediation theme, note an additional economic function: if instead of investing in a company stock directly, I do so via investment in an equity fund or superannuation scheme, the fund (etc.) may become a large shareholder in the company, simply because of the financial weight it has derived by pooling the resources of so many small-time investors. Two things then happen. First, the fund's managers will acquire some clout in the company, perhaps even with a seat on the Board. Second, the fund's managers are (I hope!) expert at company analysis. So they will have both the means and the expertise to *monitor* the company's management. In effect the fund are my agents (managing my funds), monitoring their agents (the company's management). Time was when being on a Board was all champagne, private boxes at the cricket and the carefully staged group photo in the glossy Annual Report. With the responsibilities and penalties imposed by the new Companies Act, the large institutional shareholders breathing down their necks and the new breed of security analysts on the rise, the times they are a-changing.

Incidentally, in the above discussion we touched on another, minor, theme: *ownership concentration*. As you will see in Chapter 5 on company equities, the days of lots of little shareholders are passing; bigger and fewer seems to be the trend. And all manner of peoples are now holding claims on New Zealand resources. Also of note, especially as a consequence of deregulation, is the increasing openness of New Zealand capital markets, especially since deregulation. You will find in Chapter 7 that New Zealand companies managed (for a while, at least) to get cheaper funds offshore through the NZD Euromarkets. By doing so they – in effect – lowered the domestic rate of interest, resulting in a direct welfare gain for the New Zealand holders of their stock and in an enhanced capacity for physical investment. Likewise the openness of onshore New Zealand assets to foreign purchasers has had beneficial macroeconomic fallout, whatever our views about selling off the family silver. Those of us who can recall the official consents and tortuous bureaucracy in making even the simplest of overseas payments will testify personally to the welfare gains resulting from internationalisation. Most of all, however, internationalisation allows New Zealanders to extend their own investment portfolios by investing abroad. In technical terms, their investment efficiency frontier is beneficially enlarged.

Another kind of efficiency is *informational efficiency*, which refers to the idea that new information should be instantly impounded in the value of shares, or in interest rates, exchange rates and other prices. Note the emphasis on *new* information; old news is no news, so far as an efficient market is concerned – it is already incorporated into the security's price. There are those who see the informational aspect as primal in nature. For example, requiring a takeover bid to extend the same price to minority shareholders might be unnecessary if provision existed to make the bid public on reaching a certain limit. Then minority shareholders would know what was up and have the opportunity to form their own judgement of the future of the company before the new controller can take substantive actions affecting its value. Some academics would even allow untrammelled insider trading, on the grounds that this should be reflected in rises or falls in the share price, leading the market to guess that something good or bad was about to happen; in other words, prices fully reveal information. Some neoclassical financial economists evidently place a great deal of faith in information efficiency! However, it is clearly a good thing if news is incorporated as soon and as fully as possible into the price of financial securities.

A good financial system should also exhibit *liquidity* in its traded instruments, or at least in certain bellwether instruments. This means that if you want to buy or sell something, especially on an organised Exchange, you should be able to find a counterparty without too much trouble. Liquid markets are typically characterised by low bid-ask spreads, which means that there is not much of a gap between what a dealer would quote to buy from you versus to sell to you. Persistently large bid-ask spreads are often viewed as a market inefficiency. Another sign of illiquidity is that reported trades are very 'spotty' in their incidence. It is very important to have liquidity not only in the spot markets (i.e. buying or selling the physical item like a bond or a stock), but also in the derivatives markets (e.g. an option written on a stock, or a stock price index). For example, in major financial centres, swaps traders hedge their temporary exposures by means of bond futures. In the New Zealand market, there are indeed bond futures traded, on the New Zealand Futures and Options Exchange, but the volume is still very spotty. So for his hedging needs, the swaps trader will have to use a physical bond, which is a bit awkward, for a number of reasons. Overall, liquidity is indeed a problem in the New Zealand market. It is a function purely of our size and not at all a commentary on the financial sophistication of the major players.

Finally, the fallout for deregulation has included a greatly enhanced financial sophistication on the part of investors, borrowers, managers, financers and all who are connected directly or indirectly with the capital markets. If you are reading this book, you are doing so because you want to understand better the New Zealand financial system and its possibilities. The explosion of derivatives in recent years is one sign of this growing sophistication, no matter that some hiccups have accompanied it. Financial ideas now are light years ahead of the rather limited understanding even as late as the fifties. World-wide financial deregulation has accompanied and been accompanied by, an explosion in financial technology and financial understanding. Some New Zealand corporates have it and some do not.

1.3   Information

Information is the life-blood of financial markets. It is therefore no accident that the markets have so wholeheartedly embraced on-line news services such as those provided by Reuters or Telerate. Low-tech sources of information also continue to be important: the business pages of newspapers, press releases by government departments and good old market gossip and rumour. Each dealing room will have a schedule of forthcoming economic announcements and dealers will frequently take positions in advance of announcements, especially if they concern the IER ('interest rate and exchange rate') nexus. And even more especially if the information content of the announcement is likely to be high, for example if people are a bit uncertain about the likely value of a Consumer Price Index (CPI) or current account figure. Behind all the ongoing news is also an imperative for market players to develop an overall perspective on economic trends and here the economic weeklies or monthlies can play a valuable role.

Trader screens play a special role in the dissemination of information. There are a number of networks operating in New Zealand or available here: examples are Reuters, Telerate, Bloomberg, Equinet, Future Source, ADP; and even teletext on your home TV screen. Some offer a real time facility, wherein you can observe prices and trades as they unfold. Others offer more historical data, or software based on such. In the financial markets, the big three in New Zealand are of the former category. Reuters and Telerate are broad spectrum, while Bloombergs tend to concentrate more on fixed interest markets. Many dealing rooms will subscribe to more than one, if they have a fancy enough computer platform to allow this. Generalist networks such as Reuters or Telerate will allow the user to access both general news screens, provided by the networks themselves and dedicated screens provided on the network by particular companies or organisations. For example, the New Zealand Futures and Options Exchange provides several screens, detailing current quotations or ranges for each of their products as well as a composite screen. There are codes for each screen: Reuters uses letter mnemonics, e.g. 'wasp' for guess what, while Telerate uses numbers. Each user will have a contract with the network that covers a specified bundle of screens and limitations on the number of users for different screens. In addition, private screens will be available. These might be screens containing the swap or bond rates quoted to corporates by a major bank and access would be limited to those corporates. Or brokers might have their own screens, access to which is limited to their favoured customers or price-makers.

The on-line information networks are in one sense rather like electronic newspapers. A newspaper, however, is almost a public good. How many times have I picked up and read today's copy of the *Sydney Morning Herald* left thoughtfully for me on the ferry seat? But the screen networks also offer private informational goods, as they can restrict access to designated screens, either by payment of a special fee, or by absolute restrictions on access. This combination of exclusivity with the public good aspect makes them unique. In the language of game theory, they are co-operative organisations with side agreements among members as to private coalitional benefits.

Dealing rooms, with their ranks of traders and screens, are a common sight on national news, following some major economic announcement. If you are a corporate client, you will find your bank's dealing room a diverting post-prandial perambulation, if you can persuade them to let you past the security doors. Note the screens, two or more, in each dealer space. Notice the dealer, watching the cricket scores on one of them. Observe the telephones and the squawk boxes, which are client microphones to favoured brokers. Listen carefully to the rational and learned discourse across desks. You will learn many new expressions. Truly, the dealing rooms are the basal ganglia of modern capitalism.

1.4   Further Reading

On the historical side a very useful short account is:

Wallace, R. (1990), 'Agricultural Reform: The Macroeconomic Environment', in Sandrey, R. and Reynolds, R. (eds), *Farming Without Subsidies: New Zealand's Recent Experience*, Wellington: MAF, G.P. Books.

Section 1.1 above draws heavily on the Wallace treatment.

For an entertaining version of the background, the politics and personalities and the precise sequencing of reform, read:

Douglas, R. and Callen, L. (1987), *Roger Douglas: Toward Prosperity*, Auckland: David Bateman.

Another very personal account of the wild New Zealand eighties is:

Newland, O. (1994), *Lost Property: The Crash of 1987 and the Aftershocks*, Auckland: Harper Collins.

Mr Newland is a bit short on detail, and Henry James he ain't, but the book is graphic on shock-horror as to how easy it all was – at first. An enjoyable read.

For a more analytical account of deregulation by professional economists, see the collection of essays:

Bollard, A. and Buckle, R. (eds) (1987), *Economic Liberalisation in New Zealand*, Wellington: Allen and Unwin.

Also, a forthcoming book with a much later vantage point:

Bollard, A., Lattimore, R. and Silverstone, B. (eds), (1996), *A Study of Reform: The Case of New Zealand*, Amsterdam: North Holland.

The Reserve Bank of New Zealand publishes a review volume from time to time, concerned mainly with monetary matters. At the time of writing, the most recent is:

Reserve Bank of New Zealand (1992), *Monetary Policy and the New Zealand Financial System*, 3rd ed.

More systematic books on New Zealand capital markets, or aspects thereof, are hard to find. You could try:

Karacaoglu, G. (ed) (1988), *An Introduction to Financial Markets in New Zealand*, Wellington: Victoria University Press.
Layton, B. (1987), *New Zealand Futures Trading*, Wellington: Allen and Unwin/Port Nicholson Press.
Carew, E. (1987), *New Zealand's Money Revolution: A Comprehensive, Up-to-the-Minute Guide to New Zealand's Rapidly Changing Financial System*, Wellington: Allen and Unwin/Port Nicholson Press.

The Australian scene is in some respects similar to New Zealand, though you should always check to make sure of any supposed similarities – the monetary control regime, for instance, is quite different. The standard reference – a book to go to bed with (beats Milo) – is:

Bruce, R., McKern, B., Pollard, I. and Selby, M. (1991), *Handbook of Australian Corporate Finance*, 4th ed., Sydney: Butterworths.

On an ongoing basis, descriptive articles on the New Zealand financial system appear from time to time in various periodicals. The *Reserve Bank Bulletin* is a good source and the *Chartered Accountants Journal of New Zealand* sometimes has articles. An up-and-coming source that has already had some most useful articles is *Treasury Note*, the journal of The New Zealand Society of Corporate Treasurers.

Notes

1.   Attributed to Henry Ford, but probably many others before and many after. What do you think he meant?
2.   Perhaps a better measure would be debt servicing costs as a percentage of GDP (the latter representing the government's potential tax base). How would such a measure correlate with the value:GDP ratio commonly employed?
3.   Actually a little later via the Employment Contracts Act of the subsequent National government.
4.   An arrangement where a finance company lends you a certain proportion of the value of the shares you buy, against security of the whole lot. If the value subsequently rises you can borrow more. If it falls, you have to maintain the margin by stomping up extra cash (has similarities with futures margins – see Chapter 6). In the eighties, this was a new idea for Kiwi investors.

CHAPTER 2

Domestic Fixed Interest

2.1   The Interest Rate Jungle and its Animals

This chapter will deal with bonds, bills and similar instruments. The generic expression 'fixed interest' to cover these instruments is a bit confusing at times. It really refers to a coupon payment on a bond, say, which is fixed at the outset and does not vary subsequently. However, if by 'interest' is meant 'yield', then the interest rate on most bank instruments is not fixed at all, but can freely vary in line with market sentiments. Moreover, bank bills and other kinds of bills are sometimes subsumed under the fixed-interest label (as we shall do here) and in this case the label is a complete misnomer, for it is impossible to identify any kind of interest concept that could even remotely be described as 'fixed'. Indeed, rates on bank bills are an example of 'floating' interest rates. Another is the rate paid on a variable rate house mortgage, though one might describe this as a rather 'dirty' floating rate, as it may be adjusted only infrequently in response to market forces. Instead, the fixed interest market category has come to be used for all kinds of debt instruments, on some of which the interest rate is floating and for others various options exist to convert to company equity. Perhaps a better title might be 'debt instruments'.

You can see from these remarks that we are already experiencing difficulty with the idea of just what an interest rate is. In the present section we shall describe three basic kinds of interest rate: yields to maturity, zero coupon rates and implied forward rates. The coupon rate (see below) could also be described as an interest rate, but this is a rather trivial usage that can easily mislead the unwary. At any rate, a health warning before we start: the remainder of this section may be a bit technical for some, so airport bookstand freeloaders have our permission to skip straight to §2.2.

Yields to Maturity

Suppose a bond of face value $A pays a series of coupons $c every interest rate period (rests') over a lifetime (maturity) of N such periods. The bond is tradeable and its current market price is

$P. Notice that our unit of time in this example is left unspecified; there are a few wrinkles in this that we will sort out below. The 'coupon rate' on this instrument is just the coupon divided by the face value, generally expressed in terms of a percentage: $\frac{c}{A} \times 100$ per cent. The 'yield to maturity' ρ is defined by the equation:

(1) $$P = \frac{c}{1 + \rho} + \frac{c}{(1 + \rho)^2} + ... + \frac{c + A}{(1 + \rho)^N}$$

You will recognise ρ as the familiar internal rate of return on the bond. (1) multiplied by $(1 + r)^N$ results in:

(2) $$c(1 + \rho)^{N-1} + c(1 + \rho)^{N-2} + ... + c(1 + \rho) + c + A = P(1 + \rho)^N.$$

The interpretation of equation (2) is that every period you take the coupon for that period and reinvest it at a constant rate ρ. The sum of money so generated at maturity should be equal to the initial purchase price invested and compounded at the same rate ρ. If the yield ρ and the coupon yield $\frac{c}{A}$ are equal, then P=A and the security trades 'at par'. Otherwise it trades at a discount (P<A) or premium (P>A).

Par yields are often called 'swap rates', or the 'swap coupon', since they also represent the terms on which a fixed 'coupon' payment can be swapped for a series of floating interest-rate payments. Swaps are discussed in §2.5. The 'swap rate' is itself a kind of interest rate; indeed it could almost be said that the swap rate is 'the' interest rate in the market, for any given maturity N.

In practice, the coupon periods for most bonds are six-monthly, whereas interest rates and maturity are quoted on an annual basis. Another complication is that valuation may be done in between coupon dates and the coupon dates themselves may vary from 181 to 184 days (for government bonds, at least). So some form of fractional discounting is going to be necessary. The formula used by general consensus to handle all these exigencies is the so-called 'Reserve Bank Formula'.

First, the yield quotation. The convention is that the annual yield is obtained by multiplying the six-monthly yield by two. In other words, if the bonds were quoted as yielding[1] $\rho_A = 9$ per cent, then the rate used for six-monthly discounting is 4½ per cent:

$$\rho = ½ \rho_A$$

(Note that we have been a bit fast and loose here in switching between percentages and fractions – in actual discounting, ρ must be a fraction: $\rho = 0.0450$, whereas in common parlance ρ is referred to as a percentage: $\rho = 4.50$ per cent.)

The sketch below illustrates the problem with intra-period discounting. The shaded triangles represent the six-monthly rests. The current time is somewhere between the two rests indicated. At the next rest, there are (say) N periods still to run. To value the bond at time B you would just use (1) as

$$P_B = \frac{c}{1 + ½\rho_A} + \frac{c}{(1 + ½\rho_A)^2} + ... + \frac{c + A}{(1 + ½\rho_A)^N}$$

in terms of the annual yield ρ_A. However, you have now to discount P_B to get the value at the current time point 0. To do this we discount fractionally at the same rate $½\rho_A$:

(3) $\qquad P_A = \dfrac{1}{(1 \,+\, \tfrac{1}{2}\rho_a)^{a\,/\,b}} \cdot P_B \; .$

A special formula (not given here) is used when there is only one coupon to go. For versions and a discussion, see the Bank of New Zealand *Fixed Interest Strategist*, 13 May 1996.

Figure 2.1: Time Conventions in Bond Discounting

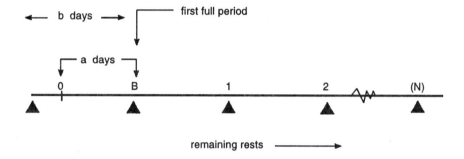

It is important to remember that the Reserve Bank formula represents primarily a convention rather than pricing exactness. If a newspaper article says that '11/06 stock yielded 8.56 per cent' on 14 January 1995, you should be able to figure out by using the RB formula and conventions, what price the stock sold at; and indeed government bonds are traded on a yield basis. A true daily yield could also be worked out by applying formula (1) above from 14 January until final settlement day in November 2006, with the unit of time chosen as a day.

Zero Coupon Rates

These are the yields on pure discount securities – those that pay no coupons. Such securities pay face-value at the end of the period and are issued at a discount, which rewards the holder. Such securities have an appeal for fundamentalist Muslims, who hold that the Koran forbids the offer of money for interest, interpreted here as coupons. St Augustine was not too hot on the idea, either.

To take the simplest case, suppose the security of face value \$A is held for one complete discounting period. Then its yield R is defined once its issue price P is known by:

$$P = \dfrac{A}{1 + R} \quad ; \text{equivalently } R = \dfrac{A - P}{P} \; .$$

If the security is being priced in the market at some point during its life (i.e. post issue), the Reserve Bank formula is:

(4) $\qquad P = \dfrac{A}{1 + \dfrac{a}{365} \cdot R} \; .$

Here a = number of days from settlement date (i.e. when the security is paid for) to maturity. The yield R is expressed on an annual basis as a fraction, e.g. R = 0.0929. The intent of formula (4) is definitional. Given face value A and the price P that the security is traded at, its annual yield R is defined implicitly by (2.4) and written up in the newspapers as such.[2] The rate R is an example of a zero coupon rate, for obvious reasons. Such rates are used in pricing securities where just a single 'balloon' payment is involved at the end of the horizon.

Notice the 'pricing' usage. Technically, R is defined once P is known (given also A and a), so the logic really flows from P to R. But the latter is also used as a pricing guide. The prevailing market yield for 90-day bills is published as R, say. So if you were interested in buying such a bill you would certainly avoid one whose price was such as to yield much less than the current R. Conversely if the asking price yielded a lot more than R, everybody would jump in on such a trader, forcing him to quickly readjust his price upwards. In this sense, bonds are priced to yield the designated yield R.

Multiperiod Rates

Suppose a pure discount bond paid 1\$ at the end of one period (in discrete time discounting). Its price would then be given by

$$P_1 = \frac{1}{(1 + R_1)} \ .$$

Here the P_1 will simply denote that this is a one period bond. Suppose now that the bond lasts two complete discounting periods. Its price-yield relationship is then given by

$$P_2 = \frac{1}{(1 + R_2)^2} \ ,$$

where R_2 is defined as a two-period yield. Evidently, if you took a sum of money P_2 and compounded it over the two periods at rate R_2 you should reach 1\$ at maturity. Note that there is no reason why R_2 should equal R_1. The two-period security is locking up your money for two periods rather than one. You might then want a greater return R_2 to compensate. Similarly, the price of a pure discount bond lasting three periods would be

$$P_3 = \frac{1}{(1 + R_3)^3} \ ,$$

and so on.

The graph of R_1, R_2, R_3 against the maturity period is called the term structure of interest rates. R_3 is a 'longer' interest rate than R_1 or R_2. We will look at the term structure further below.

The zero coupon rates R_1, R_2, R_3 refer to compounding or discounting over the complete apposite maturity period, e.g. R_3 refers to a sort of average discount rate over the entire three periods. We would define a period three marginal interest rate r_3 by the relationship:

$$(1+R_3)^3 = (1+R_2)^2 (1+r_3) \ .$$

The compounding factor $1+r_3$ is that what you would apply to the initial two period compounding at rate R_2 in order to arrive at the results of three period compounding at rate R_3. The interest rate r_3 is called the *three-period forward rate*. Similarly, the two-period forward rate r_2 would be defined by

$$1+r_2 = \frac{(1 + R_2)^2}{1 + R_1} \ ,$$

and obviously $r_1 = R_1$; for one period discounting r_1 and R_1 are the same thing and sometimes called the 'spot rate'. As the name suggests, forward rates bear a relationship to fixed interest forwards and futures, for which see Chapter 6. You can also define a term structure of interest rates in the form of the graph of r_τ against maturity τ (a 'forward rate term structure'). In many ways, this is a lot more useful than for the zeros or yields.

Zero Coupon Rates and Pricing

Let us reconsider the price-yield relationship (1). Throw away the ρs and consider how you would arrive at a price for a coupon bond. The first payment is c, due at the end of period one. If the prevailing one-period coupon rate was R_1 the contribution to period zero value should then be $\frac{c}{1 + R_1}$. Similarly the value of the second coupon would be $\frac{c}{(1 + R_2)^2}$, and so on. Then given a sequence $R_1, R_2, \ldots R_N$ over the maturity of the bond, its price should be

$$(5) \qquad P = \frac{c}{1 + R_1} + \frac{c}{(1 + R_2)^2} + \ldots + \frac{c + A}{(1 + R_N)^N}.$$

Equivalently, you would be saying that each coupon payment was itself of the character of a zero coupon bond maturing when the payment is due; similarly for the principal A.

If you had a complete set of coupon bonds available, with different maturities 1, 2, 3 ... N you could easily use a set of equations like (5) to actually compute $R_1, R_2, \ldots R_N$ if you knew what prices the bonds were currently traded for. Thus given

$$P_1 = \frac{c}{1 + R_1}$$

$$P_2 = \frac{c}{1 + R_1} + \frac{c + A}{(1 + R_2)^2}$$

$$P_3 = \frac{c}{1 + R_1} + \frac{c}{(1 + R_2)^2} + \ldots + \frac{c + A}{(1 + R_N)^N},$$

you can easily (well, a computer can) solve for $R_1, R_2, \ldots R_N$ in terms of the given prices $P_1, P_2, \ldots P_N$.

Once you had the $R_1, R_2, \ldots R_N$ you could then price any sort of fixed interest security, even ones with nonconstant coupons. Essentially you would do it by breaking the cash payments of the security up into so many equivalent zero coupon securities. Thus knowing the $R_1, R_2, \ldots R_N$ you could guard yourself against arbitragers who seek to make some money at your expense by doing the physical unbundling themselves.

Suppose you continued to price bonds on yields to maturity ρ in such a world. You could then be subject to arbitrage attack.[3] Even for very conventional coupon bonds all of period N, use of the yield to maturity is insufficient information to price them. The reason that yields are nonetheless so widely used – and zero coupon rates not used – in the NZGS market is simply that the market is incomplete in terms of the number of maturities available to calculate the zeros. One or two institutions have attempted to construct zero coupon rates from government stock, but the techniques used are so far unconvincing; a big problem is the thinness of the market, especially at the longer end (7–10 years). It is also possible to recover zero coupon rates, or approximations, from swap rates quoted in the market. Technical problems aside, there is a varying spread between NZGS and swap rates, so the latter are an important guide to NZGS zero coupon rates. Nonetheless, it is important to know something about zeros and implied forwards. If you are going to be a yield curve jockey, i.e. attempt to make money from changes in the shape of the yield curve, the zeros give a much clearer indication of where the anomalies lie in terms of maturities and a better clue as to how these might be exploited, even in terms of the available coupon bonds or swaps.

A quite different line of attack on the zeros is to obtain them from swap rates. Essentially, given a complete series of maturities, you can back the zeros out of the swap rates for those maturities. Such a calculation is indeed done in the New Zealand market. However, there may be variable spreads between swap rates and NZGS, as well as a credit spread (see below), so using one for the other may be problematical, though better than nothing.

A final algebraic note. Notice that equation (5) can be rewritten in terms of the implied forward rates as:

$$c\,(1+r_2)\,(1+r_3)\,(...)\,(1+r_N) + c\,(1+r_3)\,(1+r_4)\,(...)\,(1+r_N) + ... + c+A = P(1+r_1)(1+r_2)\,...\,(1+r_N).$$

What this tells you is that each coupon can be regarded as being reinvested on receipt at the implied forward interest rates from that date thereafter. The result should equate the initial price purchase accumulated at these rates. The equivalent version (2) above supposes that each coupon can be reinvested at a constant rate ρ. This is the 'constant reinvestment rate' assumption implied in all valuation calculations relying on yields to maturity. You can see that this does not amount to good valuation. In terms of equation (2) why should you be able to assume that all coupons can be reinvested at exactly the same rate as all the others, no matter what point in time they are received? The zero coupon valuation is much more realistic in this respect; the implied forward rates represent your best guess now as to what sort of one period rates you will be able to reinvest at, when the coupons are eventually received.

Market Jargon

As if you hadn't had enough, here is some more market jargon. Throw these words around and the job is yours!

1. *Basis Points (bps)*

As at C.O.B. 27 October 1995, NZGS 11/06 (you figure this out!) was trading at 7.16 per cent. Write this yield as a fraction, 0.0716. A basis point is 0.0001, in fractional terms. The yield for NZGS 11/96 was 7.64 per cent, or 0.0764. So 11/96 was trading at 48 basis points above 11/06. [You are entitled to feel uneasy about saying that it trades 'above', for in price terms it is effectively trading below, at a discount. Remember, however, that in the New Zealand market, all quotation is done in terms of yields rather than prices].

2. *Price Value of a Basis Point*

Regard the quoted yield as a flat interest rate or discount factor, to be applied to the future coupon flows and principal repayment of the bond. Now suppose you lower your discount factor by one basis point: thus in the case of NZGS 11/96 from 7.64 per cent to 7.63 per cent. What difference does this make to the price of the bond, viewed as the present value of all its cash flows? This difference is the PVBP. So for NZGS 11/96 it computed out at $99 per million dollars of face value. For NZGS 11/06, trading at 7.16 per cent, the PVBP was $785 p.m. A one basis point movement in yields would gain or lose you $785 for every million dollars worth of face value. You might like to reflect on why the longer dated bond has a PVBP so much greater than the shorter one. The PVBP is sometimes called 'sensitivity' or 'value 01' in the New Zealand market.

3. *Spreads*

The term always refers to one interest rate relative to another (in other contexts it can also refer to one price relative to another). It is usually expressed in basis points. Contextually it can refer to:

(a) A bid-ask spread. A bid-ask spread of five bps would mean that the dealer will buy the bond from you at five bps more than he will sell it to you. (Figure out what this means in terms of prices.)
(b) A term-structure spread. The difference of 48 bps between 11/96 and 11/06, in the example quoted earlier, is a term-structure spread: same sort of security, different maturities.
(c) A comparator spread. If a regional authority bond is trading at 50 bps above a NZGS of the same maturity, this is such a spread. In this particular case it would be regarded as a 'credit spread'. Similarly, a spread between (the coupon on a) swap and a reference bond often exists, altering daily from the forces of demand and supply. (If you do not understand this, start to worry only after you have read the section on swaps.) A comparator spread can also refer to cross-country comparisons of bond yields, suitably adjusted or hedged for exchange rate changes. In all cases, the bonds have to be of the same general class and maturity.

4. *Duration*

This is a measure of a bond's *economic* maturity, rather than its temporal maturity. If you hold a coupon bond, you receive a series of cash flows at various time points in the future – coupons and principal return. Duration is a weighted average of these times to receipt. The weight attached to any time is computed as the PV (as at time zero, i.e. now) of the relevant cash flow relative to the sum of the PVs of all the cash flows, i.e. relative to the price of the bond itself. So for an asset of maturity T,

$$\text{Duration} = 1 . \frac{v_1}{V} + 2 . \frac{v_2}{V} + \dots T \frac{v_T}{V} \; ;$$

where v_1, v_2 ... v_T are the PVs of all the cash flows and $V = P =$ sum of all the vs. For a coupon bond, v_1 ... v_{T-1} would be the present values of coupon payments and v_T would be the present value of the final coupon plus the principal.

For a zero coupon bond, you can verify that its duration is just equal to its maturity. But for a coupon bond, its duration is less than its maturity. Generally, duration measures the interest sensitivity of the value of a bond – the higher its duration, the greater its interest sensitivity. Intuitively, the 'longer' (in economic terms) is the bond, the more it is exposed to changes in the discount rate used to value it.

A related concept is *convexity*, which refers to the curvature of the plot of bond price against yield, or equivalently to the way in which duration itself changes with the bond's yield or discount factor. As an investor, you want a bond with higher convexity, for this means that as the yield rises the bond decreases in value by less, whereas as the yield falls it increases in value by more. Such properties are a consequence of higher curvature. On the other hand, what if you were a borrower?

Figure 2.2:   Illustrating Convexity: Which Twin has the Toni?[4]

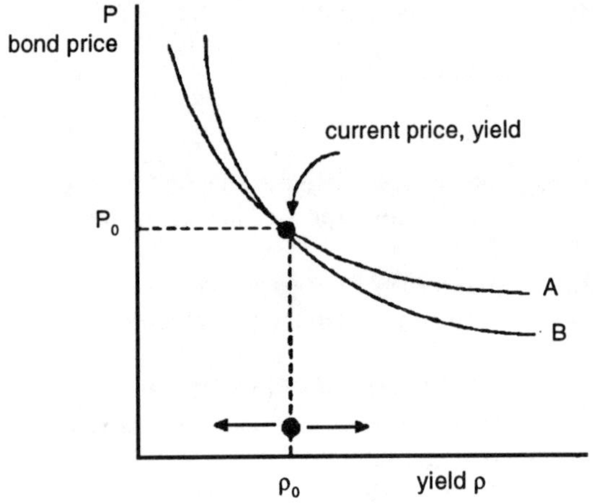

Duration, in particular, comes in all sorts of flavours, depending on just how you do the present values and other matters. It is an important tool in many areas of financial management.

The Term Structure

As mentioned earlier the term structure is a graph of interest rates against maturity. Ideally this should be a plot of the zeros or implied forwards (R_τ or r_τ) against maturity τ. In the New Zealand scene one is generally forced to graph yields for maturity (vertical axis) against maturity time (horizontal axis). Henceforth we shall use the term 'yield curve' interchangeably to refer to zeros, forwards or yields against maturity. Notice that the yield curve is an ex-ante graph; we do not graph yields actually achieved historically over securities of lifetime τ, but those yields currently priced into the market for securities of length or maturity τ, looking ahead to its sequence of cash flows. A curve in which yields are higher for longer-term than short-term securities is called a 'normal' curve. If shorter-dated yields are higher than longer-dated, this is an 'inverted' curve. Look at column 2 of Table 2.1 below. Was the yield curve for government stock normal or inverted (or what?) at 27 October 1995?

In general, there are two predominant influences on the shape of the yield curve:

(a) *Expectations*

Here the expectations basically refer to expected future 'spot' or 'floating' (one-period) rates. The idea is that the current τ period ahead forward rate r_τ is supposed to be a predictor of the one-period rate τ periods hence.

(b) *Risk*

If you view r_τ as a prediction of the spot rate i_τ at actual time τ ahead, there will usually be a prediction error; investment decisions made now on the basis of r_τ will be correspondingly wrong. The further ahead, the greater one can expect the error to be and hence the greater the pricing penalty that ought to be applied to r_τ. One would therefore expect to observe r_τ higher the longer is τ, or equivalently the graph of r against maturity τ to rise with τ.

A 'normal' term structure is therefore one for which expectations, if downwards, are at least not pronounced and risk considerations prevail, so that the entire curve slopes upwards. However, if people expected short-term interest rates to be high for a while, then decline, this expectations profile could overwhelm the normal risk effect, creating an inverted curve.

Other explanations for the slope of the term structure have been proposed in the earlier economics literature. Examples are hypotheses as 'liquidity preference' (a natural preference for short-term rather than long-term assets) and 'market segmentation' (the slope is due to the differing economic weight of those whose business is naturally in one or other maturity area). However, with the rise and rise of deregulated capital markets, such explanations are these days losing weight. Most people now think in terms of expectations and risk as the two major factors. However, term-structure dynamics remains one of the areas of New Zealand financial economics least studied by academics and the researchers and the most poorly understood by the markets, considerable recent theoretical development notwithstanding. My own feeling is that expectations are extremely important, risk is important, segmentation has historically been important and who knows about liquidity preference? Nobody has ever explained what it really means; the most reasonable explanations relied on a segmentation effect arising from market incompleteness, but this is becoming less important with time. We come back in §2.5 below to the surprising empirics of the recent history of New Zealand interest rates.

Bond Returns

Yields should not be confused with *returns*. If a bond is currently yielding nine per cent, that is what it would return you on the constant reinvestment rate assumption (a big 'if'), were you to hold it for the remainder of its life. But suppose you wanted to hold the bond, or did hold it, only over a set period of time, say a quarter or a year. What would the actual return be? The return components will be (a) any coupon paid over the holding period; and (b) the change in the price of the bond – what you sold it for less its purchase price; or simply, the capital gain component. When you add the two together, the results when expressed on an annual basis will often be wildly different from the original yield to maturity. Table 2.1 illustrates for government stock over the month October 1995.

Table 2.1: Making (or Losing) Money in Bonds

Govt. Stock issue	Yield at close 27/10/95 %	Monthly return: October 1995 %	Year to 27/10 %	Turnover week 27/10 $m
11/95	8.28	0.74	8.00	0
11/96	7.64	1.56	9.59	181
7/97	7.29	2.20	10.88	161
7/98	7.15	2.95	12.14	133
2/00	7.13	3.81	13.37	538
2/01	7.14	4.16	–	22
3/02	7.16	4.23	14.06	38
4/04	7.15	4.44	15.39	121
11/06	7.16	4.80	16.56	88

Source: NBNZ Treasury.

Compare columns 2–4 of the table. You will see first, that yields are no guide at all to actual returns – which indeed could quite easily have been negative; and second, that the actual returns are evidently quite volatile. October 1995 was a great month in a good year (to date).

For the purposes of stockmarket and other studies, yields or returns on government bonds or Treasury bills are often regarded as a 'risk-free' benchmark against which share returns are measured (see, for instance, the CAPM model of Chapter 5.2). As Table 2.1 shows, this can be highly misleading; great care must be taken in defining the holding period and assumptions before any kind of return can be regarded as effectively risk free. While OECD governments do not usually suffer from credit or default risk (though one or two are starting to look a bit shaky), any kind of yield or return on their bonds will vary, simply from market demand and supply. A more consistent portfolio approach would be to regard them as a risky asset just as you would a company share or any other investment. Indeed, such a philosophy underpins the entire theory and practice of fixed interest portfolio management.

2.2   New Zealand Government Bonds

Issue

Government bonds are issued by the New Zealand Debt Management Office (NZDMO), a division of the Treasury, although the mechanics of the issue process are handled by the Reserve Bank. Apart from refinancing expiring issues, there are two primary reasons for issuing government stock:

(a) to finance the government sector borrowing requirement (GSBR)
(b) to provide continued liquidity in the market for government stock previously issued; and in particular, in the case of certain 'benchmark' stocks, to provide a physical underpinning for trading in futures, options and other derivatives based on government bonds in the NZOFE (New Zealand Options and Futures Exchange) and OTC (over the counter) markets.

As the name suggests, the GSBR arises in response to the cash budget deficits of government. In the bad old days this used to be financed also by the issue of money (borrowing from the Reserve Bank) but this is no longer considered financially correct. Very recently, the government has been running large budget surpluses which will be devoted in part to retiring some of the (large!) stock of outstanding government bonds, starting especially with overseas debt. For the moment – i.e. until more overseas debt is retired – issue is expected to continue at around \$2bn for 1996. The intent thereafter is apparently to issue further debt only in response to the exigencies of portfolio management, i.e. changing the maturity spectrum according to views about the likely course of interest rates. The implications of this for the liquidity of the local bond market are not altogether clear. But then, anything could happen in an MMP world.

Currently the maturities on issue range from 11/95 to the most recent addition, 11/2006, which carries an eight per cent coupon and was made with the express intent of preserving the liquidity needed for the 10-year bond futures contract. Table 2.2, column 2, gives the face values on issue as at August 1995. Evidently, eight issues account for the bulk of liquidity, though they are well spread out over the maturity spectrum. And some of these are 'hotter' than others. The last column gives the amounts expressed in present value terms, where the respective yields have been used as the discount factors. Each pv has been expressed as a percentage of the sum of all present values, i.e. as the total value of all government bonds on domestic issue. These figures constitute the weights for the CS First Boston bond index, which is an attempt at a 'representative' yield for all government bonds. JP Morgan also publishes an index of bond yields. The economic meaning of such indices is not clear, but they are often used for portfolio benchmarking purposes.

Table 2.2:   NZG Bond Holdings August 1995

Maturity	Issue amount (nominal) $m	August 1995 Foreign holdings		CSFB PV Weight (%)
		Amount	% of issue	
11/95	2,475	856.1	39.6	7.9
10/96	302.8	27.9	9.2	–
11/96	2,449	516.6	21.1	12.0
7/97	1962.7	239.3	12.2	10.2
7/98	2,449	573.3	23.4	11.2
2/00	2,736	522.9	17.4	14.5
2/01	600	0.0	0.0	3.3
3/02	2,512	600.8	23.9	14.1
4/04	3,044	1525.1	50.1	14.2
11/06	1,302	413.2	24.6	11.0
Other				
(10/96, 6/99, 9/01)				1.6

Source: NBNZ Treasury.

Recently 2–3 different lines have been offered at tender, at about $300m per tender. The DMO determines the maturities, coupons, volumes and timing of the tender in response to the exigencies noted above and to the requirements of debt portfolio management, which include altering maturities (technically, duration) depending on views taken about the likely future slope of the term structure curve. Ideally, the coupons on new issues should approximate current yields, for the latter become questionable guides to pricing for deep discount or premium bonds.

The actual issue process is managed by the Reserve Bank, who issue an invitation to tender one week before the date of each tender, in terms of the pre-existing prospectus for such issues. The invitations are advertised and appear on Reuters (RBZI) and Telerate (39979). Normal bidding closes at 1.15 p.m. on the day of the tender and the results are announced at 2.30 p.m. Settlement can be either via Austraclear (see Chapter 3) for member institutions, by bank cheque or by personal cheque if suitable securities are lodged with the bank, or if the bank can grant a daily settlement limit to the purchaser.

In the old days, 'coupon' stock meant that you clipped off a coupon and sent it in for payment of the coupon $ amount. Such 'bearer bonds' are in fact still used in the Euromarkets, where anonymity is both valued and available. In New Zealand, government stock is 'inscribed' stock and the Reserve Bank runs the register. When you sell bonds on the secondary market, you advise the registry of the name and address of the new owner. Coupons and any principal repayments are paid for value 15th of the month. The Register closes 10 days before this, with the holder as of the 5th qualifying for the coupon but not thereafter (the stock becomes 'ex-interest'). The Reserve Bank is both registrar and paying agent.

Finally, New Zealand Government stock is rated by Moody's and Standard and Poor; the credit rating has improved in recent times along with the government's budgetary position. The current (November 1995) rating for domestic stock is AAA with S.&P. and Aa2 with Moody's. For overseas issued stock, the ratings are slightly lower at AA and Aa2, respectively. This is the highest rating for any bond issues on the local market. [Or to be more precise, the equal highest rating – there are two other organisations whose debt is also issued and traded locally that have an AAA rating. Can you can name them?]

Holders

The demand for New Zealand Government stock is primarily institutional in nature. On a long-term holding basis demand comes from fund managers of various kinds: those operated by local banks, insurance companies, independent private fund managers and statutory funds such as the Accident Compensation Corporation, the Earthquake Commission, the Government Superannuation Fund and the National Provident Fund. The commercial funds run dedicated fixed interest funds, which are ipso facto large holders, but even more balanced funds include large portfolio holdings of government stock. Government bonds are also held as an active part of portfolio management by banks and other financial institutions, especially by managers of derivatives books because of futures illiquidity. The tender is dominated by large fixed-interest specialists, who break up acquired blocks into smaller parcels and retail off to smaller or less specialist institutions, funds or individuals. The specialists notify the RBNZ registry of the sales and the new owners replace them on the register for the relevant parcel of bonds.

Referring back to Table 2.2, columns 3 and 4, you will see that an appreciable portion of the domestic NZGS issues are held offshore, about 27 per cent of it when totalled over all the issues. If you added in overseas issues of NZGS, the proportion is even larger, about 40 per cent. This is an important element of the capital account in the balance of payments. It reflects the large current account deficits that New Zealand has run in the past.

Traders

There are eight liquid stocks actively traded in the New Zealand market; you will find their yields quoted in the newspapers every business day. Most liquidity is associated with three-year and 10-year stock. The trading is mediated by *pricemakers*, mostly banks and investment banks. Most will quote on up to $5m parcels. Table 2.3 below lists dealers and pricemakers in both the bond and bill markets. Note that not all the dealers are actually pricemakers.

Table 2.3: Dealers in New Zealand Bond and Bill Markets (as at mid-1995)

Dealer	Bond market	Money market
AMP Society (New Zealand Branch)	*	
ANZ Banking Group (New Zealand) Limited	*	*
ASB Bank Limited	*	
Bain and Company Limited	*	
Bank of New Zealand	*	*
Bankers Trust New Zealand Limited	*	*
Citibank NZ	*	*
CS First Boston New Zealand Group	*	
Hong Kong and Shanghai Banking Corporation	*	
The National Bank of New Zealand Limited	*	*
Trust Bank New Zealand Limited	*	
Westpac Banking Corporation	*	*

Source: RBNZ [Potter (1995), RBNZ *Bulletin* Sept.].

As the name suggests, a *pricemaker* stands ready to buy or sell securities up to its stated limits. It is they who carry the market and make its liquidity in the day-to-day sense. Prices are quoted in yield form (see above) and in terms of points; recall that a basis point is the last of the two decimal places quoted for percentage interest rates. (In the U.S., on the other hand, quotes are in terms of prices rather than yields.) Pricemakers will quote a two-way price, i.e. a price (yield!) at which they will bid to buy from you and one at which they will offer to sell. A normal spread between the two is five points or so. This will widen in times of uncertainty.

A *broker* is essentially a middleman, who has good client contacts, carefully cultivated. On receipt of a client expression of interest, the broker will ring around the pricemakers for the best price. The pricemakers have their own corporate (retail) dealers, but it is considered highly unethical to go behind a broker's back when the source of the order is suspected. Many other institutions are actively in the market buying and selling government stock, sometimes on behalf of third parties. There are, in turn, two sorts of brokers. *Screen brokers*, as the name suggests, operate via Reuters or Telerate screens to bring buyers and sellers together. On the longer end New Zealand Fixed Interest Securities Ltd and G5 Financial Services are the screen jocks on bonds, bills and interest rate derivatives. *Non-screen* brokers operate via telephones/fax, etc. and deal mainly in bonds. SBC Warburg (formerly Buttle Wilson), Cavill White, Garlick and Co. and Jordan Sandman Were provide services of this kind.

Market Dynamics

The quoted yield is rather like a price, except that it is an inverse price – it goes down when news is good and up when news is bad. Notice the usage; the things that affect bond yields are *news*. Moreover old news is not news – only happenings that are unexpected by the market and therefore not already priced in, will move bond prices and yields. As we will see in Chapter 7, a prime influence on bond yields is changes in international interest rates. As well as these, however, a host of domestic and international news events will shift the market.

In Appendix II we reproduce (with their kind permission) yield graphs for five-year stock constructed from seven years of news events by the Treasury of the National Bank of New Zealand. You will notice how much the general level of interest rates has changed over the seven years. Then as an exercise in understanding the market, ask a friend to read out the news events and try to guess which way (if any) the events moved the market and how much. Is there a board game here?

2.3   Other Coupon Bonds

Two other large(ish) bond markets exist in addition to government bonds: (a) the semi-government market and (b) the corporate bond market.

The Semis

Strictly, the term 'semi' for 'semi-government' is used in New Zealand if at all, only for the state-owned enterprises, at the time of writing down to four: Government Property Services, Airways Corporation, Electricity Corporation of New Zealand (ECNZ) and Transpower. In the present study, however, we will follow overseas precedent by enlarging coverage to include regional councils (as the Auckland Regional Council, say), territorial councils (e.g. the Auckland City Council) and special purpose authorities such as museum boards, airports, all but two of the national ports and a dozen publicly owned energy companies. The latter grouping we shall refer to as the local authorities (LAs). Perhaps arbitrarily, we will lump a small amount of CHE debt with the corporate debt, considered later.

Collectively there is about $1.9bn of LA debt, most of it in the form of debenture stock. As one would expect, the largest borrowers are generally the large regional and territorial councils of the main centres, faced with expensive infrastructure to build and maintain. The ability of LAs to issue and manage debt was severely circumscribed by the 1956 Local Authority Loans Act, which required new loans of any significance to be tied as to maturity and scheduling with an underlying project and to be vetted and approved by the Loans Board, set up under the Act. The requirements have in recent years been increasingly circumvented by the Authorities setting up LATEs (local authority trading enterprises), which have some independence in the issuance and management of loan funds. For example, they can and do issue floating rate (promissory) notes, as well as debt stock. If the Local Authority Reform Bill now before Parliament is enacted, July 1996 will see a new order, in which many of the 1956 controls are removed. Council treasurers will be able to use derivatives to manage their portfolio and can borrow freely in accordance with an approved risk management policy. However, they will still have to borrow in New Zealand dollars.

LA stock varies enormously in liquidity. The large authorities tend to issue large tranches of debt – for instance the Auckland Regional Council issues debt in lots of $500,000, generally to funds and banks, by means of a tender process through a broker. On the other hand, there are hundreds of small issues of purely local appeal, with a correspondingly limited secondary market. Possibly because of liquidity problems, LA stock is issued – and trades – at a hefty premium above government stock of similar maturity. Even large LAs have a 'penalty' of 15 bps for one-year stock and 40–50 bps for longer maturities. The margins get even higher – 80 points or more – for smaller authorities. Table 2.4 gives some indicative margins for broad classes of loan stock.

Table 2.4:   Indicative Spreads Over NZGS

Local Authority and Telecom Margins to NZGS (As at Close Friday 27 October 1995)						
Issuer	0 to 18m	1997	1998	1999–00	2001–02	2003–04	2005+
City Councils	+20	+25	+37	+45	+51	+60	+70
Regional Councils	+22	+32	+42	+50	+57	+65	+75
Electric Supply Athy	+30	+40	+55	+65	+75	+80	+95
Govt Gteed Health Bd	+15	+20	+25	+30	+30	+40	+40
TeleBonds	+15	+20	+30	+35	+45	+50	+55
Telecom Eurokiwis	**	**	+25	+30	+40	+45	**

Source: NBNZ Bond Weekly 30.10.95.

Turning to the true 'semis', the big New Zealand issuers are ECNZ and Transpower, in that order. The debt portfolio of ECNZ is second only to that of the government. They currently have $1.57bn. public stock issued in New Zealand in three maturities (/96, /01 and a small amount in /09) and $250m in short-term paper. Their New Zealand debt trades at 10 bps or so for short maturities (rated AA-) and 35–45 bps further out (rated A1+). Recent policy since 1994 has seen a shift towards issuing offshore, with eight issues spanning Euro USD, Yen, Swiss Franc and DM, from notes to medium-term eurobonds. By swapping back into NZD they can achieve an interest rate of only 5–10 bps over New Zealand Government stock. We will see in Chapter 7 how this is done.

Transpower, the other big semi borrower, has a total of $1.7b. debt at nominal value. They issue both domestically and in the Euromarkets. Much of the total is made up of $1.1bn of stock owed to the government which will be refunded in the near future by the issue of additional debt into the local and overseas markets.

Prognosis is for further expansion of the LA market, as councils issue new debt to finance decaying social infrastructure. According to the story, we are nearing crunch time in the '40-year sewage and water cycle'. The projected amount is about double the present total in 5–10 years' time. Following the Local Authority Reform Bill, we shall almost certainly see more active management of LA debt, with use of the derivatives market and more marketable parcels of debt. The result will hopefully be to improve the rather unnecessarily expensive margin in yield over government stock.

Other Government Bonds

1. *Kiwi Bonds*

These are for small holders; $250,000 is the upper limit for holdings of any one issue, while the minimum investment is $1,000. They come in a range of maturities from six months to four years and coupons can either be paid out quarterly or compounded until maturity. Their issue yields are set at a margin below government bonds of similar maturity. Currently there are about $0.6bn. on issue, so they are quite popular with retail investors.

2. *Government Coupon Strips*

These are simply the coupons on government bonds, sold as an instrument in their own right by financial institutions holding the underlying bonds. The coupons can be sold collectively, or can themselves be 'unbundled' into individual coupons. Current amounts in the market are small. However, they are potentially important as a way of completing the market in different maturities.

3. *Inflation Indexed Bonds*

In its original version this golden-oldie was discontinued in 1984, but is still around. The general idea is that both coupons and principal are indexed to the consumers price index. The government has recently announced that it intends to resurrect the idea. These will be very long-term bonds with nominal or face value continually adjusted for inflation; coupons will be a fixed percentage or the adjusted value, so they themselves will automatically change. Oops, your author has just been overtaken by events. A $75m tender took place in late November 1995. They are 20-year bonds with a coupon of 4.5 per cent and the principal adjusted for inflation. Market estimates are for a secondary market yield of 4.6 to 5.25 per cent. By the time this book appears you will have been able to see how good these estimates were.

The Corporate Market

Bond or bond-like corporate borrowings come in a variety of forms, often distinctly creative. The main types are:

1. *Unsecured Notes*

As the name suggests, these are generally coupon bonds of up to five years maturity, with no specific security as backing. They are issued by companies with good credit ratings and are governed by a trust deed and trustee company. The deed may offer additional protection such as limits on total secured liabilities, which rank ahead of the notes, or conversion rights to debentures if any subsequent charges are made on the company's assets. Various kinds of negative pledge may further limit the ability of the company to issue securities or make other changes that rank ahead of the noteholders.

2. *Convertible Notes*

These are notes carrying an option to convert after some specified time to ordinary shares at stated conversion ratios. New Zealand convertibles have maturities of five years or less, but longer dated issues are quite common overseas. There is much room for creativity in the design of such issues, with the help of your friendly investment bank who may also act as underwriter. For instance the conversion option may be detachable in the form of a warrant. Or conversion may be to another company's shares. The valuation of convertible notes is not straightforward; in addition to the debt component, one has to attach a value to what may be a long-dated conversion option. Tax aspects can also be a bit tricky.

Because of the option to convert to equity, convertible notes share some of the characteristics of the latter. They rank behind all other liabilities and they are commonly listed on the Stock Exchange. The NZSE currently quotes nine convertible note issues:

Table 2.5:   NZSE-Quoted Convertible Notes

| Share | CONVERTIBLE SECURITIES | | | | | | | |
	Quote Buy	Sell	Last Sale	No. Sold (100s)	Interest c/unit	Maturity Date	Conversion Terms	Yield on Interest
A Barnett $1 notes	148	150	148	–	8	11/12/96	•1: 1	5.4
Brierley 85c notes	108	109	108	1969	7.65	30/6/98	•1: 1	7.1
DB 85c notes	88	94	90	100	5.95	30/6/96	•1: 1	6.6
Defiance $1 prefs	176	185	175	–	18.5	9/1/02	•1: 1	10.6
Macraes 250Ac notes	195	250	205	2	21.49	15/9/98	•1: 4	10.4
Nat Gas $1 notes	198	199	198	215	10.5	14/10/97	1: 1	5.3
NZ Pet 25c notes	22	24	22	500	1.25	1/7/98	•10: 1	5.7
Seabill $1 notes	93	94	93	4480	9	27/6/99	•1: 1	9.7
Short Prop 85c notes	87	–	86	–	6.375	31/12/98	•1: 1	7.4
St Lukes $1 notes	110	112	112	165	8.7	1/4/99	•1: 1	7.8

Convertible Securities: • Final conversion date.

Source: *New Zealand Herald*, 2 November 1995.

3. *Debentures*

This is transferable loan stock, sometimes listed on the Stock Exchange, secured over assets of the company; the security may be either over specific assets or more usually, a floating charge over all assets of the company. Debentures are often long term in nature; maturity dates of 10 years are quite common. Like other forms of corporate debt there is a trust deed administered by a trustee company. Debentures are most commonly public issues, but may also be institutional private placements, or alternatively 'family issues', which are issues to holders of the company's existing securities (shares, convertible notes, etc.). Most are issued at par and take the form of traditional coupon stock, though zero coupon issues have been made overseas. The debentures of companies with a strong credit rating, or access to such via ownership arrangements, are sometimes listed on the NZSE. Nonetheless, secondary trading is still thin, on the whole.

Debentures have historically been the favoured form of non-bank corporate loan raisings in New Zealand. Finance companies have been regular issuers (see Chapter 4) as have a variety of industrial companies and other bodies down to the local bowling club. If you are able to, get hold of the NBNZ *Bond Market Weekly*, or a similar publication from one of the other traders. There you will find a table listing prices, other details and diagnostics, like duration and spread over

NZGS, for the 70 or so well traded public and private corporate bonds on the New Zealand market. The table is unfortunately too large to reproduce here. Recently the Bank of New Zealand has constructed a corporate bond index for use in benchmarking exercises and other purposes.

4. *Mortgage-backed Securities*

In the present study we do not consider in detail the scope and nature of traditional mortgage lending, as this is not strictly a matter of capital markets as such. For the sake of completeness, however, we ought to mention the securitisation of mortgages, a feature of the U.S. capital markets and to a lesser extent Australia (e.g. with FANMAC, a NSW Government Corporation which bundles home mortgages). The idea is that mortgagees (those who fund mortgages) can bundle their mortgages and issue bonds against the bundle. If ordinary coupon bonds are issued, the cash flows on the bonds will not match the repayments of interest and principal on the mortgages and there can also be problems of early repayment of the mortgages. The originating institution may borrow or lend funds to smooth the mortgage cash flows ('enhancement', in the jargon) and the credit rating of the institution is therefore a factor in pricing of the bonds. As yet, mortgage-backed securitisation is not a feature of the New Zealand institutional scene. There is an informal market for transfer of various kinds of mortgages, but in the original form rather than enhanced. A conspicuous recent example was the sale of State Housing Corporation mortgages to a subsidiary of the Fay Richwhite group.

2.4   Bills and Related Instruments

Bills are short-term zero coupon instruments, mainly issued in connection with cash management exigencies or as a source of bridging finance. The principal categories are:

1. bank bills
2. Reserve Bank bills
3. Treasury bills
4. commercial bills
and we will also add
5. Promissory notes.

Item (2) – Reserve Bank bills – are issued by the Reserve Bank for purposes of monetary control and held only by the commercial banks. For further details see Chapter 3. Excluding this item, we will go through the rest in order.

1. *Bank Bills*

The title is a bit of a misnomer, for these are short-term debt instruments issued in the first instance by private borrowers. However, they have been accepted by a bank, which means that the bank has taken over the payment obligation from the issuer. The originator (borrower) is the 'drawer' of the bill, which has a 'payee', the party to whom the bill is specified to be paid. The 'acceptor' undertakes to pay to the person presenting the bill on the due date the face-value of the bill. The payee and acceptor are usually one and the same bank.

Bank bills can readily be sold in the market. The seller of the bill endorses the bill by signing on the reverse side and the buyer becomes the holder and will present the bill to the accepting bank on maturity.

As indicated earlier, bank bills are issued at a discount to the face value. In New Zealand they are issued with 30-, 60-, 90- and 180-day maturities. All maturities are well traded in the secondary market with the 90-day the most liquid. It is therefore possible to buy bank bills on the secondary market to any maturity less than 180 days and therefore to 'fill in' the yield curve at the short end. Most banks and investment banks actively make a market in bank bills, quoting the bills as a discount on a nominal face value of $100. See Table 2.3 above for a listing of market players.

Bank bills have considerable systemic importance for the financial marketplace, stemming in the first instance from both the liquidity and high credit standing of the instrument:

(a) They are widely used by corporates and banks themselves for cash management and short-term funding purposes.
(b) The 90-day bank bill rate (BBR) forms the reference rate for many (if not most) domestic floating rate debt instruments and for derivatives such as swaps that rely on a floating rate benchmark. Floating rate notes, for example, will carry an interest rate expressed as a margin above BBR, depending on the creditworthiness of the issuer.
(c) Ninety-day bills with a face value of $500,000 form the physical basis for the bank bill futures and options contracts on the New Zealand Futures Exchange (see Chapter 6).

3. *Treasury Bills (T-bills)*

Like the longer-dated bonds, Treasury bills are issued on a tender basis, by the Reserve Bank acting as agent for the NZDMO, with the same sort of information, settlement and clearing processes. However, tenders are held more regularly; every Tuesday, in fact. The amounts offered and their maturities differ from time to time, in line with the exigencies of Treasury cash management. As we will see in the next chapter, Treasury bills are an instrument for the monetary control mechanism via the Reserve Bank's open market and liquidity management operations, so their issue will also be governed by the monetary situation. The RBNZ itself sells Treasury bills as part of their open market operations ('seasonal' T-bills). T-bills come in all maturities up to one year. Current credit rating is A-1+ (S.&P.) and P-1 (Moody's).

4. *Commercial Bills*

These are bills accepted by non-banks, such as investment (merchant) banks, a large parent company (e.g. an overseas one), or finance companies. They fell out of favour for a while, overtaken as it were by bank bill facilities. However, they can be originated as part of a bill options facility in investment bank lending operations (see Chapter 4).

5. *Promissory Notes*

A.k.a. commercial paper. As the name suggests these are unsecured, so only prime corporates or semis qualify as names. Maturities range from seven to 365 days. In addition to uses in cash management they can be raised on a revolving basis to finance longer-term capital expenditures.

2.5   Interest Rate Swaps and Other OTC Derivatives

Interest Rate Swaps (etc.)

A ('vanilla') interest rate swap is an agreement between two parties whereby one pays the other a stream of fixed coupons in return for a stream of interest rate payments that are tied to a floating interest rate, usually the 90-day BBR. The swap has a notional principal value to which the coupon rate (the fixed rate) and the floating rate are applied to determine the six monthly payments and receipts for each side. Most swaps are mediated and warehoused by a bank, which stands in the middle, as illustrated in Figure 2.3. It will extract a margin fee (δ in Figure 2.3) as a small difference between the fixed payment from B passed on as the fixed payment to A.

Figure 2.3:   Vanilla Interest Rate Swap

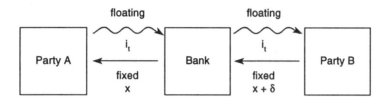

Party A is the 'receiver'; party B is the 'payer', the convention being associated with the fixed side of things. On a nominal $1 of face-value, party A would net out at a cash flow of (x-i_t) for the horizon of the swap. So every six months from now to the end of three years (if this is maturity), A would receive a fixed coupon of x, known right at the outset and pay a floating six-monthly interest rate i_t, not known at the outset. Actually the New Zealand arrangements are a bit unusual: corporates prefer to pay or receive on a three-monthly basis, whereas interbank dealing generally takes place on a six-monthly payment basis.

A swap is a financial instrument that could theoretically be bought and sold. On inception, its true market value is always zero, because no money changes hands. The coupon rate x is set so as to make the discounted value of the swap equal to zero. It turns out that x must be equal to the coupon on a bond of the same maturity and same credit rating that would be selling at par. The swap coupon is therefore identifiable as the par yield on bonds. What bonds? That is a hard one. A theoretically correct answer might be: an equivalent bond of the same maturity issued by the same bank as the one originating the swap. In practice, government bonds of similar maturities are taken as the reference yield. However, spreads between the swap rate and the yield on NZGS do vary quite substantially. The reason is that at any one time there may be substantial imbalances between those wanting to pay fixed and those wanting to receive. Such imbalances are often associated with major bond issues. So the forces of supply and demand would move the swap rate relative to any underlying reference rate. Major differences are almost always short run in character as professional market players move in and semi-arbitrage away a large spread (see section 2.7 below).

Once the swap is underway, it does acquire a nonzero value. The reason is that over time, market perceptions of the likely future course of floating rates change (remember that at real time t the best estimates of the future spot rates $i_{t+\tau}$ are the current forward rates r_τ and these change as time unfolds). Therefore in a new swap just instituted, the coupon x' would differ from that on the original swap. Discounting the difference (x'-x) gives a nonzero value for the swap over the remainder of its lifetime. This is what you would have to pay (or receive) if you wanted and were able to cancel the swap at a subsequent time.

The role of the bank is partly as arranger and partly to assume credit risk. In the *arranging function*, it will first take on one party and then look around for a suitable counterparty or combination of counterparties. In the meantime it must wear a certain amount of interest rate risk; it is exposed to market valuations of the swap, as exposited above. Bearing in mind that the valuation is just the same as a corresponding bond, minus its principal, the swap bookmaker will hedge the temporary exposure by buying or selling either bond futures (preferably) or physical bonds. The *credit risk* arises because party A (say) might default. This would leave the bank carrying the can – floating rates could in the meantime have risen enormously (which is why A might have headed for the bush) and the bank still has to pay party B. The bank will therefore need some compensation in its margin for this risk. And party B will feel much happier with the bank as a counterparty. The banks therefore fulfil a useful economic function by acting as middlemen. Legally, however, they are themselves principals in each side of the swap.

Why do swaps exist? The most popular explanation is that a corporate might have a comparative advantage in arranging one type of debt rather than the other. Party A might be better at raising fixed-rate debt (via a bond with fixed coupon), rather than floating-rate debt. So it goes ahead, raises the fixed-coupon debt and swaps the payments stream into a floating rate. Thus to Figure 2.3 we could add another arm:

Figure 2.4:   Completing the Square

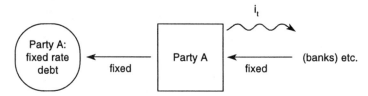

There would be a corresponding arm for Party B, who (in the story) finds it easier to raise floating-rate debt than fixed. Even if the terms on which party A can raise both kinds of debt are cheaper than for B, they can, nonetheless, achieve a solution under which they both end up better off. Appendix II to this chapter sets out a more detailed example that you can work through.

In practice swaps are also used to change the temporal pattern of a firm's cash flows to any desired shape. For instance if you wanted to write off a lot of interest against this year's income, you could arrange a swap where you paid the entire interest fee in an advance lump sum payment. See, however, later remarks about changing tax provisions. Or if you were worried as a company treasurer that the duration of your liabilities was too long, you could shorten it with a floating rate swap. In general, interest rate swaps are a very flexible and cheap way of rearranging the time profile of your balance sheet. Finally, academics have suggested several other reasons for the swaps phenomenon in the literature, but none of these attempts have gained much market credence.

The world-wide swaps thing took off about the beginning of the 'eighties, though precursors existed in the 'seventies in the form of parallel and back-to-back loans operated by British firms to avoid foreign exchange controls and FX risk. Since that time, growth has been ,massive, amounting to trillions of dollars face-value world-wide. The range has also extended to include other types of swaps: FX swaps are discussed in detail in Chapter 7. You can also have *commodity swaps*, where one payment is made accordingly to the current or spot price for a commodity and the other is a fixed price. Such swaps have been used by producers or users of gold, aluminium, oil, aviation fuel to create a fixed or known cash flow for investment planning purposes. And you can have *equity swaps*, where the floating rate is pegged to some stock index. Trading volume on these latter types is very thin, at best, in the New Zealand market. Commodity swaps have been traded from time to time on the Australian market for aviation fuel and Texas crude.

The first New Zealand interest rate swaps took place in 1985 soon after deregulation, with Southpac, Westpac and the yesterfang DFC as early players on the scene. In those early days swap margins were pretty huge and dealers drove Porsches; these days the margins are much narrower, reflecting the more mature state of the market. Swap activity usually follows debt issues, indeed many debt issues are arranged with a subsequent swap very much in mind. As well as bank pricemakers and dealers, brokers also operate in the market – having found a client they ring around the market to find the best priced counterparties.

The principal New Zealand swaps dealers are the National Bank of New Zealand, ANZ, BNZ, BT, Citibank and Westpac. There are three brokers, New Zealand Fixed Interest Securities, G5 Financial Services and Astley and Pearce. All these players are affiliated to ISDA, the International Swaps Dealers Association. Swaps users or third party arrangers include non-dealing banks such a ASB or the Trust Bank Group; finance and investment organisations such as Bancorp Treasury Services and Fay Richwhite and large corporations. In very recent times, with lower general interest rates, the large corporates have been less concerned about minimising high-interest payments, so their activity has dropped off a bit. Figure 2.5 illustrates total New Zealand interest rate swaps turnover from 1988–1993.

Figure 2.5: **Total New Zealand Interest Rate Swaps Market Turnover 1988:4–1993:4 ($NZ Millions)**

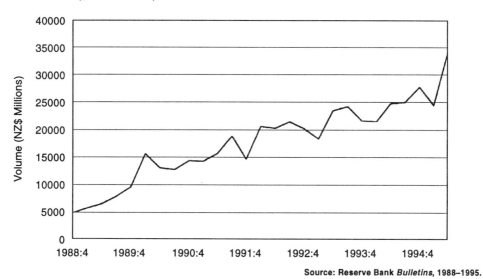

Source: Reserve Bank *Bulletins*, 1988–1995.

Documentation

Most swaps are documented according to a standard International Swaps Dealers Association (ISDA) format structured as a master swaps agreement, which can cover any subsequent swaps between the parties. The standard form agreement consists of a number of parts dealing with:

- identification of
- definitions
- payments
- representations and warranties
- agreements
- termination events and consequences
- early termination

- default events and consequences
- transfer provisions
- tax matters
- credit support documentation
- governing law
- confirmation
- assignment.

The ISDA is an international format, although British banks operate with their own, the BBA (British Bankers Association) guidelines.

Legal aspects of swaps have been spectacularly troublesome. The celebrated U.K. case of the Hammersmith and Fulham City Council, which went right up to the House of Lords, concerned the legal capacity of the servants of an organisation to enter with such agreements and indeed had wider implications than just swaps. Organisations whose founding documents and rules predate much recent financial technology may not have the specific power to enter into such arrangements. It is not sufficient to rely on implicit powers. A similar situation is in principle applicable to a number of swaps users here in New Zealand, including companies, government corporations and trust funds. The onus is very much on the arranger to ensure that the parties do have the legal capacity to enter into such swap agreements. Otherwise when interest rates go against them the parties could exit without meeting their liability, leaving the arranger to carry the can.

Contractual aspects have troubled other authorities. A recent U.S. Congress decision affirmed the legality of 'netting' on close out, which refers to the practice of making a single payment representing the netted out present value of all remaining commitments following default or termination. It seems likely that should problems arise, New Zealand courts would follow such overseas precedents.

Accounting and Tax Aspects

Swaps are usually created as off balance sheet transactions. Creative treasurers can therefore use them to change the duration of their fixed assets and liabilities, or to boost reported return on equity and return on assets. More recently, concern has arisen with disclosure requirements for such devices. Financial Reporting Standard (FRS31) 'Disclosure of Information about Financial Instruments' issued in March 1993 by the New Zealand Society of Accountants, addresses such issues. The FRS addresses general disclosure requirements, credit risk, fair value and disclosures concerning currency and interest rate risk. This is a proactive initiative on the part of the NZSA, as similar accounting standards do not appear to exist for most other OECD countries.

No specific tax rulings have yet been issued by New Zealand Inland Revenue on swaps and similar transactions. The central issue is whether one follows a 'due and receivable' basis for assessment, or an accruals type basis. The former refers to the practice of assessing simple cash flows as taxable income, or allowable losses, no matter that these might represent liabilities artificially rearranged in time with the precise object of avoiding tax. The latter refers to attempts to measure the 'true economic substance' of the income flows lying behind the cash flows.[5] In the meantime the general accruals provisions of sections 64C (2, 4) of the Income Tax Act 1993 would appear to apply. However, a more authoritative statement and code of practice would be welcome.

Credit Risk Provisions

Earlier we referred to the credit risk arising from the contingency that one side of the swap might fall out of bed. Banks, as the middlemen, would thereby be exposed. Sections 74 and 78 of the

Reserve Bank Act 1989 implement the 1987 Basle Accord on capital adequacy. The general thrust of these provisions is discussed in the banking chapter (Chapter 3). Credit exposures arising from swap transactions must be incorporated into the bank's capital adequacy rate calculation. The details involve complex rituals with counterparty factors, credit conversion equivalents, etc. and are best left to the high priests or Baal[6] himself (spot the pun).

Caps, Collars and Other Mercery

Here we will briefly cover a number of derivatives issued on an OTC (over the counter) basis; this means that they are originated and tailored on demand by a bank or other dealer. Collectively, they could be described as the OTC interest rate options market, as they all incorporate option like features and are priced and hedged using options technology. Pricing of the latter is based on the more formal exchange traded derivatives on the New Zealand Futures Exchange; for which, see Chapter 6. Reference to that chapter should also be made by readers unfamiliar with options. The five major New Zealand players in fixed interest OTC markets are ANZ, BT, BNZ, NBNZ and Westpac. The principal types of OTC instruments are as follows:

1. *Bond Options*

Options are described in more detail in Chapter 6, which is concerned with derivatives. Briefly, a bond option gives you the right to buy or sell a bond at or before some point in the future, at a preassigned price (the strike price). BNZ, National Bank, BT, Westpac and Citibank (out of Sydney) are all actions in the interbank market for bond options. At the time of writing, New Zealand Fixed Interest Securities was the only broker in the local market.

2. *Embedded Bond Options*

A callable bond contract might specify that the issuing firm can repurchase the bond at a predetermined price at any time before expiration. A puttable bond gives a similar facility to the holder. Naturally such features must be priced into the bond, the price of which can be broken down into the core bond price plus the price of the implied option. There are several callable issues on the New Zealand market. Similarly you can have early redemption privileges on fixed-rate deposits or mortgage commitments.

3. *Swaptions*

These are options on interest rate swaps, giving the holder the right to enter into a designated interest rate swap at a set time in the future. If, for instance, a swaption gives the holder the right to pay fixed and receive floating, it can be recognised as a put option on a fixed coupon bond with strike price equal to the principal value. Or if it gives the right to pay floating and receive fixed, it is effectively a call option on the equivalent bond. Swaptions are not quoted interbank in New Zealand, but are done for corporates on a 'best efforts' basis.

4. *Interest Rate Caps*

A pure cap might be where you receive the differential between floating and fixed rates, with an upper or lower limit on the floating rate. The fixed rate would be set so the value of the cap is zero at inception. Or, a cap on a loan protects the borrower from (floating rate) interest payments rising above a preassigned cut off point. If sold as part of a loan package, the implied option cost is incorporated into the interest rate charged. When the cap is provided by another institution, an up-front payment is usually required. Similarly, an interest rate *floor* has a lower limit and will carry an interest rate benefit on initiation.

5. *Interest Rate Collars*

Collars specify both the upper and lower limits for the rate that will be charged. It is a combination of a long position in a cap and a short position in a floor, typically such that the price of the cap equals the price of a floor; the facility would therefore be costless, or nearly so, allowing for margins.

In general, the OTC market is less liquid than the market for exchange-traded options. Providers may also have difficulty hedging their own exposures, perhaps ending up with a basis risk because their chosen hedges do not exactly track the instruments they are offering, as interest rates change. For this reason, spreads and margins are usually large in this market.

2.6   The New Zealand Term Structure

One can look at historical interest rates either by plotting a selection of interest rates of various maturities against time on the horizontal axis, or else by presenting annual snapshots of the term structure over a number of years. Figure 2.6 illustrates the first-time series approach, focusing on the 1993–1994 changes. Figure 2.7A is a smoothed version over July in each year, of the annual snapshot approach from 1987–1995. Figure 2.7B combines all the annual graphs into a three-dimensional surface ('manifold'). In each case, the term structure is portrayed as yields to maturity. The various graphs are all revealing, in their different ways. They show the fluctuations in the *levels* of interest rates that have occurred during the last 10 years or so. They also show the changes that have taken place in the *shape* of the yield curve.

Figure 2.6:   Time Sequence of New Zealand Term Structures

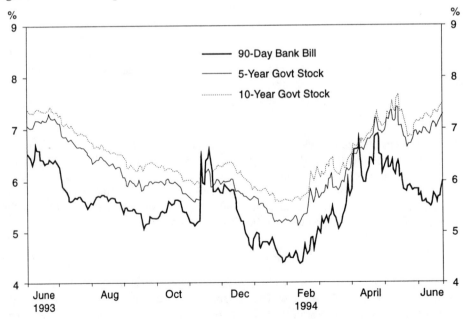

Source: RBNZ June 1994 monetary policy statement.

Figure 2.7a: Term Structure of Interest Rates: July Monthly Averages from 1987 to 1995

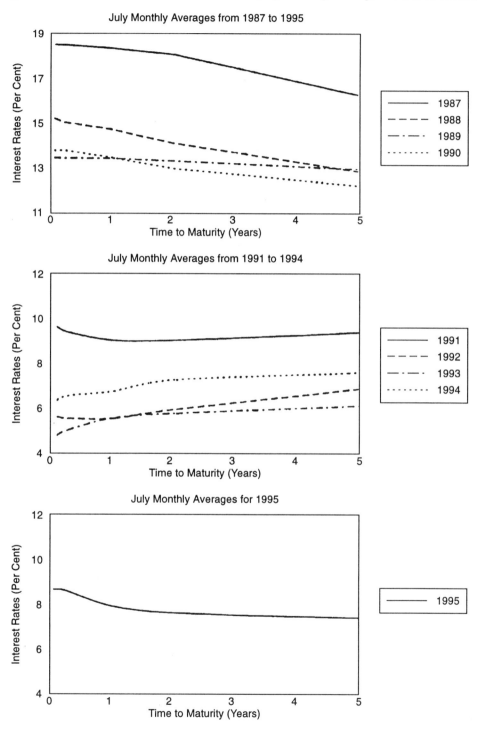

Source: RBNZ *Bulletins*, 1979–1995.

Figure 2.7b: Term Structure of Interest Rates: July Yield Averages for 1987 to 1995

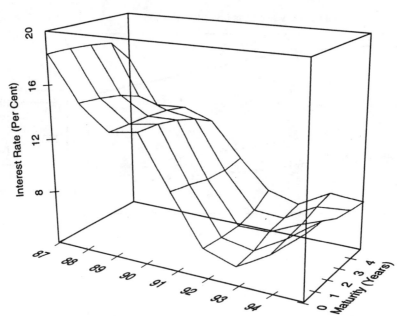

Source: RBNZ *Bulletins*, 1979–1995.

As mentioned in §2.1 above, we have to use yields to maturity on bonds (ρ) because data on zero coupon rates (R) or implied forwards (r) are hard to come by for reasons of maturity incompleteness. Actually the data are a mixture: for maturities shorter than one year the 'yields' are of the character of true zeros as they are computed by using pure discount securities (T-bills). For maturities longer than one year, coupon bonds are used, for which internal rates of return (ρ) are calculated. This is a bit like a giraffe-corgi cross. However, if we take the curves at least on rough face-value, they show a negative slope to yields against maturity from 1987 to 1990. In other words, the yield term structure was inverted over this period. Subsequently the yield structure flattened and became normal in the early part of this decade. In 1995 the term structure again inverted, with short rates higher than long rates.

The yield structure by itself is not actually very informative. As we saw in §2.1, expectations and risk bear a more natural or interpretable relationship with the implied forward rates; we want the rs instead of the ρs. But one can show that provided the securities do not trade at too deep a discount, the yield for any maturity T can be interpreted as a weighted average of the r(τ) for $\tau \leq$ T. This means that the true forward rate structure 'lags behind' the yield structure. Figure 2.8 is a graphic illustration for the particular case of a humped yield curve. You can see that the forward rates curve crosses the yield curve at the point of hump. Beyond that it declines at a faster rate.

Using such insights one could certainly say that in 1987 and just after, the forward rate curve must have been even more negatively sloping than the yield curve, for longer maturities. Such a state of affairs is clearly not due to risk, which would dictate that people need to be rewarded extra for holding the marginal maturity. Instead the negative slope must refer to expectations of lower spot rates 1–5 years hence – we recall that the implied forwards are in a sense market certainty equivalents for future spot rates. It would be a useful research exercise to prepare

Figure 2.8:   Kiwi Humps: Schematic Term Structure

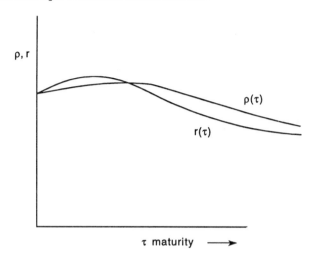

historical forward rate curves off market swap rates and verify the above references directly. As mentioned earlier, market swap rates have a varying basis spread over NZGS, but the exercise would nevertheless remain 'highly indicative', in burospeak.

Subsequent history showed that spot rates (e.g. the BBR) did indeed fall dramatically, from 20 per cent down to five per cent in seven years or so; before subsequently rising. So the market seems to have been justified in its expectations. Pundits would attribute this to expectations about the decline of inflation both in New Zealand and internationally. High short-term rates have also been viewed as a signal of Reserve Bank action via OMOs and jawboning, to push down inflation and/or strengthen the exchange rate. Inversions are thus a sign of a tight money regime, which accords with the 1995 experience. Others would attribute the very high short-term rates in 1987–1988 to stresses in the financial markets associated with the incipient collapse of large players. All of these explanations seem jointly to have merit, perhaps along with a degree of segmentation between long and short maturity sectors of the market.

The term structure will be revisited in Chapter 7, where we shall consider in more detail the ways in which overseas interest rates impact on local rates. We have to do this, for domestic economic scenarios are increasingly insufficient in themselves to explain movements in either the level of interest rates or the shape of the term structure.

Real Interest Rates

Finally, we will look at real interest rates, which are the nominal rates less the rate of CPI inflation. The idea is that the real interest rates should ideally approximate the real return on physical capital. Nobody quite knows what the latter (the marginal physical productivity of capital) actually is, numerically, but it presumably cannot change all that quickly. So if real interest rates look abnormally high relative to their long run history, this could be a signal that they will drop (i.e. either the nominal rate will drop or – in a less likely scenario – the nominal rate will stay constant while the inflation rate increases). A real rate of return of, say, 10 per cent would be regarded as exceptionally high.

Figure 2.9 portrays recent real rates, both for New Zealand and two of its reference currencies. Figure 2.8A is the real five-year rate and Figure 2.8B is the real 90-day BBR.

Figure 2.9a: Real Long-term Rates: Us versus Them

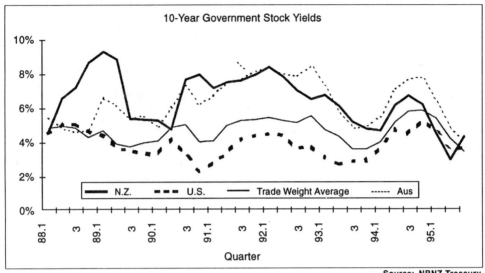

Source: NBNZ Treasury.

Figure 2.9b: Real Bill Rates: Us versus Them

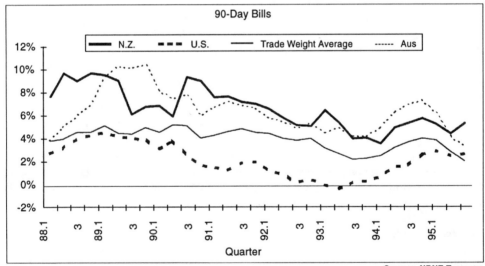

Source: NBNZ Treasury.

2.7   Bond and Swap Trading

After reading the foregoing, you will know many of the ingredients of the fixed-interest recipe.
To make the dough rise, however, you knead some of your new-found knowledge. That requires
further discussion of how in practice dealers and traders do make money – or lose it. A rough sort
of activity classification might proceed as follows:

1. *Broking and Parcelling*

This covers day-to-day activities such as making a market in bonds and living off the bid-ask spreads. Less routinely, parcelling up and retailing off major new issues and repackaging operations such as stripping coupons off government stock.

2. *Basic Speculation*

By this we mean taking more or less simple open positions based on predictions of future interest rates; either overall levels or else movements of yields at some particular maturity. Out and out speculation by private individuals is often done via bond futures, which require a much smaller cash outlay and less registration hassle. But the immense leverage involved does require *huevos*. To be consistently successful at this sort of play is a rare skill. It entails a good understanding of the economic factors that drive interest rates at different maturities. It requires an even better understanding of market sentiment and how other players will react to events.

3. *Spread Trading*

(a) Credit Spreads
   Changes in the credit rating of a corporate or an issue will usually impact on the corresponding bond price. Most major bond traders or fund managers have dedicated credit watchers, who never read a newspaper without a pair of scissors in hand and for whom the very rumour is realisation.

(b) Swap Spreads
   Swap basis trading is essentially making money from changing spreads between the swap rate and the comparator rate, usually taken as the rate on NZGS of a similar maturity. This apparently innocuous recipe in fact amounts to a fascinating witches' brew of market players and their interactions, of which we give here an account that by no means does it justice.
   Suppose that a large bond issue or bunched issues, say $250m or so, suddenly hits the market. It could take place locally, or more probably in the Kiwi Eurobond market (Chapter 7). However, the issuer wants a floating-rate obligation, not fixed. So it arranges a swap with Bank A, whose dealers see it coming but cannot hide. Bank A pays the issuer fixed and starts looking around for another party from whom it can in turn receive fixed. In other words, there is suddenly a large market demand for 'pay fixed'. The problem is that other market players know the situation, having observed the issue. They will want to take a receive position in advance of A, i.e. pinch A's potential payers. If they can do so, they receive, then wait for swap rates (more precisely, margins over NZGS) to drop. The freeloaders will then look to pay at the new lower rate. They have made money from the margin (receive – pay). Poor old A is caught by the dropping rates.
   There may also be a bit of accompanying dynamics from NZGS rates. Swap traders hedge their temporary exposures – until they can arrange an offsetting fixed side – by buying or selling bond futures.[7] As an exercise, you could ask yourself: Would A buy or sell bond futures? What about a freeloading bank B trying to climb in on the action? So there may also be movements in NZGS rates. However, these are not a vital part of our current story.
   At any rate you can see from the above that there are plenty of opportunities both to lose money and make money by trading swap spreads. Woodducks do not survive long.

4. *Riding the Yield Curve*

Shapeshifters are alive to configurations of the term structure that they think are unusual or temporary. The basic idea is to adopt self-financing positions, going long in one maturity region and short in another.

Consider, for instance, Figure 2.10, which is actually an exaggeration of a yield curve shape that developed in late 1995. You will notice that curve ABC has a sag in the middle. This is an unusual shape and you bet that it will not last – you are picking that the yield curve will straighten out, either coming down at the ends (A,C) or up in the middle (B), or possibly a combination of both. As a dedicated shapeshifter you could try to take advantage of the space-time warp in a number of ways.

Figure 2.10: Making Bags from Sags

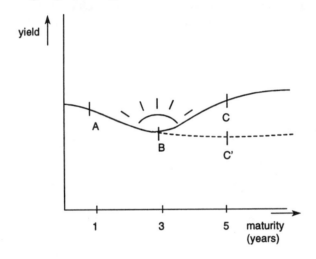

In New Zealand you would probably operate via physical bonds. Suppose you went long in bonds of maturities A and C and short in bonds of maturity B (a butterfly sort of position). Going short means that you sell the bonds without owning them. If a private individual, you will probably accomplish this by means of a buyback agreement – the dealing bank sells you the bonds with an agreement to buy them back, minus their margin, at a later date.

Having taken up such a self-financing position, your profit exposure in terms of yields is some weighted average of ρ_B-ρ_A and ρ_C-ρ_A. Suppose, for instance that the price of bonds at A rises, so that ρ_A falls and the price of bonds at B falls, so that ρ_B rises. Then the difference ρ_B-ρ_A is up and you have won. [What happens, for instance, if the sag presaged a general inversion to ABC?] On the other hand there are plenty of possibilities for this sort of play to go wrong; you might like to figure out some possible adverse movements of the yield curve.

Alternatively, you could – as a dealer – operate via swaps. What would happen if you arranged two swaps, pay at B and receive at A? And finally, much the same sort of thing could in principle be done by operating with bond futures.

The cook's tour just completed has omitted explicit mention of arbitrages. An arbitrage is the opportunity to make money for certain without the outlay of any money: a financial free lunch. Some of the plays we have surveyed come quite close, especially one or two of the swap spread operations. Very temporary opportunities for arbitrage between classes of instrument, e.g. bond futures and the physical bond, can and do arise, but as you would expect, are closed off rather quickly.

By now we should have disabused you of any notion that fixed interest means fixed. There is still a popular impression that hot money is made and lost only on the stockmarket. If anything, the truth is the reverse. To use the description immortalised in Lewis's *Liars Poker*, bond traders are the big swinging dicks of the financial community, with big swinging egos to match.

Notes

1. Here the subscript A stands for 'annual'. Nothing to do with the principal sum A.

2. For mathematicians, suppose you break the maturity (one year, say) up into N subperiods (e.g. N could equal 365 days). Thus the price $P = A/\left(1 + \frac{R}{N}\right)^N$. Now let N→∞, which amounts to finer and finer compounding intervals. Then $P \to Ae^{-R}$. The annual rate would then be recognisable as the rate of continuous compounding or discounting. In such terms, the value of the security described in connection with (2.4) above would be $A \exp(-R \times \frac{a}{365}) \simeq \frac{A}{1+\frac{a}{365}.R}$. So the R in the Reserve Bank formula can be interpreted as the instantaneous rate of compounding, or an approximation to it.

3. For instance, suppose you have two bonds X and Y of the same maturity N, face value A, but one has coupon c, the other 2c. The correct pricing relationship between the two is easily shown from (2.5) to be:

$$P_Y = 2P_X - \frac{A}{(1 +R_N)^N} .$$

If you tried to price Y off the yield ρ (for maturity N), your price would be

$$P_Y = 2P_X - \frac{A}{(1 + \rho)^N} .$$

You would be correct only if $\rho=R_N$; there is no reason to expect this to be the case.

4. Definitely an 'in joke' for geriatrics, this. A 50s–60s ad wherein you were supposed to guess which of the twin young ladies had used Toni on her hair. Uneducated males had no clue – both twins looked exactly the same. Also, please do not write about duration having to be modified duration when measuring interest rate sensitivity. Yes, I know; but we will leave this to the special courses in financial risk management.

5. On this, see Bowden, R.J. and Tiwari, J. (1996), 'True Income Components and the Taxation of Fixed Interest Derivative Securities', *Pacific Journal of Accounting*, in press. The NZFOE also publishes a booklet on taxation advice.

6. Baal-Habal was the original Canaanite (BC 1400) God of fertility and storms. Seems a good sort of deity for the financial markets. For the long history of the subsequent transformation of Baal, see Karen Armstrong's monumental *A History of God*, Mandarin paperback. You should know this.

7. If you are lucky, in the New Zealand market. Often physical bonds are used as hedges, because of the thinness of the futures markets. One problem with this is that you need a lot more capital to buy the physical, diminishing the economic attractiveness of swaps dealing.

CHAPTER 3

THE MONEY MACHINES

3.1   Introduction: The Role of Banks

Banks are a natural starting point in our survey of capital markets players, for they are pivotal in the operations of the financial system.

(a) Collectively, they facilitate the principal payments system of the economy. Indeed, apart from gold dust, cigarettes (in POW camps) and other mediums of exchange, there is virtually no other. Such clearing mechanisms that exist for special purposes are ultimately piggy-backed on bank accounts, and even distrustful pensioners who keep their wealth inside their mattresses generally do so in the form of banknotes created by the Reserve Bank as one element of the banking system. More general and effective forms of money are simply the medium in which banks transfer titles to purchasing power and individuals store it. Thus banks are about money and payments.

(b) Banks are an important financial intermediary. They take in savings from surplus players in the form of deposits and lend out the proceeds to other, deficit players. In doing so they may transform the maturity structure. For example, banks fund mortgages, usually regarded as longer term in nature, from short-term liabilities such as demand deposits, certificates of deposit and wholesale money market instruments. Such maturity transformation is regarded as one manifestation of socially valuable financial intermediation. Whether or not this stylised fact is indeed technically correct and whether its nature or extent has changed over time, is an issue addressed in Chapter 4, section 2.

(c) As an extension of their intermediation role, banks either create or underwrite many of the tradeable instruments that enable funds to slosh smoothly between surplus and deficit units. The leading example is bank bills; another is certificates of deposit (see later). As we saw in Chapter 2, the economic role of banks in the case of bank bills is to attach their guarantee of payment in case the issuer should default; the strength of this guarantee derives from the same sources that underpin the integrity of the payments system. Without that support, short-term funding would cost more than it does – the risk reduction constitutes a form of economic efficiency.

(d) Banks also do lots of other things, generally associated with financial services. The most important of these for our present purposes is to create a market and deal in foreign exchange. Of course, one could regard this as a natural extension of their role in the payments system.

The present chapter is primarily concerned with the payments system and the role of banks therein. Other aspects of banking operations will be discussed in Chapter 4, which considers bank assets and liabilities in more detail and Chapter 7, which is about foreign exchange, a market in which banks are important players. Bank operations as such are not of prime concern to us – for this see textbooks such as Shanmugan *et al.* (1994). For the role of banks and money creation in the macroeconomic system, the reader can consult any macroeconomics text or else books on money and banking. For now, read on.

3.2   The Players

Private Banks

Below is the list of registered banks in New Zealand as at September 1996. (To these we will later add the Reserve Bank.) Two things stand out. First there are now lots of banks, compared with 10 years ago. Second, nearly all of them are majority-owned offshore, as branches, subsidiaries or majority shareholding – the BNZ, for instance, is now a subsidiary of the National Australia Bank and ASB has a 51 per cent shareholding by the Commonwealth Bank of Australia. Indeed, the minnow Taranaki Savings Bank remains the only New Zealand-controlled bank. Some banks on the list are minor in terms of their local operations, but very large internationally, indeed some do not offer a retail operation at all. Four of the older (ignore the formal registration dates) banks account for the bulk of banking business in New Zealand; you will have no trouble in recognising which.

Table 3.1:   Registered Banks in New Zealand as at September 1996

Name	Reg. Date	Country	Banking Group
Multipurpose Banks			
ANZ Banking Group (New Zealand Limited)	1/4/87	Aust.	Australia and New Zealand Banking Group Limited
Bank of New Zealand	1/4/87	Aust.	National Australia Bank Limited
The National Bank of New Zealand Limited	1/4/87	U.K.	Loyds Bank Plc
Westpac Banking Corporation (B)	1/4/87	Aust.	Westpac Banking Corporation
Wholesale Banks			
Bankers Trust New Zealand Limited	21/6/88	U.S.	Bankers Trust New York Corporation
Banque Indosuez (B)	28/3/91	France	Banque Indoseuz
Barclays Bank Plc (B)	7/12/88	U.K.	Barclays Bank Plc
BNZ Finance Limited	23/1/91	Aust.	National Australia Bank Limited
Citibank N.A. (B)	22/7/87	U.S.	Citibank NZ
Primary Industry Bank of Australia (B)	11/5/89	Aust.	Rabobank Nederland N.V.
The Hongkong and Shanghai Banking Corporation (B)	22/7/89	U.K.	The Hongkong and Shanghai Banking Corporation
Mainly Retail Banks			
ASB Bank Limited	11/5/89	Aust.	Commonwealth Bank of Australia
Countrywide Banking Corporation Limited	3/12/87	U.K.	Bank of Scotland
Post Office Bank Limited[1]	11/8/89	Aust.	Australia and New Zealand Banking Group Limited
Trust Bank New Zealand Limited	21/12/89	Aust.	Westpac Banking Corporation
TSB Bank Limited	8/6/89	N.Z.	TSB Limited

1.   Post Office Bank Ltd is a member of the ANZ Banking Group, but operates under a separate banking registration.
(B)   Banks registered in New Zealand as branches of overseas incorporate banks.

Basic source: RBNZ *Bulletins.*

The table represents a snapshot frozen in time; a similar snapshot five years hence will almost certainly not look the same, as some players exit and others merge or are taken over. The 1994 snapshot reflects a major upheaval starting about 1985 in the regulatory system that controlled financial intermediaries; itself part of the financial and economic earthquake that followed the 1984 election. The Reserve Bank Amendment Act (1986) resulted in the liberalisation of bank registration requirements from April 1987. Prior to this time, the establishment of a bank required an empowering Act of Parliament. Now any organisation in the business of deposit taking and lending could become a bank, provided it had also a minimum of $30m in issued capital with at least $15m fully paid up and could satisfy the Reserve Bank that it had good standing and expertise in banking. It could also be a branch of an overseas bank (unlike Australia where until recently the overseas bank had to set up a subsidiary). Within a year of these regulations, 10 new banks were registered. Later events saw takeovers or sales to overseas interests of banks such as the ones referred to above, or the purchase of the Post Office Bank by ANZ. More or less simultaneously with this reform, the government removed (in May 1988) the special status of trustee savings banks, in particular, revoking the government guarantee on their deposits, requiring the trustee savings banks to become incorporated companies, with fewer restrictions on their areas and modes of operation. With similar reforms to building societies and other deposit taking institutions, the aim was to create a level playing field on which all financial institutions could compete for deposits and offer loans and other services.

On the face of it, opening up the banking sector to foreign competition did indeed promote competition. Bank margins, calculated as net interest (on loans, minus on deposits) fell steadily from about 1990 onwards from about 3.2 per cent to 2.7 per cent, only rising again from mid-1994. Simultaneously the sector as a whole shed about 4,000 staff, the entry of new banks notwithstanding. And the steep rise in problem loans from 1989 could itself be regarded as a manifestation of competitive pressures to lend on what were in retrospect not the best of projects and purposes, a fallout also from distortionary internal incentive schemes for bank staff. However, a more precise treatment of bank profitability and competition remains to be accomplished. It could be noted, for example, that the decline in the interest margin was very small relative to the steep decline in market interest rates over the period 1990–1994; so that bank margins, as a proportion of the interest cost to borrowers, in fact soared. Be all this as it may, the geomorphology of banking changed abruptly from 1987 onwards. Later on we shall look at other regulatory changes, in connection with such matters as bank prudential supervision and monetary control.

The Reserve Bank

The Reserve Bank of New Zealand is not an old institution and not even original. It dates from 1933, whereas an earlier central bank, the Colonial Bank of Issue, briefly arose and fell from 1850–1856. Like most if not all central banks the RBNZ has two primary responsibilities, connected (i) with the issue of money and monetary control and (ii) with the prudential supervision of banks. From time to time, central banks – and the RBNZ is no exception – have encompassed other objectives and other operations. However, the combination of the deregulatory changes from 1984 and an explicit piece of legislation, the Reserve Bank Act of 1989, have pared the role of the RBNZ down to the two functions given above, plus a few other bits and pieces such as the issuing agent for government stock and a certain amount of registry activity. These latter roles are covered in other chapters; here we consider in detail only the monetary and prudential supervision aspects.

The most public side of the 1989 Act (which was effective 1 February 1990) concerned the conduct of monetary policy. The effect of the Act was to assign priority in conducting monetary policy to the control of inflation; prior to this, the Bank was required to encompass other objectives such as employment or growth. Under the 1989 Act, the success or otherwise of

RBNZ policy actions was rendered more unequivocal by being expressed in terms of the rate of inflation. The Minister of Finance, in conjunction with the Governor of the Bank, fixes and announces to the public a numerical inflation target over a five-year horizon. Currently the policy target is a range of 0–2 per cent inflation in the consumers price index. Allowances are made for extraneous or exogenous influences such as changes in individual taxes, in the terms of trade, local body changes and also interest rates. (Actually interest rates are far from exogenous!) Indeed, these 'allowances' have given rise to the publication by the Bank of two distinct inflation series: 'headline' inflation, which is the inclusive figure and 'underlying' inflation, which removes the effects of interest rates and exogenous shocks of the kind just mentioned. The policy targets agreement can be altered by Order in Council, in which case new policy targets have to be announced within 30 days. Otherwise, however, once in place the PTA gives considerable autonomy to the Governor in the conduct of monetary policy; far more so than prior to the Act, when responsibilities were divided, unclear and often gave rise to acrimony in the relationships between the Reserve Bank and other sources of policy advice such as the Treasury. The current PTA is reproduced as the appendix to this chapter.

Prudential Supervision

We shall return (Section 3.4) to the monetary policy issue in some detail. Less central to our present purposes but nonetheless of considerable practical importance, is the other principal role for the RBNZ, namely the prudential supervision of banks. Just prior to the Act, the government decided (March 1989) to implement – through the RBNZ – the Basel (Basle) Committee's recommendations on bank capital adequacy, in this respect confirming supervisory practice established from 1985 onwards by the RBNZ itself and followed in many other countries around the world. The Basel Committee's prescriptions start with the definition of two 'tiers' of capital:

Tier 1:   ('core') capital which comprises items like paid up ordinary shares, nonrepayable share premium account, general reserves, retained earnings not specifically earmarked, non-cumulative irredeemable preference shares; and minority interests in subsidiaries conformable with the foregoing;

Tier 2:   ('supplementary') capital, consisting of items like term and perpetual subordinated debt, asset revaluation reserves, cumulative or limited life redeemable preference shares, mandatory convertible notes and general provisions for doubtful debts.

Generally speaking, Tier 1 capital carries no redemption obligations, creates no fixed charges and is not earmarked for specific projects or assets. Tier 2 capital does carry obligations of one kind or another, but these can be deferred. A further subclass of Tier 2 capital is created that must not exceed 50 per cent of Tier 1 capital.

The basic idea is that the banks must keep Tier 1 capital to at least four per cent of its risk weighted assets and the combination of Tier 1 and 2 to at least eight per cent. Risk-weighted assets are established by applying the following weightings:

0 per cent	Cash and short-term government securities
20 per cent	Loans to other banks, local authorities
50 per cent	Loans against residential mortgages
100 per cent	Commercial lending.

A more precise treatment of the above can be found in textbooks on banking or in the notes to bank annual accounts. Thus a bank can be all gung-ho in attracting retail deposits but this may not be too much use without further capital augmentation.[1]

In addition to formally implementing the Basel recommendation, the 1989 Act set the tone and boundaries of current Reserve Bank supervision. Thus another strand established prudential limits: on overnight foreign exchange exposures (not more than 40 per cent of capital); on exposures to a single borrower (not more than 35 per cent); and limits on how much a bank can lend to its owners. Further requirements related to accounting and auditing requirements; the RBNZ monitors these together with an overview of internal controls and liquidity. A later (1991) provision in the aftermath of the DFC collapse required the banks to inform the RBNZ when their exposure to any one sector of the economy exceeded 10 per cent, with an upper limit of 35 per cent. The Reserve Bank also has general powers to investigate a bank's affairs and can recommend the appointment of a statutory manager if doubt as to solvency has arisen.

A more recent guideline statement by the Reserve Bank (December 1994) represents something of a change in the philosophy of bank supervision. While some formal limits such as the eight per cent capital adequacy are retained, the general thrust is towards requiring maximum public disclosure of a bank's financial affairs, certainly of key indicators such as capital adequacy ratios or credit ratings, but encompassing also statements about large or related party exposures. More controversially, the guidelines called for disclosure of interest rate risk in each maturity bucket. The banks regard this as commercially sensitive information. The Reserve Bank has agreed to allow more time to work these objections out of its new disclosure regime, which will be introduced in late 1996.

The general idea of all this is that public disclosure is a source of financial discipline in itself. The Reserve Bank would remain in the background unless a general or 'systemic' threat emerged to the entire banking system, if necessary even allowing the doubtful bank to fail. It has often been supposed that the Reserve Banks of both Australia and New Zealand underpin commercial banks with formal guarantees. This is not the case. Recent history has shown that local banks can and do fail. The proper role of the Reserve Bank is to forestall failure as much as possible, and where it occurs, make it as painless as possible for the depositors of the bank and to prevent any systemic threat.

3.3   The Payments Mechanism

Money

Table 3.2 shows money and credit aggregates for the New Zealand financial system. On the most elementary level, note the distinction, sometimes fudged in the popular press, between 'money' and 'credit'. The former refers to means of payment, the latter to loans or instruments of borrowing. In this chapter we shall mainly be preoccupied with the left-hand column, referring to types of money.

The items totalling to M1 in the left hand column constitutes the narrow – and technically more correct – definition of money. 'Money' can itself be divided into (i) 'high-powered money' or the 'monetary base', which consists of notes and coin and settlement balances held by the banks with the Reserve Bank and (ii) demand deposits held by the public at the banks. Other more embracing definitions of 'money' really refer to liquidity. Thus the items M2 and M3 add in balances held by the public in the form of deposits at call with other financial institutions and term deposits held with the banks as well as other financial institutions. The M1, M2, M3 hierarchy can be regarded as reflecting degrees of liquidity. In former years, policymakers paid a great deal of attention to these monetary aggregates, often going so far as to extend monetary targeting – the idea that M should not grow faster than a preassigned rate – to the more inclusive definition of liquidity instead of just M1. Monetary targeting is less fashionable now, but remains essential in regimes of high inflation, where one of the first

Table 3.2:   Money and Credit Aggregates, June 1995

Money Supply[1]	$Millions	Credit Aggregates	$Millions
Notes and Coins held by the Public[2]	1,341	**Claims on Private Sector by:**	
		M3 Institutions	88,166
Total Transaction Account Balances[3]	10,058	Other (Reserve Bank)	2
		Less Inter-Institutional Claims	8,024
Less Inter-Institutional Transaction Balances	35		
Less Government Deposits	18	**Private Sector Credit**	**80,144**
		Marketing and Stabilisation[4]	1
M1	**11,319**	M3 Institutions[5]	5,134
		Reserve Bank[6]	2,139
Total Other Call Funding	21,181	Coins in Circulation	171
Less Other Call Inter-Institutional Funding	1,894	**Domestic Credit**	**87,889**
M2	**30,606**	**Net Overseas Assets of:**	
		M3 Institutions	-7,916
Total Term Funding	50,898	Reserve Bank	296
Less Inter-Institutional Term Funding	8,482	**Net Other Assets of:**	
Less Government Deposit	1,088	M3 Institutions	-5,887
		Reserve Bank	-835
		Inter-Institutional Discrepancy[7]	-1,614
M3	**71,934**	**M3**	**71,934**

1. Institutions covered are the Reserve Bank, registered banks and other M3 Institutions.
2. Notes and coins on issue from the Reserve Bank minus until money of all M3 Institutions.
3. Balances that are subject to chequing and/or 'EFT–POS' facilities and/or in sweep accounts.
4. Reserve Bank advances and discounts to marketing organisations plus export credits, less marketing stabilisation deposits at RBNZ.
5. M3 Institutions' holdings of government securities (book value) less government deposits
6. Reserve Bank holdings of Govt. securities (book value) and N.Z. coin plus advances to the state, less Govt. deposits
7. The difference between M3 funding and M3 claims; this discrepancy may be caused, for instance, by timing differences and items in transit.

Source: *Banking in New Zealand*, Reserve Bank of New Zealand, updated.

prescriptions is to restrict the expansion of the money supply. Even in such interludes, however, the target should more correctly be formulated in terms of M1, the actual means of payment.

In particular, close attention and control should be devoted to the high powered component, the monetary base. The inflationary problems arise when the government funds its expenditure programme by borrowing from the central bank. When this happens, the settlement accounts of the banks grow, because the central bank is the government's banker, so cheques drawn by the government and deposited by recipients into the private banks result in transfers from the central bank to the private bank settlement balances. These funds represent bank resources against which they can proceed to lend. By a multiplier process involving lending and the redisposition of lending into banks, the new reserves are 'multiplied up' into new demand deposits (see any elementary macro textbook for the details). The collective extent of this multiplying up process is limited only by the amount of reserve that the banks wish to keep on hand as settlement balances with the Reserve Bank. This amount is sensitive to interest rates (for exactly which interest rates, see below), which means that there is not a mechanical 'reserve multiplier' translating reserves into demand deposits and M1. Nevertheless, for the government to finance its expenditure programme by borrowing from the Reserve Bank is potentially a dangerous expedient. The money so created represents an injection of 'outside wealth', in the sense that the private sector discounts or ignores any potential future tax obligation arising from the necessity or desirability of repayment of the government's loan (an 'anti-Barro' position, this). Expansions of high-powered money are as near as one can get to dropping money from helicopters. It is no accident that all the great inflations of the past have been associated with this form of public financing. Milder inflations have sometimes been associated with the expansion of high-powered money in other forms, such as the gold discoveries of the nineteenth century.

The Payments System

The predominant form of private payment in our society is the transfer of demand deposits. Hitherto this has usually been done in the form of cheques. In current MICR technology, the recipient bank passes the cheque through a magnetic reader, at which stage an operator also adds to the account information the value of the cheque. The encoded information as to account and amount is passed to the paying bank. So is the cheque itself. The snail-mail character of the latter requirement, i.e. to physically move the bill of exchange, slows the whole clearing process down enormously and moves are afoot to amend the relevant legislation (Bill of Exchange Act 1908) to enable electronic clearing. In the meantime, note the growing popularity of EFT-POS, which accomplishes the same thing directly; about 15 per cent by value of all demand deposit debits are of this character. Apart from the convenience of direct clearing, there is clearly less risk of default than with conventional cheque clearing.

Other forms of settlement are associated with special purposes and players. *Austraclear*, which is run by the Reserve Bank, is a settlement system for money market securities; members include banks, dealers and other financial institutions. Transactions are confirmed when both buyer and seller enter identical details into the system. Settlement takes place at about 4.30 p.m. on the same date, following confirmation by the buyer's bank. The four major banks also have a dedicated system used to settle the New Zealand dollar leg of FX transactions, called KITS (the 'Kiwi Inter-bank Transfer System'). Settlement is overnight or weekend. In other chapters we shall look at the settlement process for special markets such as the futures and stockmarkets; these are not really monetary clearing mechanisms.

Inter-bank Settlement Processes

The above covered how banks transfer their depositors' funds from one bank to the other. Now we come to consider how banks settle up the surpluses or deficiencies among themselves that will arise on a day-to-day basis. The starting point is the flow of notified debits generated by the MICR technology (or EFT-POS, etc.). These are recorded by a data processing company (ISL Ltd, actually owned by the banks), operating under the auspices and rules of the New Zealand Bankers Association and at the end of the day – actually well on into the evening – a net figure is arrived at for each bank that is a member of the clearing system, against every other member bank. At this point the system goes to sleep for the night. In the morning, the net differences will be settled by transfers between *Bank Settlement Accounts*, which are the balances in special accounts held at the Reserve Bank. Such balances do pay interest, but currently at only 65 per cent of the 180-day bank bill rate, so they are not in themselves profitable. However, they cannot be in overdraft. If a bank's settlement pool balance will otherwise be negative, it has to find reserves from somewhere and this is expensive. Hence there arises a motivation to keep reserves on hand in the form of the settlement account with the Reserve Bank and this is in itself a brake on the lending process referred to earlier. However, it is time to look in more detail at the whole settlement and reserves process and all the wheeling and dealing associated with it, for this process is intimately bound up with interest rates and the whole business of monetary control.

Good Morning New Zealand!

By 7 a.m. a bank's cash dealers will be on the job. They will know the extent to which the bank's exchange settlement account is in the red. Indeed they may have had an inkling the previous afternoon and if so might at that time have attempted to borrow on the overnight cash market. However, this morning is here, they are in the red and they need exchange settlement cash. First recourse is to ring up their counterparts in other banks, to find out whether they are in surplus and would be willing to lend. The Reserve Bank has to be informed of such interbank lending or borrowing of reserves. However, it is quick and relatively painless – extortionary rates are not charged, if only because even cash dealers have memories. All interbank transactions should be completed by 8.45 a.m.

If a bank cannot obtain sufficient funds from other settlement banks – for example because the system as a whole is in deficit – then they must get the funds from the Reserve Bank itself. They must sell ('rediscount') Reserve Bank bills back to the Bank. Only Reserve Bank bills with 28 days or less to run are eligible for the discounting process. The rediscount window is open from 8 a.m. to 9.20 a.m. Such purchases are in multiples of $1m and settlement can be by Austraclear if the bank is a member. It should be completed by 9.30 a.m. It is by setting the price at which the bills are bought (the 'rediscount rate') that the RBNZ can set the tone for short-term interest rates in the economy as a whole.

Final settlement of the exchange settlement accounts follows when the Reserve Bank has confirmed the settlement pool figures and the interbank borrowings and lendings. A final cash position will be shown on the dealers screen ('RBZA' for Reuters, '39971' for Telerate). It should be noted that all this above activity, though taking place this morning, is for value the previous day, preserving what is otherwise a technical factor – that the banks' settlement accounts are not allowed to be in deficit as the result of any day's activities.

With all the settlement scurrying done, cash dealers can then devote their whole attention to chasing overnight deposits from cash-surplus corporates or financial institutions, or loaning it out to deficit units. The money market settles down to thoughts of lunch.

The Government Float Tender

Although the government runs a day-to-day account with one of the commercial banks, the Reserve Bank is the government's primary banker and the daily flows of government payments and receipts out of and into the Crown Account, are therefore also flows of reserves into and out of the banks' exchange settlement accounts. They constitute a wildcard that the Reserve Bank has to neutralise. On a day-to-day basis it does this by advancing one-day loans to the banks, for value the previous day. These are advanced on an unsecured basis up to specified limits; security is required for advances in excess of these limits. The unsecured basis is a special feature of the government float tender arising from the 'unforecastability' of government payments and receipts, so far as the banks are concerned.

Between 7.30 and 7.50 a.m. the Bank announces on screen the amount available for tender; this represents the government revenue deposited to the public account the previous working day, adjusted for transactions that have no liquidity impact. The Banks' cash dealers bid for an amount and an interest rate. The minimum interest rate acceptable is 90 basis points below the RBNZ one-day discount rate (for which, see above). Bids are allocated in order of descending interest rates and the overall results appear on traders' screens by 8.15 a.m.

Note that the government float tender should not be confused with the tendering process for government securities, which is also run by the Reserve Bank. For details of this, see Chapter 2.

Real Time Gross Settlement

The description earlier given for the inter-bank settlement process describes the system as of the time of writing (late 1996). By early 1997, the banking system is expected to implement a new clearing system called the 'real time gross settlement system' (RTGS). The essence is that the Reserve Bank will be able to move settlement cash between paying and receiving banks' exchange settlement accounts in real time, as and when the underlying customer transactions occur. The '7 a.m. washup' might therefore lose much of its force, or even vanish altogether. For some details, see the article by Helen Walshaw in the September 1995 *Treasury Note*.

In general, a real time clearing system has a number of advantages. Perhaps chief among these is a reduction in systemic risk to the banking system. As the system now works, a given bank could at some particular point be in hock to the other banks for $2b or so, simply because of the 'lumpy' character of inter-bank flows. By the end of the day such large one-way positions almost always net out to a much lower net indebtedness, to be dealt with the following morning. However, if a bank fails, the clock stops dead at a particular moment of history. Suppose it was at that moment when the failing bank owed the rest of the system $2b! A real time system should help to prevent such scary systemic scenarios. It should also enable corporate treasurers to access quicker value for their transactions. As yet, experience still has to be acquired in the operations of the RTGS.

3.4   Monetary Control

The settlement mechanism as described in §3.3 is the medium through which the Reserve Bank implements monetary control. Generally, monetary control can operate via one or both vectors: (a) the amount of money in circulation and (b) interest rates. Recent policy emphasis has shifted away from (a) (monetary targeting), in favour of (b). However, quantitative restrictions on the money supply are certainly present, on an ongoing basis. This is indeed implicit in constraints on the obtainability of reserves in the form of cash settlement accounts. For instance, only a limited supply of Reserve Bank bills is available for discounting. Currently only two tenders, of fixed amounts, are offered in any week and the 28-day rule for discounting further limits the effective amount available for discounting. Availability constraints of this kind, however, are all a bit academic; the system would have to be down by an awful lot before everybody tried to rediscount all their eligible Reserve Bank bills!

Control of the amount of money on issue is also implicit in the Reserve Bank's *open market operations* (OMOs), which are part of the overall liquidity management operations of the Bank. It can enter the money markets to buy or sell Treasury bills. If it buys T-bills, its payments for the bills are ultimately credited to the banks' exchange settlement accounts, while if it sells bills the banking system loses cash. The Bank also operates sellback agreements, which are effectively loans secured against government securities (usually T-bills); this is indeed the preferred medium for cash injections.

An ongoing function of OMOs is to smooth out fluctuations in high-powered money. For instance, if a net flow of cash from the government is expected over the coming week, the Reserve Bank will step in and sell T-bills by tender on the Tuesday to offset the forecasted flow. Other sources of variation that must be neutralised if the Bank is to achieve its settlement cash target ($20m) are settlements on other government stock or bill tenders, changes in the demand for notes and coin, voluntary Reserve Bill discounting by the banks and FX transactions by the Reserve Bank. Thus if the Bank forecasts a net cash injection of $50m for today and yesterday's closing cash balance was $10m, then OMOs will sell $40m worth of securities, leaving a targeted $20m for cash remaining in the system. In general, the Reserve Bank invests significant resources in the cash forecasting business and takes pains to let the market know these forecasts. Figure 3.1 is a sample contrast of net cash injections (NPSI) with the neutralised cash position (NCI), showing that the investment appears to be worthwhile.

Figure 3.1:   Keeping the Patient Calm: Liquidity Management Operations

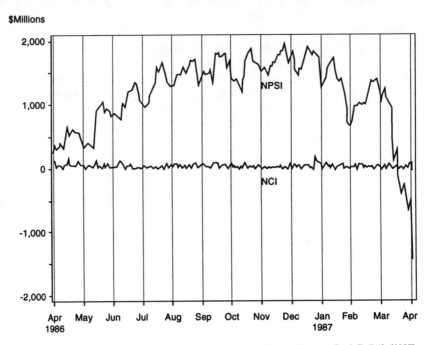

Source: *Reserve Bank Bulletin* (1987), vol. 50, no.3.

Interest Rates

The obverse side of monetary quantity is the level of interest rates. If banks find themselves short of settlement cash and have to front up to the Reserve Bank's discount window, they can expect to take an interest rate penalty (about 0.9 points above market cash rates). Even the prospect of such shortages can create anticipative behaviour in which banks compete actively for cash, either on the overnight market or else by selling T-bills or bank bills on the open market. The result of any or all of these actions is higher short-term interest rates.

In principle, several policy actions are available to the Reserve Bank if it should decide that a firming or easing is necessary:

(a) OMOs based on T-bills, especially in accepting or rejecting bills in the new issue process;
(b) Changing the supply of Reserve Bank Bills by new issue, buying back or by deciding not to resell previously discounted Reserve Bank bills back to the market;
(c) Changing the discount margin (–) or the rate paid (+) on settlement cash;
(d) Changing the cash settlement target;

(e) If supply of cash is involved, changing the mix between outright purchases of Reserve Bank bills and sellbacks, which are loans using bills as securities. (The former is usually regarded as more restrictive in nature.)

In practice, however, basic policy settings such as the cash target or discount rate are only rarely altered. An exception was a significant lowering of the overnight cash target in mid-1995, from $20m to $15m, on the 11th August and then to $5m on the 25th. In general, OMOs are used more as a means of achieving a cash target fixed and known in advance, than of forcing banks to conform to a new cash target, in line with the Bank's policy of encouraging informational certainty rather than uncertainty in the market. Policy measures (b) and (e) are sometimes used as a signal to the market that the Bank is not entirely comfortable with existing monetary conditions. One is left with the most frequent policy measure as:

(f) Jawboning, or Open Mouth Operations (OMOOs).

The idea here is that statements by the Governor or other senior Bank staff are extremely influential in the market. Market players react to the apprehension of further policy (say) by bidding up cash or bill rates. In doing so they obey the behest of the Reserve Bank without any overt actions by the latter. The markets sneeze when the Reserve Bank says they should have a cold.

3.5   Policy Games

It is probably fair to say that with the demise of active fiscal policy in recent years, the burden of short-term economic policy has shifted onto monetary policy. Moreover, the nature of the monetary policy has changed, away from the explicit targeting of monetary aggregates towards the control or attempted control of interest rates. And the goals of policy have themselves changed – at least in emphasis – towards a primary preoccupation with inflation and only secondarily with a concern for other indicators of economic welfare such as the employment rate. Thus the inflation/interest rate nexus is seen as central. Into this nexus the NZD exchange rate enters both in the role of an economic indicator of likely inflationary pressures and, in the form of the real exchange rate (see Chapter 7), as an important economic price with employment implications. Although other economic indicators do from time to time enter into the thought processes of the Reserve Bank and other policy initiatives, their impact on financial markets is ultimately vectored via the reality or apprehensions of one of the three panic buttons of New Zealand financial policy, namely inflation, exchange rates and interest rates, the IER nexus.

It could be said that the objective (target) is an inflation rate in the range 0–2 per cent; the instrument is interest rates; and the primary indicators are inflationary expectations, on the one hand and the NZD exchange rate on the other. According to conventional market wisdom, the Reserve Bank establishes from time to time a 'comfort zone' for the exchange rate, primarily the trade weighted index, for which see Chapter 7. Expectations – at an unchanged policy setting – for the exchange rate are in the comfort zone if they are consistent with the policy targets for inflation, bearing in mind that a depreciation of the exchange rate is a stimulus, via the cost of imports, to consumer price inflation. If the exchange rate is in danger of falling out of the comfort zone, then the Reserve Bank will act to raise short-term interest rates which also acts directly on the demand for non-tradeable goods, which also appear in the CPI. As we saw in §3.4, interest rate policy is usually vectored through OMOOs.

Expectations of a weakening of the exchange rate could either reflect concerns about the causal effect of internal inflationary expectations produced by a state of excessive internal demand, or on the other hand could reflect rises in overseas interest rates. The NZD might weaken on both counts. Hiking up short-term interest rates could fix both problems, the former by dampening down domestic economic demand and the latter by making it more attractive to hold NZD denominated securities. Either way, the direction, at least of policy action based on interest rates would be clear.

Implicit economic modelling of this kind is built into market anticipations and behaviour and governs reactions to economic events not formally part of the IER nexus. Consider, for instance, an impending announcement of the current account figure in the New Zealand balance of payments. Such announcements are ticked off as dates to watch in the dealing room calendar. The market will already have formed a expectational range for this forthcoming figure. Market players will also have a simple economic model wired into their neural circuits, interpreting the current account figure in terms of the IER nexus. A larger than expected current account deficit would be taken to indicate a state of excess demand in the economy and potentially a threat to the exchange rate. Dealers would be anticipating Reserve Bank action in such a contingency. So, the current account result is published and it is worse than prior market expectations. Cash and other fixed interest dealers immediately move on to the defensive, bidding down the price of bills and driving up the cash rate. They do this not necessarily on the immediate expectation of any economic consequence of note, but instead on apprehensions of Reserve Bank toughspeak (OMOOs), or even on apprehensions of Reserve Bank action (OMOs, etc.)

For the primary motivation of the market in such circumstances is not the pursuit of economic rectitude but to save ass. The object is to predict market behaviour and market prices. To this end commonly agreed interpretations and apprehensions acquire imperative force. Because the Reserve Bank's behaviour is thought to be widely understood and predictable, its pronouncements acquire a driving force in the market. It is, on the face of it, remarkable that Reserve Bank OMOs, which concern just a few million dollars, could drive a market in short-term securities that is many times larger; and even more remarkable that the mere threat of OMOs, cash targets and other policy actions could have the same effect. Truly a case of a small tail wagging a large dog.

Note

1.   A common error in bank simulation games played by students at the University of Waikato.

CHAPTER 4

Deposit-taking Institutions and Related Intermediation

4.1 Introduction

The previous chapter on banks and payments did not consider bank balance sheets and what they represent in terms of financial intermediation, so we shall have to look at this in more detail; in doing so we shall also touch on certain off balance sheet items and functional roles. Thus the present chapter returns to banks, but treats less miraculous aspects, regarding the banks as more or less ordinary financial intermediaries, rather than Iscarii (sorry, J.R.R.) stewarding the operations of the monetary system.

As the focus has shifted on to financial intermediation in general, we shall look at other important players, at least part of whose role is concerned with intermediation: the Merchant Banks (aka Investment Banks), Finance Companies, Credit Unions, Building Societies and Life Offices and Superannuation funds. [We could have gone further and considered cash management trusts or even investment trusts of various kinds, but this is enough.] As we shall see, legislative changes accompanying deregulation have directly or indirectly caused dramatic changes in the business volume and/or modus operandi of these institutions. The desire to create a level playing field that characterised much of this legislation has seen the untrammelled forces of competition shift deposit taking and lending business towards the banks, leading the other deposit-taking institutions either to become banks themselves, or else to attempt a sharper definition of the services they offer. So far as savings (more generally than just deposits) are concerned, the same desire not to discriminate among different forms of savings has whittled away certain advantages held by superannuation funds, which have also diminished in importance.

Although we will be dealing here with all sorts of DTIs, it is important to see the wood rather than just the trees. Why do such institutions exist? Such financial intermediation has several angles: all of them represent economic value added by the role of institutions in achieving what primary agents cannot do for themselves, either individually or collectively.

(a) *Maturity transformation.* If surplus units mainly want to lend short in the form, say, of demand deposits – but deficit units want to borrow long, then the DTIs can take advantage of the fact that not all depositors will want to withdraw their funds at the same time and thereby achieve the required maturity mismatching, more or less as a statistical artifice. There is, however, another sense of the word 'maturity' that deals with the more technical concept of the *duration* of assets and liabilities. In this sense, the maturity mismatching is more problematical – see section 4.2 below.

(b) *Contract tailoring.* The DTIs can easily tailor any specific borrowing requirements – interest payment basis, length of the loan, principal repayment provisions (credit foncier, balloon, etc.).

(c) *Risk enhancement.* The latter word refers to making things better, in this jargon. Credit risk is the big thing here. If I, as a surplus unit, lend out my meagre capital in a block, a default will wipe me out. Spreading default risk by dividing up my capital into $1 loans makes no kind of transactional sense. Nor do I have the informational capability to adequately *monitor* the credit risk; perhaps I could buy insurance against it, but at what cost? DTIs solve all these problems as a matter of course. They are big enough to be able to spread credit risk over economic-sized loans and also to spread monitoring costs over a large number of loans. And hopefully they are big enough and smart enough to hire risk management experts.

Indeed, the success of banks in handling credit risk enables them to offer guarantor facilities in their own right, as when a bank accepts a commercial bill. This is a day-to-day function that attracts public attention only when the unthinkable occurs and a bank is in danger of collapsing through lack of public confidence. Paradoxically, the ructions associated with such collapses are a measure of the economic value associated with banks (and some other DTIs) in their normal day-to-day operations.

There are other sorts of risks faced by DTIs: liquidity risk, which refers to the possibility that you have to be able to meet calls of various kinds; interest rate risk, which refers to the income or valuation effects of interest rate changes (both in the level and shape of the term structure); and exchange rate risk. As well as handling these, the DTIs should be big enough to take advantage of general diversification risk, which means that you can switch your portfolio to any optimal proportions between different classes of assets to achieve any desired stochastic profile for your overall portfolio return; as between, say, expected return and variance as a risk measure.

Some of the angles (a)–(c) are effectively invisible on superficial examination (which is what we are limited to here). Other aspects, such as portfolio diversification, will be readily apparent in what follows. All the above kinds of economic function and enhancement are dealt with more or less on an ongoing basis by financial institutions. Indeed, their financial management, in both precept and practice, is light years away from once upon a time. That is why there are entire courses and diplomas devoted to financial institutions management and related areas.[1]

4.2   Banks Again

Table 4.1 is a balance sheet for a New Zealand bank (for reasons of space we could not list them all, so we chose this one because of the degree of detail provided in its 1994 annual accounts). You will see many of the assets and liabilities that we have already treated under monetary mechanisms or else in the work on fixed interest. Note the relatively minor assets component 'Central Bank balances', reinforcing our early remarks about tails wagging dogs in the monetary control context. Although the bulk of the bank's assets are loans and advances, roughly matching its retail deposit liabilities, the bank is also heavy in cash and liquid securities. The distinction between 'trading' and 'investment' securities is widely made in New Zealand financial institution accounts and refers to a tax-driven maturity distinction. It does not seem to have any real economic basis.

Table 4.1:   New Zealand Bank Balance Sheet

Assets		$000
Cash and short-term moneys		239,576
Cash on hand and in transit	3,468	
Central Bank balances	11,097	
Balances due from other banks at call	142,328	
Money market placements	82,683	
Trading securities		919,437
New Zealand Government and local authority securities	47,924	
Treasury bills	169,515	
Reserve Bank bills	54,686	
Bank bills and certificates of deposit	518,367	
Other trading securities	128,945	
Investment securities		439, 170
New Zealand Government and local authority	348,757	
Other investment securities	90,413	
Net loans and advances	6,357,386	
Properties intended for sale	14,868	
Investments in associates	519	
Future income tax benefit	10,765	
Fixed assets	145,703	
Other assets	68.376	
	8,195,800	
Less general provisions	(27.760)	
Total assets		8,168,040
Liabilities		
Deposits		7,486,659
Retail	6,207,837	
Negotiable certificates of deposit	411,328	
Balances due to other banks	20,223	
(excl. negotiable CDs)		
Other money market deposits	847,271	
Other liabilities		136,834
Accrued interest payable	67, 111	
Accounts payable	60,723	
Provision for dividend	9,000	
Loan capital		77,238
Shareholders funds		223,358
Revenues		243.951
Total liabilities and capital resources		8, 168,040

Source: Trust Bank, 1994.

What about maturity transformation? As remarked on several previous occasions, it all depends on what you mean by maturity, Here we shall interpret it in the more technical sense, concerned with duration, a measure of the time that you are locked into a security before you can adjust its interest rate.[2] If you are locked in, a general increase in interest rates will sharply diminish the value of your assets. In fact, most bank mortgages in New Zealand are floating rate, as are most bank liabilities. On the face of it, this means that banks do not really engage in much maturity transformation (in the technical sense) and also that they should be reasonably protected against interest rate shifts. They make their money by means of margins between rates on assets and rates on liabilities. As yet we do not (to this author's knowledge) have a scientific treatment of how bank margins vary with interest rates or with the business cycle generally, although various informal accounts exist.

Having said all this, let us undo it. In fact, a lot of the important action in bank balance sheets takes place off it. Chief among the off-balance sheet items are interest rate swaps. Suppose an adventurous bank wanted to take an interest rate position; it thought, for instance, that interest rates were going to fall. It could enter into swaps where it received fixed and paid floating. The net effect of this – to the extent that it was done – would be to replace the floating interest rates on its assets (on balance sheet mortgages) with fixed rates. However, the rates on its deposits are still floating. So it has generated a mismatch. The bank's value will rise if interest rates do fall across the board, but it can be badly burned if it gets the direction wrong.

Should banks take open positions of this kind? We do not answer that one. However, it is obviously of importance that bank treasuries have expertise and senior management and the Board the rudiments in interest rate and FX risk management. Among the securities industry, bank stock analysts should also be aware of such a dimension. The problems with a bad or underperforming loan book have received massive public exposure. A good bank stock analyst should also understand the rudiments of interest rate risk management and the potential for things to go wrong. The annual accounts of banks should contain enough information – in particular a maturity breakdown of assets, liabilities and swaps – to enable such judgements to be made, even if they are back of the envelope in character.

At any rate, back to the financial intermediation. We have seen that the verdict on maturity transformation is mixed; it is partly a matter of definition and partly a matter of operation. What about other intermediation angles? Most New Zealand banks are heavily into home mortgages, which are statistically pretty bombproof. Even though the odd loan will fail here and there, there are many of them and most homeowners are reliable bets. The historical problems have arisen where a heavy component of bank lending has been concentrated into just a few large developments or to finance takeovers or other share market plays; or where lending has been concentrated in a particular industrial (including agriculture) sector. Most New Zealand banks have learned the diversification and other lessons of the eighties well in respect of lending. However, their interest rate risk management can be critically viewed in one or two cases.

4.3   Building Societies and Credit Unions

These are co-operative deposit-taking institutions, governed by their own acts: the Building Societies Act 1965 and the Friendly Society and Credit Unions Act 1982, respectively.

(a) New Zealand *Building Societies* are 'permanent societies', as distinct from the older 'terminating societies' which were essentially devices to recycle members funds into loans on a lottery basis and are now prohibited. They are funded by shares, deposits and a smaller amount of debenture stock, primarily less than one year in maturity. Shares are operationally just as ordinary redeemable deposits, although they rank in security as an equity share. Security apart, the only time things get interesting in this respect is where the building society is taken over or converts into a bank. The 'deposit shares', if we can call them that, are also title to the accumulated reserves of the Society and those who treated them merely as passbook deposits lost out if they closed their accounts or ran down their deposits before such changes. They had in effect undervalued their deposit shares. Building Societies also have ordinary deposits of various kinds, ranking ahead of share deposits in security. Generally, they rely heavily on retained earnings for capital. On the assets side, the predominant activity is residential mortgages and a lesser amount of other types of lending: personal loans, farming and commercial mortgages. They also run a variety of other services, not of concern to us here.

The collective assets of New Zealand building societies have sharply diminished from $2.8 billion in the late eighties to only $800m at the end of 1993. This is at least partly because some large building societies converted to banks in the late eighties.

(b) *Credit Unions* are small in total assets (not more than $150m collectively) but large in number (about 150, at last count). You can see from this that the typical credit union is a rather small co-operative associated with a place of work or some interpersonal association. The latter provides their funding base in the form of demand and time deposits, on much the same security and equity basis as building societies. Although some of the larger credit unions are flourishing, they are reportedly concerned at the onerous burdens placed on their (honorary) directors and administrative staff by legislative developments such as the Privacy and Financial Reporting Acts of 1993 and a Justice Department requirement for prospectuses to be lodged every six months.

Possessed of an interesting history, both building societies and credit unions are now financial minnows and look set to remain so. They do not have economies of scale on their side. They may, however, retain a competitive niche that ultimately derives from the co-operative principle.

4.4 Investment Banks

The titles Merchant Bank and Investment Bank are virtually synonymous. The former is the earlier designation, while the latter term is a more recent import from the U.S., so far as naming is concerned. The key difference is probably historical[3] in nature: merchant banks were primarily concerned with commercial bills and trade finance, while the expansions of advisory and other fee-based activities, underwriting and securities trading have been viewed as the hallmark of investment bank activity. Other writers have viewed the key characteristics of investment banks as a willingness to trade in the financial markets on their own behalf, i.e. as principals. The naming issue is hardly worth bothering about: of the 30 companies listed as investment banks and the 26 as merchant banks in the 1994 New Zealand Business Who's Who, 10 appeared on both lists and very possibly more might have appeared if they had thought about it. In deference to current usage we will use investment banking to cover all of them.

In general financial history, merchant banks evolved from the activities of merchants of stature who started adding their name to trade bills, increasing their tradeability to investors with surplus funds. From there it was a short step to start holding the bills themselves as an investment and funding them from short-term deposits, or else simply to make a market in the bills, on-selling them to other investors and living off the margin. Thus evolved the commercial bill markets and the deposit-taking behaviour of the investment banks. In recent times commercial bills have largely been superseded by bank bills, for a number of reasons – uniformity of credit risk, liquidity and simple legislative opportunity. Nonetheless, the type of activity – taking in short-term deposits and onlending them or else using them to trade – has continued to flourish, with a recent impetus from the world of takeovers, mergers, project finance and other fee-based activities. In New Zealand, as in Australia, investment banks owed much of their expansion to controls implied on trading banks back in the regulated era. For example, trading banks were unable to offer short-term interest-bearing deposits (see Chapter 1).

Investment banks typically have very short-term deposit books, with the single biggest tranche placed at 24-hour call. Most lenders are individual companies with temporarily surplus cash; some investment banks can source their funds from trading bank owners or shareholders, an obvious advantage. They operate from a relatively low capital base and rely on high volume turnover with low margins.

Although they may be for terms of up to five years, the typical financing facilities from a investment bank have short durations, in the technical sense of frequent adjustments in the interest rate. The loan will have regular rollovers, at which the interest rate can be changed, generally off a benchmark such as the bank bill rate plus a margin, depending on the customer and purpose. Moreover the facility may contain an option to convert the advance into a bill of exchange (the 'bill option'). Under this arrangement, the borrower draws a bill which the bank has previously agreed to purchase; the bank accepts the bill when it is drawn (recall that acceptance means giving a guarantee). When the bank exercises the option, the borrower has technically repaid the loan to the bank, but of course remains liable to whoever owns the bill. The merchant bank can, if it wishes, now sell the bill, or alternatively pledge it as collateral to investors who require security. Either possibility is beneficial in balance sheet terms. For a detailed treatment of the bill option, see Skully *et al.* (ibid., ch. 1.4, pp. 195–197).

Investment banks offer a number of other market-related activities.

(a) They arrange and underwrite promissory note issues, syndicated funding and other types of debt issue for private and public borrowers;
(b) They have treasuries that generate margin and other income by buying and selling fixed-term and FX-based instruments. You will find some of these players listed in the fixed interest chapter and elsewhere;
(c) They advise on mergers and takeovers, a major source of fee-based income in recent years. They can also underwrite new stock on fixed interest issues;
(d) Like finance companies, they may be involved in lease finance, on much the same terms as to risk;
(e) They may offer advice and arrange project finance, which sometimes involve novel risk-sharing arrangements between borrowers and private lenders;
(f) They may lend on property of various kinds, including real estate developments, using their expertise in risk management to protect themselves against the funding mismatch problem and the credit risk entailed. As with leasing, creative financing can see tax benefits from the project passed through to the investment bank.

You will find further reference to the activities of investment banks in the chapters on fixed interest, FX and elsewhere.

4.5   Finance Companies

Finance companies actively raise funds from the general public via deposits, secured debenture stock and sometimes unsecured notes, on terms varying from at call to five years. Their borrowing is covered by trust deeds and supervised by trustees. On the assets side, funds are generally lent to finance hire purchase sales, leasing, general working capital needs for industry, physical capital and property. They continue to hold significant quantities of government and local authority securities as portfolio diversification, even in the post-deregulation era.

In recent years, finance companies have faced stiff competition from banks, with a sharp decline in their share of overall loans and advances in the economy. There has also been a niche rearrangement, perhaps as a consequence. Thus while the more traditional breed and spectrum companies continue to exist, other companies have specialised. For example, dedicated areas may cover corporate, import, export, commercial real estate, car, mortgage, personal or inventory finance; leasing or hire purchase and debt factoring (buying receivables); security, commercial bill or wholesale money market dealing; shipping or rental services; and financial services relating specifically to the motor, rural or health care sectors. In respect of the latter, the companies may be set up as the financing arm of industrial or rural activities; for instance, Fisher and Paykel Finance or Toyota Finance have obvious parentage. Elders Rural Finance belongs to New Zealand Rural Services Ltd. Other finance companies are owned by banks: National Australia Finance belongs to the NAB; UDC Finance Ltd to ANZ and AGC to Westpac.

Generally speaking, finance companies operate in the higher end of the risk spectrum in their lending and charge accordingly. They have smaller loan sizes than banks, concentrate on secured lending and often provide point-of-sale finance through third parties. Deregulation has thus seen the finance companies settle into what seems to be an equilibrium niche, even if not nearly as large in terms of market share as hitherto.

4.6 Life Offices and Super Funds

Though not quite so obviously deposit-taking institutions, the life offices are channels of saving so we shall treat them here as financial intermediaries. As well as offering traditional insurance products like whole of life or endowment policies and their cover, the Life Offices were – and still are – heavily involved in offering and managing superannuation schemes. Because of the long-term contractual nature of this business, the life offices were one of the few institutions required even in the post-deregulation era to continue to hold government securities as a sort of reserve ratio; legislative requirement is for at least $500,000 in market value, deposited with the Public Trustee. Like the banking sector, the New Zealand Life Insurance and related business is heavily concentrated, with the six largest companies (AMP, National Mutual, Colonial Mutual, NZI, Tower Corporation and Prudential) writing 75 per cent of the life business and together with the state schemes (Government Super Fund and National Provident Fund), controlling most of the super business.

Superannuation funds were casualties – wounded but not fatally – of tax changes announced in 1987. Super scheme members could no longer make tax deductible contributions, employee contributions were now taxed on fringe benefits; and the investment income earned by life offices was to be taxed. The basic idea was to bring super schemes into line with other savings plans that did not have the benefit of tax advantages. The extra tax revenue – about $800m – was jolly nice for the government, but the initial fallout saw five per cent of all super schemes terminated and an estimated $500m in terminations or lost sales. The value of retirement super schemes declined from $11.6b in 1985 to $11.0b in 1991. Accompanying these changes was a movement away from defined benefit schemes, where the fund or employer promised on signing up to meet specified payout levels, to defined contribution schemes which are simply a fancy way of saying that you get out no more than what you put in, plus earnings and minus fund expenses and taxes.

The net result of all this was a shift in comparative advantage away from the life offices to the emerging unit trust movement (see Chapter 5). In many ways this was a good thing, for it frequently amounted to a kind of unbundling. People could now make up their own personal portfolio of investment classes, of life insurance types, or of management expenses, rather than having to accept a single package covering the lot.

4.7   Before and After Snapshots

Figure 4.1 is a revealing comparison of loans and advances from various classes of financial intermediaries, between 1984 (with deregulation just getting under way) and 1995 (with the shakeout more or less complete). Similar sorts of figures would result had we portrayed deposit or other common liabilities. Evidently the level playing field legislation has resulted in a major shift of the financial centre of gravity as between different classes of institution.

Figure 4.1:   Market Shares Before and After Deregulation

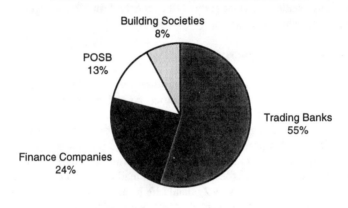

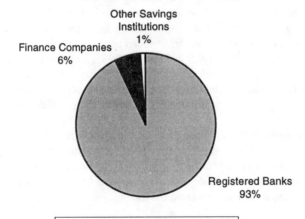

Notes

1. Nor does the above list exhaust all the economic value or potential of DTIs. Their size often enables general economies of scale in operations. Together with the large number of 'clients' they serve, this also allows 'economies of scope'. This expression looks like trendy managerial gobbledygook and possibly is; it refers to the idea that by some sort of association your depositors may also be interested in your investment trusts or even your life insurance policies as offered by an associate or subsidiary. One-stop financial shopping and so forth. (Hmm ...).

2. Suppose you have a series of cash flows $c_1, c_2 ...,$ to which you are to apply a discount factor ρ. The value of the cash flows is then

$$V = \frac{c_1}{1 + \rho} + \frac{c_2}{(1 + \rho)^2} + ... = v_1 + v_2 + ... \quad , \text{ say.}$$

The (Macaulay) duration is then

$$d = 1.\frac{v_1}{V} + 2.\frac{v_2}{V} + 3.\frac{v_3}{V} + ... \quad .$$

In other words, d represents a weighted average of the times to receipt of the cash flows, with the weights as the proportion of total present value attributable to the cash flows. A better measure is Fisher-Weil duration; which uses zero coupon rates $R_1, R_2 ...$ instead of ρ [see Chapter 2 for the distinction]. The importance of F-W duration is that if your portfolio of cash flows has weighted d=0, then the portfolio is immunised against parallel shifts of the term structure curve (i.e. its change in value would be zero).

3. Culture corner: can you name a prominent and tragic Shakespearian merchant banker? Who was his client, what was the transaction and what was the default penalty?

Chapter 5

Equities

5.1 Introduction

This chapter will be principally concerned with ordinary shares of public companies; in other words, titles to ownership of companies and participation in dividends and other forms of distribution (bonus or rights issues, capital dividends and the like). It should, however, be noted that other forms of equity scrip exist that have similar characteristics as to tradeability and privacy, such as units in investment or property trusts. We ought also to mention preference shares, which have characteristics of both equity and debt. Moreover, some forms of debt carry entitlements to convert to ordinary shares. Thus there are no hard and fast distinctions to be made between equities and other forms of security, at least from the point of view of pricing, tradeability or security.[1] Instead, the New Zealand Stock Exchange currently lists all sorts of securities as well as ordinary shares: preference shares of various kinds, equity warrants; and debt instruments such as convertible notes, capital notes, unsecured notes, debentures, equity options, instalment receipts and miscellaneous registered or bearer bonds. It also lists some overseas securities, mainly equities. However, there is quite enough to study in respect of common or garden type equities, so apart from a brief historical note on preference shares, we shall limit consideration in the present chapter to ordinary shares, or to titles to funds that invest in such shares.

Although the share market has not seen the deregulatory upheavals of other markets, the last 15 years or so have certainly witnessed some notable milestones and events. On the legal front perhaps the most important development has been the introduction in April 1988 of the imputation regime for company dividends, according to which dividends in the hands of taxpayers have franking credits, i.e. they can be set off against tax paid on other personal income, provided they are paid from income on which company tax has already been paid. Effectively it means that dividend income is free of personal income tax for most resident taxpayers. This ended a longstanding whinge about the 'double taxation' of dividends. On the institutional front we have seen developments such as the introduction of screen trading by the New Zealand Stock Exchange and improved arrangements for off-market transfer of stocks run by private registry managers. The stockmarket crash of October 1987 entered economic history, as did the collapse from over-gearing and other causes of some high-profile investment trusts and companies in the aftermath. Perhaps such changes and events are part and parcel of a deregulation era, effected by the same causes and affected by the deregulatory changes themselves. Moreover, there is continuing public debate about the proper role of the Securities Commission and associated regulatory legislation of the securities market (in respect of such things as insider trading, takeover offer provisions, etc.), so that matters are still far from settled as far as the environment for equities is concerned. Nevertheless, we are – perhaps temporarily – in calmer waters than at the start of this decade.

5.2   Generalities: Pricing and Return

Suppose that an ordinary share is priced at P_0 at the start of this period and will be priced at P_1 at the end of the period. It will also pay a dividend D in the hands of the receiver (ignore tax for the moment). The return r on the stock is then defined by

(1) $(1+r) P_0 = D + P_1$.

[For simplicity we have ignored the transaction costs (in New Zealand, brokerage; in other countries also stamp duty on the transfer) that would have been incurred, had this been an actual transaction, buying the share at P_0 and selling it at P_1]. Now suppose that we are at the start of the period and we do not know what D or P_1 will yet be. We cannot therefore compute an actual return. However, we can take mathematical or subjective expectations of both sides of (1). As P_0 is known, $E P_0 = P_0$ and we can recast (1) into:

(2) $$P_0 = \frac{ED + EP_1}{1 + \theta} \quad ,$$
           where $\theta = Er$.

In this guise, the return equation becomes a pricing equation. The term Er is reinterpreted as a *required return*. Given the perceived riskiness (measured, say, by their estimated standard deviations) of the unknown D and P_1, investors will require a rate of return θ and therefore be willing to pay P_0 as defined by (2); they discount the expected payoffs for D and P_1 by means of a rate of return θ that incorporates their attitude towards risk. The influences that might determine θ are discussed further below.

Thus we have two equations of importance: an ex-post return equation (once we know D, P_1) and an ex-ante pricing equation (in which we do not). Both these equations can be developed a little further.

Returns and Indexes

Reconsidering equation (1), D could be taxed in the hands of the holder (if, say, dividend imputation did not hold for some reason). So, too, could the capital gain implicit in P_1 versus P_0 if the holder was a short-horizon sharetrader – in other countries the capital gain would automatically attract capital gains tax. In that case we would simply redefine r, applied to the post tax D and price gain, as a *post tax* rate of return. We could also get a *real* rate of return by deflating D and P_1 by the CPI at time 1 relative to time 0.

A more general way of looking at equation (1) is to note that the value of the investment at the end of the period is $V_1 = D + P_1$, compared to the value at the beginning $V_0 = P_0$. The rate of return r is then defined by

(3) $1 + r = \dfrac{V_1}{V_0}$.

We can see immediately the real rate of return idea. If the rate of inflation is π, say, then V_1 has value only $V_1 / (1+\pi)$ in period 0 dollars, so that the real rate of return (r_* say) is obtained from

$$1 + r_* = \frac{V_1}{(1 + \pi) V_0} = \frac{1 + r}{1 + \pi} ,$$

or approximately $r_* = r - \pi$.

Equation (3) is useful for other purposes. As well as dividends, companies can also distribute value – or just windowdress – by means of bonus issues, rights issues, capital dividends and other forms of capital changes. These should also be factored into the return. Leaving it as just dividends and end of period price would be grossly misleading if, say, the company split its shares into two during the period! Handling such charges with the V formulation is easy, at least in principle. You simply reinvest all proceeds, real or implied, back into the shares and compare end of period value with beginning of period value.

Suppose, for instance, that the company announced a stock split: for every share you had you now have two. Of course, the price should (theoretically) drop to half. But this change would not affect the value of your end-of-period holding V_1 at all, so that r is unchanged. Or to take a harder example, suppose there is a one-for-three rights issue. This means that for every three shares you hold you receive the right to buy another one at a stated price, which is usually below the market price. The right therefore has a value and indeed rights are generally traded in the period before the subscription is due. To get the true return including the right, we imagine that the right is sold and the proceeds used to buy further shares of the company at the ex-right price. Thus V_1 is augmented by the implied proceeds of the right, leading via equation (3) to the correct definition of the holding period return. In such V computations, note that all these imaginary transactions should be self-funding – in the above example you would not physically subscribe to the new shares, as this would involve you stomping up extra capital. Instead you generate your own capital by selling off the rights.

Measured or statistical returns generated in the above way form the basis of *accumulation indexes*, which represent an attempt to measure the wealth-generating effects of shareholding correctly. The rate-of-return measure can be multiperiod. To get V_N after N periods, we imagine that all the dividends $D_1, D_2 ... D_N$ are reinvested in the stock. The augmented stock holding then has value V_N at the end, being the final number of units times the price P_N. The geometric average rate of return – the one usually employed – is then defined by

$$(1+r)^N = \frac{V_N}{V_0} ; \text{ or } r = \left(\frac{V_N}{V_0} \right)^{\frac{1}{N}} - 1 .$$

An equivalent statement is that if we start with V_0 and invest it compound at rate r we should end up with V_N. Accumulation indexes are sometimes also used to generate true returns from holding bonds – you reinvest each coupon as it is received by buying further bonds at the price then ruling. This is the correct way to compare stocks and bonds as investments.

Benchmark Returns: CAPM and So Forth

Stocks on portfolios of stocks are often judged in terms of just two dimensions: their average returns (μ, say) and their standard deviation of returns (σ say). The idea is that high average or expected return μ is good, but is often accompanied by high variance (σ^2), which is bad, as investors prefer a quiet life. By combining stocks into portfolios in various proportions, you can engineer a portfolio of any desired μ and σ within the limitations of what you can achieve from the given set of underlying stocks. Figure 5.1 shows the kind of thing you might achieve from just three stocks (marked as × on the μ, σ diagram). The shaded area represents the possible combinations of expected return and standard deviation you could achieve from portfolios made up of stocks A, B and C.

Figure 5.1:   Feasible Portfolios and Efficient Set

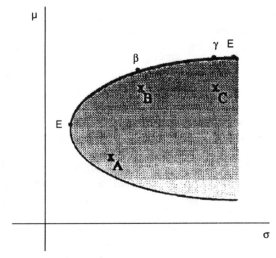

The dark shaded frontier EE is the *efficient frontier*, as it represents the achievable portfolios that maximise expected return μ for any given σ. You will note that by combining stocks you can do much better than the stocks themselves. For instance portfolio β is better than security B because it has better expected return for the same 'risk' σ; similarly γ is better than C. We will come back to the efficient frontier in various contexts.

Returning to just a simple stock, in order to judge its performance we need some kind of benchmark. It is not sufficient to judge it simply by its historical average return, because it might have wobbled around an awful lot – had a high variance. Looking ahead to potential investment in this security you would like the high expected return (just judging on the past) but you would not like the high anticipated variance (σ).

One idea is to measure the performance of the stock by the return $\frac{\mu-\rho}{\sigma}$; here μ and σ could be either the ex-ante (expected) average return and standard deviation respectively, or the historical estimates and ρ is the risk-free investment rate (the bank bill rate, say, if your horizon is short or, more problematically, the government bond rate, if it is long). The trouble is that the standard deviation σ is not necessarily a very good indicator of the stock's risk. This looks odd, in terms of earlier remarks. The trick is that you could get a stock with a high σ that was nevertheless very valuable in the context of an overall portfolio. How could this be? If its return was negatively correlated with most or all of the other stocks in your portfolio, this would tend to mean that in hard times, when those other stocks might perform badly, the stock in question would tend to perform well. So it acquires value from its covariance properties with other stocks, or with the market in general.

This is the basis of the famous CAPM model of Lintner, Meckling and Sharpe. The value does not quite stem from its covariance, as mentioned above, but from its regression coefficient on the market, $\beta = \sigma_{rR} / \sigma_R^2$, where r is the stock's return, R is the return on the 'market portfolio'; $\sigma_{rR} = \text{Cov}(r, R)$, and $\sigma_R^2 = \text{Var}(R)$. Given its beta, the stock should be priced so that its ex-ante expected return μ is given by

(4) $\mu = \rho + \beta\,(ER-\rho)$,

where ER is the expected return on the market and ρ is as above, the risk-free rate. Thus if its beta was negative ($\beta < 0$) because $\sigma_{rR} < 0$, you should have the stock being priced so that $\mu < \rho$. You would be prepared to pay a premium for the stock, so that it would yield even less than the risk-free rate. Of course, this would be nonsense if you were simply holding such a stock by itself. It is not nonsense in a portfolio context. Such a stock would be an extreme version of a 'defensive' stock. An 'aggressive stock' would be one for which $\beta > 1$. Such stocks are procyclical with respect to the market. Consequently they attract a pricing penalty – recently in a higher yield, relative to the risk-free rate, by a fraction of the 'market risk premium' (Er-ρ).

Empirically, there is little question that the historical fit of the CAPM model to observed returns data is just awful. Indeed the author knows of no correctly formulated statistical test, either at home or abroad, that has ever accepted the CAPM hypothesis. Does this mean that the theory is a disaster ('CAPM is dead', etc.). Not necessarily, for several reasons.

(a) The underlying portfolio theory is formulated in terms of the ex-ante ('before the event') investor knowledge about expected returns and covariances of returns. The empirical fit is based on estimates of expected returns and covariances generated from past observed returns. Even then, the expected returns must not be simple historical mean returns, but must represent the best predictors of future returns – a bit more complicated. At any rate, *ex-ante* and not ex-post return distributors. Not the same thing.[2]
(b) It might be that many or most investors are simply in error in their portfolio selection. Or that some use better information than others.
(c) Technical conditions such as constraints on short selling, the latter a vital part of the CAPM theory. (Indeed there are such constraints – a common one is that you have to deposit the short-sale proceeds plus a security deposit with your broker. This affects the market portfolio.)
(d) And in spite of all, CAPM cannot be dead because we have no other decent theory of the benchmark, usable for such purposes as obtaining a discount rate for capital budgeting.

There are other theories of the benchmark. For instance the APT (arbitrage pricing theory) represents a rather similar idea, where pricing penalties can arise because stocks are exposed to distinct common factors (such as an exchange rate or macroeconomic factor). A nice idea, but its empirical performance is even more dreadful than CAPM.

5.3   The New Zealand Stock Exchange

The buying and selling of equities entered in the technological gee-whiz era in 1991, when the traditional open cry pit with its chalk and blackboard props were superseded by a national computerised screen trading system. Trading is now carried out by entering offers and bids at terminals in the broker or trader's office. At about the same time, technology finally caught up with the share transfer and accounting processes, starting in 1988 with broker to broker accounting

(BBA), from which exchange members could service their day-to-day obligations and extended in 1992 with electronic transfer of securities, the FASTER system. We will look at some of the details of these operations shortly. They have clearly expedited the trading and settlement of securities.

In doing so, we may question how far they have also improved the economic function of the market, which is to act as a discovery point for the value of companies. This role may not entail much physical turnover at all – theorists sometimes imagine a world in which, following some news event, prices are bid up to reflect the fresh information with not a single security changing hands. Perhaps the big difference is in the creation of a single national market, in which a broker in Eketahuna, were there such, would be on a similar informational and executional footing as far as the trading process was concerned as would his counterpart in Auckland. (Of course, his informational flow may continue to be deficient in ways associated with nice lunches, golf games and other informal exchanges.) If this is so, then one could say that the new trading processes have allowed informational deepening and therefore a larger pool of potential traders. It may also be that the trading execution process, which is more orderly, means that no potential bids are inadvertently missed; or that potential offerors or sellers among the traders have a greater window of time and opportunity to register their bids and offers and have them executed.

The NZSE is owned by its members, with a Board of Directors as the governing body. Its operations are regulated by the Sharebrokers Act Amendment 1981, which came into effect in 1983. The 1981 Act, which replaced the Sharebrokers Acts of 1902 and 1908, also created the NZSE itself, from a collection of four regional Exchanges. Two sorts of rules come under the purview of the Act: (a) the *business rules*, which govern the operations and procedures of the Exchange; and (b) the *listing rules* which impose requirements on companies that wish to list or remain listed – information disclosure, voting rules, takeover rules, directors' duties and board composition, nature of business and so forth. Following a landmark case (NZFP v. NZSE 1984), the consensus of legal opinion is that the NZSE rules have the status of contract law, but not much more. This, in spite of a requirement under the Act that the rules be approved by Order in Council and gazetted. In other words, the public interest does not extend to an interpretation of the rules as statutory law, or even to their subjection to general administrative law, which might be expected to arise from an interpretation of the Exchange as a public body. The NZSE is free to vary the listing rules, even as to a matter of private contract with specific companies. This in turn has caused disquiet as to a possible clash of the public interest with the interests of the Exchange itself and its members in expanding business, or holding on to its existing listings where a large company may decide to list offshore instead.[3]

The Trading Mechanism

The general sequence of events in screen trading for equities is as follows. A customer places an order with his or her broker listing the company, the desired number of shares and any limit as to the prices he is prepared to pay or accept. The broker enters the details into the computer terminal, highlighting the company and inputting an offer price and quantity. Orders at the same price appear on the screen in a queue with latest last. The resulting screen might look like this:

| Ports of Auckland | | | | | |
| BUY | | | SELL | | |
Broker	Quantity	Price	Price	Quantity	Broker
ACCS	500	213	214	2T	ORDW
CVLA	1T	213	214	500	JSWA
AMSA	1T	212	215	5T	BWCA
FRAA	10T	211	215	20T	AMSA

As you can see, there is no action going at these bid or offer prices. Suppose, however, that broker ORDW dropped their sell price to 213. Trades with ACCS and CVLA, in that order, take place and ORDW is able to offload 1,500 shares.

For ordinary trading, orders must be placed in minimum quantities:

Price	Min. Q
0.25c	2000
shares	
26.50c	1000
51c– $1	500
$1– $10	100
$10 +	50

Smaller lots are referred to as odd lots and specialist odd lot brokers will buy these up at the going market price and combine them into marketable parcels. In former times there could be a price penalty for oddish lots, but this is now not the case, so that if one sold 1,599 Brierley shares the same price would be obtained for the total number of shares.

Apart from odd-lot brokers, there are no other specialists. Large overseas markets such as the NYSE often have specialists in certain company stocks or types of stock, who stand or 'make a market' in the stocks, buying and selling on their own account to do so. Such specialisation is not a feature of the New Zealand scene. In general, liquidity tends to be rather spotty, with only the largest companies constantly traded. Table 5.1 ranks companies by market capitalisation and gives corresponding trading volumes and rankings for 1994. Such tables will always change: the CCH volume, for instance will look a bit different for 1995, following the acquisition of a controlling interest by International Paper. However, note the very large influence of Telecom, both on the Top 10 (32 per cent of capitalisation) and on the Top 40 (24 per cent by capitalisation). This ought to give one pause in the use of NZSE indices: market views about just one company can significantly influence the indices and swing derivatives defined on the back of such indices. Other stocks can be only thinly traded. From the observational point of view, one should in many cases be a bit cautious about interpreting the price published in the newspaper as being current going prices for the stock and in research, studies on returns or prices, 'thin trading corrections' should be considered.

Table 5.1: The Top 10 Swingers, 1994

Company	31/12/94 Market Capitalisation ($bn)	% Top 10	1994 Value shares traded ($bn)	Ranking of trades
1. Telecom Corp. NZ	9.636	31.8	1.975	1
2. Carter Holt Harvey	5.411	17.8	1.503	3
3. Fletcher Challenge (non forestry)	5.386	17.8	1.774	2
4. Brierley Investments	3.003	9.9	1.055	4
5. Goodman Fielder	1.664	5.5	0.172	12
6. Lion Nathan	1.462	4.8	0.551	5
7. Air New Zealand A ordinary*	1.008 }	5.8	0.172	13
B ordinary	0.761 }		0.187	(10)
8. Wilson and Horton	0.881	2.9	0.524	6
9. Trust Bank NZ	0.728	2.4	0.122	18
10. Fernz Corporation	0.682	2.2	0.214	9

* The ordinary ordinary Air New Zealand shares are the B shares. The A shares have to be owned by New Zealanders and traded in New Zealand

(Source: NZSE *Review of Trading*, 1994)

The Settlement Process

After the screen transaction is consummated, a contract note is sent to the buyer requesting payment, while the seller is sent a security transfer form, which is returned together with the share certificate. When the latter arrives, the selling broker enters the documents into FASTER using a client inward transfer to the share registry manager, electronically transferring the shares to the broker's transfer account. The broker-to-broker accounts (BBA) claim of delivery initiates the transfer of shares from the selling broker to the buyer broker, with the corresponding payment between brokers made through the stock exchange settlement system. BBA sends a broker to broker transfer to the share registry, which automatically transfers the shares between the broker. Finally the share registry system prints new certificates and delivers them to the new shareholder on receipt of the client outward transfer from the buying broker. Figure 5.2 illustrates the whole process.

Figure 5.2:   FASTER Flow Diagram (courtesy NZSE)

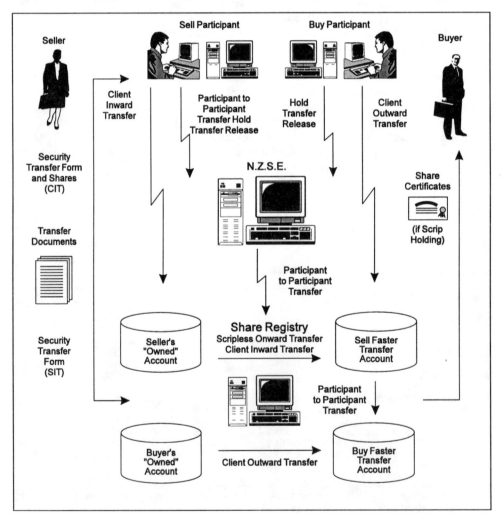

Market Indexes

The most widely quoted index of stock market prices is the NZSE-40, which has a base value of 1,000 as of 1 July 1986. Stocks entering the Top 40 index are selected on the basis of their market capitalisation (i.e. number of shares on issue times their current price). The weights in the index are based on capitalisation. The index composition is reviewed every quarter, at which time the average market capitalisation over the previous six months is used to obtain the weights as well as the stocks that enter the index.

The NZSE-40 comes in two forms, a capital and a gross index. The capital index is not adjusted for dividends and incorporates only the capital value of the shares to holders. End-of-day prices relative to opening prices are used to obtain a weighted proportional price change for the day and this is applied to the previous days' index to obtain the index as of the close of the current day. The gross index, on the other hand, does allow for dividends, capital changes and other payments to shareholders, as well as changing prices. It therefore corresponds to an accumulation index, as described in §3.2 above. Notice that the capital index might therefore be affected by the stock of a very large company going ex-dividend.

The capital index is the one generally referred to as 'the' NZSE Top 40 index. In August 1995 the NZSE-10 replaced the Top 40 index as the physical basis for share index futures (Chapter 6) on the New Zealand Futures and Options Exchange. Such a development will certainly project the Top 10 index into the limelight a little more. The NZSE publishes many other indices. The NZSE-30 Selection Index applies to the Top 30 companies with the largest capital available to small shareholders, computed by 'removing' large shareholders, defined as those holding more than 30 per cent of the issued share capital. In a joint venture between the New Zealand and Australian Exchanges, the trans Tasman 100 index was introduced in early 1996; the index includes 13 New Zealand stocks. The general idea is to 'unify' the Australian markets in the eyes of offshore investors. The Exchange also prepares 21 sectoral indices for different industrial classifications. The property index, in particular, is often used to proxy the real estate market. Finally, there is the small companies index, NZSE-SCI, of potential interest to market inefficiency experts and others.

5.4   Floats, Mergers and Takeovers

New or original equity can be raised in several ways. The precise technicalities and legal aspects will not concern us here, but origination has a role to play in capital markets, so that a brief coverage is in order. New equity can originate in company floats, bonus issues and rights issues. Starting with the latter two, *bonus issues* in their simplest form entail giving existing shareholders additional shares on a pro-rata basis. Such issues are essentially a formal capture by shareholders of company reserves and represent a way of creating formal capital at a stroke; often used as a consequence in takeover defenses. Sometimes bonus shares are issued as part of a dividend reinvestment plan. *Rights issues* enable the company to actually raise funds for investment, etc. by offering new shares to existing shareholders. Typically these are issued at a discount. The holders can elect to either subscribe or else to sell the right to subscribe by the specified date. The theoretical value of a right is just the ex-right price less the subscription price, adjusted by the number of rights needed to buy one share – thus for a one-for-five rights issue you would have to divide by five. Rights are an important investor reward and are often quite liquid securities on the NZSE during their brief life.

Floats (New Issues, IPOs)

Floating a company, i.e. public, is a long story we cannot do justice to here. The process starts with preparation of a prospectus, which must conform to a format and contain specified information: it must contain an investigating accountants' report and provide details of any special shares or derivatives, property to be purchased from the proceeds, particulars of all material contracts entered into in the preceding two years, benefits paid to promoters and information about the nature of the proposed activities and the purpose of the issue.

A second decision is whether to have the issues underwritten. The underwriter, or underwriting panel, generally large sharebroking companies or investment banks, agrees to purchase any shortfall at the issue price. The nature of the implied insurance against under-subscription to the issue will depend upon any 'outclauses', which specify circumstances that will let the underwriter off the hook; things like a general stockmarket crash. Underwriters charge for the risk involved. In the Telecom float, for instance, the underwriting fee was 3½ per cent. Add to this brokerage fees (1½ per cent or so) and the glossy sharemarketing campaigns and the costs of flotation can be pretty considerable. They typically range between 1.2 per cent to six per cent of the issue value. An additional implied cost is a $75,000 good behaviour bond with the NZSE, required to enable the Exchange to investigate any future regulatory breaches.

Not included in the above is a further hidden cost: the *underpricing of IPOs*. A considerable amount of overseas research work has shown that there is a fairly consistent tendency for the issue price as set by the company and agreed with the brokers and underwriters, to undervalue the company, in the sense that when finally listed on the Stock Exchange, the stock sells for a premium over the float price. This has been confirmed for New Zealand by Cheung *et al.*,[4] who showed that from 1979 to 1991 the average excess return earned by investors who subscribed at the offer price and sold at listing was 28 per cent. Various hypotheses have been advanced to explain this, not all of them terribly convincing. In the New Zealand case, it may simply be a reflection of the very large premiums (100 per cent or so) that occurred during those extraordinary 1986–1987 years.

All in all, it seems that the new issue process is economically not all that efficient. The underpricing of IPOs violates market efficiency, which says that the prices of all securities should on the average correctly reflect all available information; or in the present instance that the float price should represent a rational (unbiased) prediction of the listing price unless good reasons can be found otherwise. And the various costs involved in the float process seem at times to be extreme, leading one to consider whether the interests of future shareholders have been adequately accounted for.

As one might expect, floats are pro-cyclical. When the sharemarket is buoyant, the new issues float on the wave. Apart from this aspect, there is a constant change in the listings on the NZSE as companies come and go, overseas companies list or delist and debt or derivatives appear or disappear. Truly Heraclitean[5] in nature.

Share Buybacks

It might be apposite at this point to mention the mirror image of share issues, which are buybacks of some of its outstanding shares by the company itself. Share buybacks became legal under the Companies Act 1993 and one or two companies have since moved to either buy back shares or announce an intention of doing so. The practice is very common in the U.S.; for example Coca Cola bought back 2½ per cent of its issued shares in 1995 and is expected to buy back a further two per cent in 1996. In terms of basic corporate finance theory, share buybacks should not alter the market value of the firm; and indeed in the absence of corporate taxes, a buyback financed by the issuance of debt should not even alter the price of the firm's remaining shares. The most common motive appears to be to signal to the market that management thinks the company is undervalued. Sometimes buybacks are used as a defense against hostile predators – the company can compete with the raider and any debt used to finance the buyback may act as a further disincentive.

A useful piece of jargon: 'Treasury stock' is the name given to shares bought back but not cancelled by the company. This can be quite a cheap way of subsequently raising capital, as the stock can be sold without the need for a prospectus. In general, tax and other matters arising in respect of buybacks can be quite complicated.[6]

Privatisations

A substantial volume of new tradeable equity originated in the late eighties and early nineties with the privatisation of former state-owned enterprises (SOEs) which in turn represented an earlier (1986) commercialisation, and in some cases splitting, of nine government corporations. By the end of 1992, 15 SOEs or significant parts thereof, had been sold for a total of $11.3b: they were the Bank of New Zealand (47 per cent), Petroleum Corporation, New Zealand Steel, Development Finance Corporation, Post Bank, Shipping Corporation, Air New Zealand, Rural Bank, State Insurance, Synfunds, Gas Supply Contract (Maui Gas), Government Printing Office, exotic plantation cutting rights (56 per cent), Telecom, and Housing Corporation mortgages.

Many issues of principle were involved in public asset sales of such magnitudes, but the only ones considered here are those of underpricing and efficiency of the issue process. Even this is not as simple as it first appears. Partly this is due to the somewhat tortuous events surrounding the issue process in some cases (e.g. Petrocorp). Partly it is a matter of the difficulty in valuing an enterprise that had not hitherto operated in a fully commercial way – some operations subsequently showed very substantial profit growth and share values. Considering only the immediate listing impact of the public component of the offerings, the experiences of underpricing or otherwise seems to have been mixed. The Petrocorp public offer for 75m shares was oversubscribed at $1.25 and listed on August 1987 to close at $1.75 at day's end, representing an underpricing of 33 per cent, slightly more than the Vos and Cheung average quoted earlier, but of course still suboptimal. The Air New Zealand public float was issued at $2.40 and listed at $2.75, which represents good pricing. In cases such as Telecom, both the public float and listing came after initial institutional tendering, so that it is rather difficult to judge the precise extent to which the initial sale price to those institutions represented underpricing.[7] Whether any general tendency to underpricing existed for the sales and floats of SOEs remains an interesting exercise in economic history, one with perhaps some relevance for any remaining sales of public assets.

Mergers and Takeovers

On the average, about 12 companies are deleted from the NZSE each year due to takeovers or mergers. Such activity tends to be correlated with the general stock price index, but the association is imperfect and appears to be dominated by periodic episodes of rushes of blood to the head. The historical data tend to suggest three waves, the first peaking in the 1890s, the second in the 1920s and the third in the 1950s. A more recent peak was between 1986–1989. Of course most, if not all, of these extreme periods will be recognised as general stockmarket booms. Figure 5.3 portrays takeover activity over the last 25 years or so.

Are takeovers economically efficient? Financial economists often study the share price reaction to mergers and acquisitions. The most usual overseas finding is that on announcement, takeover targets shows abnormal positive returns, while bidders are unaffected. This sort of

Figure 5.3:   Takeover Activity

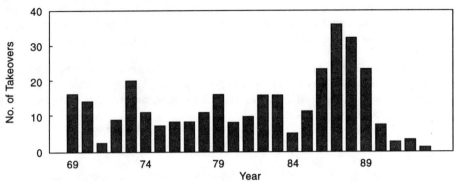

finding has been verified by Amery and Emanuel[8] for New Zealand over the period 1968–1985, although their findings were not perhaps as marked as many overseas studies. They found also that unsuccessful targets experienced negative abnormal returns for the post-outcome period, indicating that permanent increases in value relied on the two firms combining. More recent New Zealand studies support the idea that the source of gains in takeover stem primarily from the identification of underpriced target companies. If so, the gains would appear to accrue primarily to shareholders of those target companies, rather than necessarily to shareholders of the companies doing the taking over.

It should be noted that the above methodology relies on the identification of abnormal returns. To do this requires a benchmark, in other words a 'normal' return. The role of the benchmark is generally supplied by the CAPM, for reasons outlined in §3.2 above. The studies therefore inherit any potential weakness of the CAPM model as a description of reality.

Legal aspects of takeovers in New Zealand have become a real bunfight. Leading the regulatory charge, almost since its inception in the late 1970s, has been the New Zealand Securities Commission, aided from time to time by the Institute of Directors. Heavies in the other corner, against further regulation, include Business Roundtable, the Treasury and Reserve Bank and the Exchange itself. Caught somewhere in the middle, as hapless referees, have been successive governments. Those in the white pants favour an Australian-style takeovers code. This entails a control threshold (20 per cent or 30 per cent) after which the bidder has to stand in the market and offer a fixed and common price to any other shareholders who wish to sell. Those in the red pants want no code at all. The most recent (1994) compromise, if one can call it that, is the current NZSE listing rules, which allow company shareholders to choose one of three alternatives: *Option 1* is a standard three-day 'notice and pause' provision required of a takeover bidder, which has to publicly signal its intentions; the idea being that it is nice for the corporate victim to have some warning that a rape is in prospect. *Option 2* is a variant under which a longer (15 days) notice and pause applies to insiders only, with a report from independent directors. *Option 3* incorporates a minority veto against takeovers. Watch this space for further developments. It will be interesting to see if the market values companies differently according to which of the takeover rules they adopt.

The hooha has centred around whether existing or proposed takeover rules unnecessarily impede market efficiency. There is a case to be made for no code whatsoever. As mentioned above, takeovers have empirically constituted a source of wealth for target shareholders – and the threat of takeover can concentrate board members' minds on the business of maximising shareholders' wealth through business operations, rather than grandiose projects of dubious economic value, or whiteshoe perks and inflated fees for themselves and the company executives. A problem acknowledged by all is that in the past, takeovers have occurred that were immensely damaging to minority shareholders, the Bond Corporation takeover and cash stripping of Bell Resources being a widely cited example. However, code opponents argued that this is really a matter for protection of shareholder rights under the Companies Act, placing their faith in the then new Companies Act 1993, as well as further protection under the Securities Amendment Act 1988, which prohibits insider trading and requires disclosure of large (75 per cent) shareholdings. For a more detailed review of the recent history of takeover legislation see Fitzsimons (1995).[9] Urgently needed is a good theoretical discussion of all the issues involved.

5.5 The Market Observed

Historical Performance

Figure 5.4a portrays accumulation indexes for the stockmarket, one-year government stocks and the rates of inflation. It will be recalled that for the first two, such indexes are calculated by imputing a reinvestment of all earnings (dividends, etc. for stocks, coupons for bonds) into the asset concerned. In the case of equity stocks, the index is constructed by market value weights and includes most of the publicly listed New Zealand companies over the period. As well as dividends, the effects of bonus issues, rights issues and stock splits are all incorporated. For government stock, the total annual return is defined as the yield to maturity on one-year government stock. In other words, the constant reinvestment rate assumption is made. Accumulation indexes of this kind can be viewed as measuring the wealth generated by investment in the security. Note that the vertical scale on Figure 5.5 is logarithmic so that equal intervals refer to a doubling of wealth. The corresponding accumulation for the CPI could be interpreted as a wealth deflator necessary to get back to real (more precisely beginning of period) wealth equivalents. Figure 5.4b portrays the effects of an explicit inflation correction.

Figure 5.4a: Accumulation Indexes for Equities, Bonds and Inflation

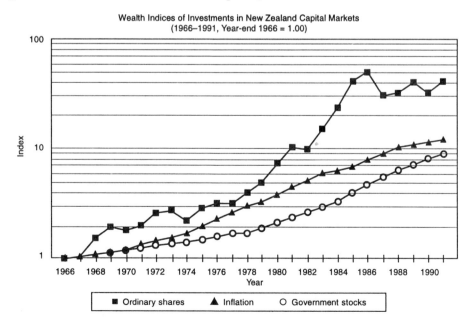

Wealth Indices of Investments in New Zealand Capital Markets
(1966–1991, Year-end 1966 = 1.00)

Figure 5.4b: Real Rates of Return: Equities and Bonds

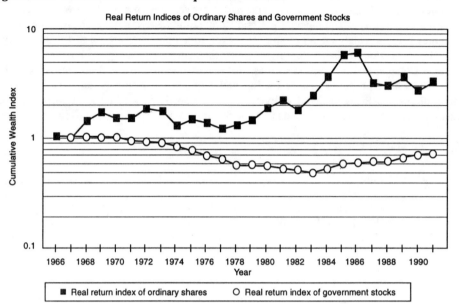

The equity index exhibits most of the shocks, upwards as well as downwards, experienced over the period by the local and international economies. The effects of the 1973 oil shock are obvious in both graphs. The stockmarket more or less kept pace with inflation over the subsequent years of that decade. The effects of the deteriorating New Zealand current account in the early eighties and restrictive policy measures (price-wage freeze and financial controls) in 1982 are registered. On a scale writ larger, so too are the events of 1984 ('Rogernomics'), all of which was very much liked by the markets. And, of course, the world-wide 1987 crash is there.

On the face of it, equities looked a clear winner over fixed interest (or at least the one-year version thereof). One should not, however, be quick to conclude that the former therefore represents a better investment. Figure 5.5 shows that the returns – measured as annual per cent changes in the accumulative indexes – differ in their variability. Over the period, the standard deviation of returns for shares and bonds were 27.25 per cent and 5.05 per cent, respectively.

This suggests that there ought to be some sort of risk premium for investing in equities. Looking again at the annual rate of return on bonds, we are probably reasonably safe as a first approximation in regarding the return on one-year government bonds as risk free. The general problem is not so much about the probability of default, negligible even over the difficult seventies, as about the possibility of capital losses resulting from falls in the bond price. These are probably minor for any reasonable patterns of investment in one year bonds. If we provisionally accept this, then the difference between the equity and bond returns can be called a market risk premium, or *equity premium*. In nominal returns, the average returns on equity and government stock were 19.47 per cent and 9.37 per cent, respectively, suggesting a pretty hefty risk premium of 10.1 per cent.

There are reasons to think, however, that this risk premium might be too large. It all depends (or it did on the historical evidence!) on the investor's investment horizon, whether it is short or long. Over the longer term the increased annual variability of equities smooths itself out, so that the probability of achieving a higher terminal wealth is high enough to compensate for the smaller possibility of a terminally bad outcome (the point can be made mathematically but we

Figure 5.5:   Variability of Equity and Bond Returns

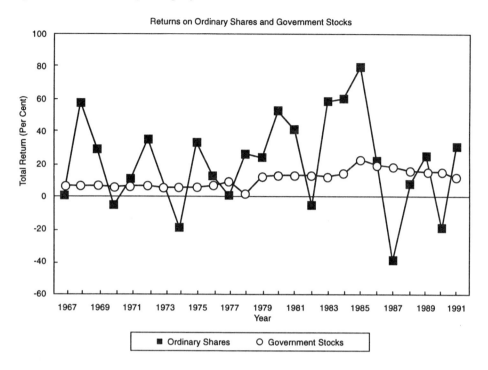

Figure 5.6:   International Comparisons

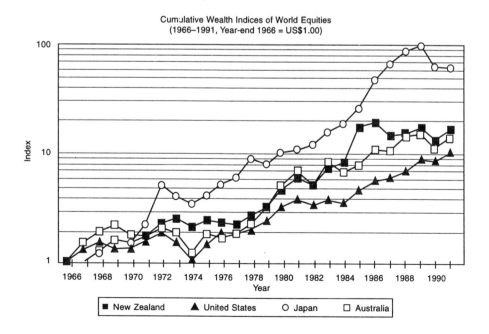

shall not do it here). If this argument is accepted, a corollary would be that stockmarket prices are too low, at least in the sense that they offer better than apparent investment prospects for longer-term investors, less worried about the shorter-term bumps and grinds. Evidently there is room for much enjoyable argument about the equity premium.

Finally, Figure 5.6 is an international comparison. The accumulation indexes (wealth) end up about the same in nominal terms for the United States, Australia and New Zealand, but chickenfeed in comparison with equities investment in Japan, although the very recent experience of the Japanese market has been much less happy. It will be interesting to draw similar graphs for certain South-East Asian countries 10 years hence.

Summary Ratios

Two ratios commonly employed by analysts are the dividend yield and the price to earnings ratio (P:E). If share prices are correctly based on fundamentals such as prices and future earnings (a big 'if') then the P:E ratio will reflect not only current earnings but the growth opportunities for future earnings (or more correctly, future dividends in the hands of shareholders). On this account, high P:E ratios indicate companies regarded as having exceptional growth prospects –

Figure 5.7: Comparative P:E Ratios – New Zealand versus Oz

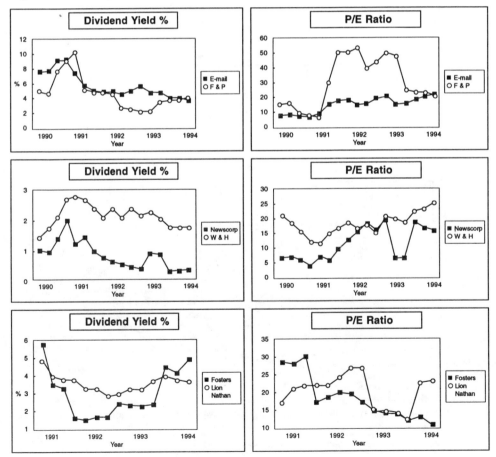

sceptics might also say, companies that are fashionable speculative plays. New Zealand P:E ratios are historically low by comparison with Japan, but appear to be rather higher than our nearest neighbour, Australia. Figures 5.7A, B, C are a short times series comparison between New Zealand and Australia of companies in corresponding industries, namely white goods (Fisher and Paykel versus e-mail) media (Wilson and Horton versus Newscorp) and brewing (Lion Nathan versus Fosters). The graphs suggest that both P:E ratios and dividend ratios tend to be higher for the New Zealand companies. Such comparisons are fraught with hazards; Newscorp, for instance, is a much more diversified group than Wilson and Horton, exposed also to international influences and perhaps, Fairfax might have been a better Oz company to use. However, the topic deserves further work. Some stylised explanations for international divergencies do exist; for example the astronomical P:E ratio of many Japanese companies has been attributed more to their ownership of real estate in Tokyo than to stunning growth prospects.

Stockmarket Efficiency

This usually refers to informational efficiency, which is the idea that prices should react very quickly to new information and therefore impound that information on an ongoing basis. (The other kind is 'operational efficiency', for which see §5.3). Unless you possess information superior to the general market you cannot hope to consistently make anything more than 'normal returns' (e.g. as suggested by the CAPM model) on a stock or group of stocks. On this basis, insiders could consistently make money if securities laws allowed them to trade. If a market were 'strong form' efficient, not even insider traders could hope to make money. The idea is that if inside information became available, insiders would immediately post a new bid price for the stock. When this appears on the screen, other traders would instantly realise that something was up and raise their offer prices to the point where even insider traders could not hope to profit from the purchase. This sort of world is only found in naïve neoclassical theory; in practice insiders do make pots of money and altruistically allow their families to enjoy it while they spend time in jail. However, some academics think that insider trading should be freely allowed.

Most if not all of the New Zealand studies are tests of general efficiency (technically 'weak' or 'semistrong'). Various kinds of tests have been applied, such as:

(a) 'Random walk' tests. It has been supposed that if the market is efficient, stock prices should follow a random walk, which means here that percentage changes in prices should be uncorrelated from one period to the next. The reasoning is that stock prices should react only to changes in information and the latter are by definition not predictable from one period to the next. The random walk hypothesis is true (under the informational hypothesis) for a stock that pays no dividends; otherwise an accumulation index should be utilised and a special meaning attached to the change – these precautions have not been generally followed in the empirical studies.

(b) 'Filter rules'. These are mechanical buy/sell rules based on the recent stock price movements. If the market is efficient, you should not be able to consistently make money by employing such rules.

(c) 'Events studies'. The efficient markets expectation is that no abnormal returns can be made after the release of new information such as the announcements of bonus or rights issues. They can possibly be made before its release if insider trading is afoot, or if on the other hand the announcement is simply a formality and the event has been widely anticipated. The calculations of excess abnormal returns needs a benchmark, usually the stock's CAPM pricing. The test itself is usually done in terms of cumulative excess returns, taken over a horizon of some weeks before the event to some weeks after it.

(d) 'Anomalies'. The idea here is that daily returns can be consistently and predictably higher at certain times of the year or certain days of the week.

Generally speaking, the results of research on the New Zealand market support the hypothesis that it is informationally efficient. Filter rules do not seem to work and no excess returns can be made after public announcements.[10] Some recent student work at the University of Waikato suggests that – in contrast to reports overseas – return anomalies also do not feature strongly here. You could not hope to make much, if any, money by trading on Mondays, in January, or around annual holidays.

On the other hand, there is anecdotal evidence that insider trading has been profitable (the market is not 'strong form' efficient). Concern has been expressed in many quarters at the effectiveness of our securities laws, especially in situations where a significant proportion of companies have a controlling shareholder, or from non-compliance with accounting standards which make it difficult to make informed judgements about the risk/return characteristics of investment policies or plans. In summary, one could say that the New Zealand market is probably weak-form efficient but strong-form inefficient.

5.6   Share Ownership

Concentration

Increasing concentration of share ownership both here and overseas is now well documented. Analysis of 10 large New Zealand companies for which sufficient ownership data exist – namely: Carter Holt Harvey, Fernz, Fisher and Paykel, Fletcher Challenge, Mair Astley, Milburn, Sanford, Wilson Neill, Wilson and Horton and New Zealand Refining – showed that in 1983 small holders (5,000 shares or less) accounted for 90 per cent of total holders and accounted for 25 per cent of shares, whereas in 1993 small holders were 80 per cent of total holders and accounted for only five per cent of shares. Large holders (50,000 or more) accounted for 0.49 per cent of total holders in 1983 and still only 1.5 per cent in 1993, yet increased their fraction of shares held from 47 per cent to 84 per cent over the same period.

The patterns of large shareholdings have also changed over the period. The data are for the same set of companies as above. Data limitations restrict us to the Top 10 shareholders for 1983 and the Top 20 for 1993. The results are portrayed in Table 5.2a for 1983 and Table 5.2b for 1993. Nominee companies are holdings registered under a separate company name acting on behalf of the real owner(s). Their share has increased from three per cent of shares held by the Top 10 in 1983 to 37 per cent in 1993, a major change even given the data limitations. Insurance companies have evidently diminished in importance and investment companies increased, as have personal holders. The rise of nominee companies reflects the growing importance of equity trusts, which we consider below.

Table 5.2a: The Pattern of Large Share Holdings 1983

	No. of Holdings	% of Total Holdings Held by Top 10	No. of Shares Held	% of Total Shares Held by Top 10
Personal	12	17.91%	6,508,377	3.36%
Nominee Cos.	5	7.46%	5, 149,049	2.66%
Insurance Cos.	29	43.28%	131,279,587	67.80%
Investment Cos.	3	4.48%	13, 144,492	6.79%
Other corporate	17	25.37%	37,032,832	19.13%
Trustee Cos.	0	0.00%	0	0.00%
Other	1	1.49%	500,000	0.26%
TOTAL	67	100.00%	193,614,337	100.00%

Table 5.2b: The Pattern of Large Share Holdings 1993

	No. of Holdings	% of Total Holdings Held by Top 20	No. of Shares Held	% of Total Shares Held by Top 20
Personal	17	8.50%	120,410,375	4.26%
Nominee Cos.	69	34.50%	1,034,702,492	36.64%
Insurance Cos.	40	20.00%	339,232,323	12.01%
Investment Cos.	27	13.50%	941,487,342	33.34%
Other corporate	23	11.50%	285,789,437	10.12%
Trustee Cos.	12	6.00%	69,501,051	2.46%
Other	12	6.00%	33,148,974	1.17%
TOTAL	200	100.00%	2,824,271,994	100.00%

International Aspects

1. *Overseas Ownership of New Zealand Stocks*

Capitalised at about NZD44b., New Zealand makes up only about 0.2 per cent of the Morgan Stanley International World Index. Nevertheless, since the mid-1980s, with the liberalisation of exchange rates and foreign investment rules we have witnessed increasing foreign ownership of New Zealand companies; and vice versa, increasing portfolio investment by locals in overseas markets. Few regulations now deter foreign investors in equity. Non-resident investors are subject to a 33 per cent withholding tax on dividends and in most cases imputation tax credits are not available to them. However, if less than 10 per cent foreign shareholding exists, the withholding tax can be returned in the form of a supplementary dividend. Investors then have to pay tax in their own countries. Recently, the Inland Revenue Department has proposed to remove the 10 per cent foreign shareholding limit.

Apart from the factors mentioned above, additional stimuli to foreign ownership have been occasioned by publicity given to privatisations of public assets and by offshore listing facilities (see below). Examples of the former are Telecom (64 per cent foreign owned), the former Power Boards and Air New Zealand.

Table 5.3 is a breakdown of the shareholding of 10 large New Zealand companies with foreign and domestic holdings. It shows that about 40 per cent of the total market capitalisation attributable to these companies is foreign sourced, conforming to anecdotal evidence in the market. Because the New Zealand market is dominated by a relatively few large public companies, overseas penetration is easily achievable.

Table 5.3:   Capitalisation Breakdown: Foreign v. Local

Rank	Company	% Foreign	Mkt Cap (M)	Foreign Cap
1	Telecom	0.64	$9,675	$6,192
2	Carter Holt Harvey[1]	0.41	$6,423	$2,633
3	Fletcher Challenge	0.2	$5,400	$1,080
4	Brierley	0.25	$3,361	$840
5	Goodman Fielder	0.55	$1,940	$1,067
6	Lion Nathan	0.06	$1,643	$99
7	Air New Zealand	0.24	$1,138	$273
8	Fernz	0.24	$1,148	$276
9	Fletcher Forest	0.1	$814	$81
10	INDP Newspapers	0.52	$465	$242
	Total		$32,007	$12,783

Therefore per cent of foreign ownership = $32,007 / $12,783
= 39.94 per cent

1.   Prior to the acquisition of a controlling interest by International Paper.

Overseas holdings are also facilitated by the listing of various New Zealand companies on offshore exchanges. The matrix below lists the New Zealand stocks quoted on various foreign exchanges. Fletcher Challenge, in particular, is quoted in all five countries.

Table 5.4:   New Zealand Stocks Quoted Overseas

Company	Australia	Hong Kong	Japan	London	U.S.A.
Brierley	*	*	*		
Carter Holt Harvey	*	*	*	*	
Fletcher Challenge	*	*	*	*	*
Fletcher Forests	*	*			
Kiwi Gold	*				
Lion Nathan	*	*			
Macraes	*				
NZOG	*				
Telecom	*	*	*	*	

Listing overseas is expensive if full registry service, etc. is desired. For this reason New Zealand companies listing in the U.S.A. operate via American Depository Receipts (ADRs). These are negotiable certificates issued by banks, who run the corresponding register. The certificates are generally traded on an OTC basis, the interestingly named 'pink sheet market'. The benefits to New Zealand companies of this sort of scrip trading is that they do not thereby have to satisfy the onerous disclosure requirements necessary for a U.S. stock exchange listing. ADR trading may involve a bundling together so that the value of a share concurs roughly with U.S. size share values. Thus one Telecom share traded in the U.S. is worth the equivalent of 16 Telecom shares traded on the NZSE; for other companies, one ADR is worth 10 shares on the local bourse.

2. *New Zealand Ownership of Overseas Stocks*

The counterpart of the listing of New Zealand stocks overseas is the listing of foreign stocks on the NZSE. A variety of Australian and U.K.-based stocks are listed. Some have only 'courtesy' listings and are not traded here on a regular basis. Others, like Goodman Fielder and the Guinness Peat Group are consistently in the NZSE Top 10 by turnover on value, doubtless because they have appreciable New Zealand interest on their registers. The Appendix to this chapter lists all such companies, trusts, etc.

3. *Trading times*

The NZSE is the first exchange to open and close each day. It opens at 9.30 a.m. and other exchanges, starting with Australia at noon, open throughout the day and night New Zealand time:

	NZ time
New Zealand market open	9.30 a.m.
Australia opens	12 noon
Japan (Nikkei)	1.00 p.m.
Hong Kong (Hang Seng)	2.00 p.m.
London	9.30 p.m.
U.S.A. (Dow Jones)	2.30 a.m.

These time differences potentially give rise to arbitrage possibilities, in which stocks bought in New Zealand could be sold later in the day in another country; this sort of thing is quite feasible since scrip registrations can be moved from one country to the other. Some industry analysts believe that inefficiencies of this kind can and do occur. Generally, however, we lack research status on the dynamic relationship between local and foreign equity markets.

5.7   Equity Trusts

Equity trusts are of two basic kinds.

(a) *Closed-end funds* are set up with a specific investment amount and do not accept further subscriptions. They are usually in the form of Investment Trusts or Companies, listed on the stock exchange and tradeable just like ordinary shares. There are now a dozen or so U.K.-based investment trusts currently listed on the NZSE in addition to the local Nuhaka and Opio forestry funds; Australia has about 20, the U.K. has 320, so we are small beer, but this could change.

(b) *Open-ended funds* allow continued investment in which investors buy further units. Such funds are usually managed by banks, insurance companies or investment houses. They often take the form of a unit trust or superannuation trust, where the assets are held and management supervised by a trustee company. Related investment vehicles are Group Investment Funds (GIFs) and Life Insurance Bonds. GIFs are established under the Trustee Companies Act and are often constituted by pooling smaller estates and trusts. Insurance bonds are investment-linked endowment assurance policies, already covered in an earlier chapter.

The tax treatment of the various kinds of funds is important in decisions to invest and in the compilation of final return to investors. For instance, the U.K.-listed funds are not taxed on realised capital gains which are reinvested to preserve capital growth. Local 'category B' GIFs – which can invest only in fixed or floating interest instruments – enjoy a similar privilege, indeed suffer only a 24 per cent resident witholding tax. Apart from a few exceptions, investing in real property and such, all the others are taxed at the full 33 per cent company tax rate, both on income (e.g. dividends) and on capital gains, whether accrued or actually realised. Unit trusts and GIFs (category A) offer holders imputation credits on franked income, i.e. that on which tax has been paid, but this is not available to super trusts and insurance bonds. Not surprisingly, such tax non-neutralities have produced flows between the different categories of fund.

A final informal distinction is between 'retail' and 'wholesale' funds. The former are available directly to you or I as private investors. To invest in the latter you will have to go through an intermediary such as an investment advisor, who may run a master trust to combine different client funds under a single wholesale fund. Indeed, the latter development has been an important source of recent withdrawals from retail funds, as investment advisors come under pressure on management costs. Investment advisors have in recent years become important drivers of fund inflows and outflows.

Managed funds have been the growth area in the New Zealand investment scene over the last 10 years. Figure 5.8 portrays the growth in the nineties of unlisted retail managed investments funds. At the end of 1986 there were 18 registered unit trusts; currently there are over 180, and indeed over 400 retail investment funds altogether, while access to Australia unit trusts is also readily available.

Figure 5.8:   Frolicking Funds, 1991–1996

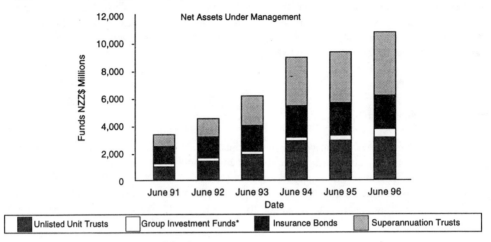

* Category A only; category B is included elsewhere.

Source: FPG Research

Fund Management

Management fees for unit trusts vary greatly but are always appreciable. They vary between 0–5 per cent depending on the asset class (zero for cash management trusts), although entry fees can usually be drastically reduced by going through a cut-price broker or financial planner; some funds also charge a rebatable up-front brokerage fee. There is an ongoing fee for managerial services, typically 1.5 per cent of the gross assets per annum. Trustee fees (0.1 per cent) may add to this. Further fees are commonly payable if the fund offers and the investor chooses to switch between classes of asset or sub-funds. There may also be exit fees, especially for mortgage trusts and the like, where investments are more 'locked in'.

It will be apparent that management fees, in the extended sense, are appreciable and most questions in the academic literature have concerned whether the fees are worth it. In practice, such fees are usually a first charge on the dividend income derived by the fund, so that capital growth is essential if the fund is to adequately reward investors on a long-term basis. If markets were informationally efficient, the fund managers should not hope to make abnormal positive returns, so that the investor would do just as well by selecting stocks according to the dartboard principle and saving the managerial fees. The problem then boils down to the detection of managerial expertise.

Most overseas studies have refuted the idea that fund managers in general have any special expertise in either stock selection (*selectivity*) or the *timing* with which they move in and out of stocks over the course of the cycle. In New Zealand, funds appear to be convergent in their choice of investments; indeed, well diversified portfolios should behave very similarly to the market return. Empirically, correlation coefficients in returns earned by New Zealand equity trusts are extremely high – of the order of 0.97–0.99. At face value, however, the high correlations are rather surprising given that some funds reportedly practise 'active' portfolio management, while others adhere to 'passive' models, referring to a policy of buying and holding the market index, or some similarly non-selective rule. Fund performance measurement is a rather subtle science, so we shall not dwell any longer on matters of historical performance. Suffice to say that apart from being a ready source of personal portfolio diversification, investment in funds is worthwhile only if fund managers exhibit special skill or enjoy superior sources of information or technology, sufficient to outweigh the tax advantages of investment on personal account in fully franked company shares, as to both dividend and capital gains. The trick, as always, is to sort out the sheep from the goats, and here investment research companies such as FPG Research or IPAC run regular reports and rankings on fund managers.

To some extent the rise and rise of equity trusts, investment companies and the like may itself create a source of extra returns that accrues as a public good to the community at large. The presence of large shareholders on company boards may act as a source of discipline and a stimulus for efficiency and expertise in corporate decisions. In other words, the increasing concentration of ownership of industry, associated with the rise of unit trusts and the like, may have positive spin-offs in terms of management rectitude. Such externalities would not necessarily show up in published return statistics or comparisons between managed and unmanaged investments.

5.8   Preference Shares

Preferred shares have fixed dividends rather like a coupon on debt. Unlike debt, however, owners do not have legal recourse in the case of default. Preference shares rank behind debt but ahead of ordinary shares. Unlike bonds, dividends paid to preference shareholders do not represent a tax deductible corporate expense and are nowadays viewed as expensive finance.

'Nowadays' refers to the post-1992 position. Prior to its amendment, the previous version of the Income Tax Act allowed for the tax exemption of intercorporate dividends. This was originally intended to prevent multiple taxation of the dividend income stream, where it was transferred between companies. However, the exemption turned out to provide a truly awesome way of avoiding (evading?) tax, the best thing available outside the Cook Islands. The trick was to create a paper subsidiary with capital provided by redeemable preference shares. The subsidiary would deposit the capital with a bank, passing back the interest earned to its parent in the form of the preference dividend, tax free in the hands of the parent. The capital for the preference share was raised by the parent via a bank loan, on which it paid tax deductible interest. Suppose, for the sake of argument, that the interest paid by the parent to the bank was the same as what the bank passed on to the subsidiary as earnings on the latter's deposit. You can see that the parent would have arbitraged the tax at the Commissioner's expense. Of course, the two interest rates were not the same, but the corporate tax saved nevertheless allowed plenty of cake to be shared between the parent company and the friendly bank. Banks were evidently also direct investors in the preference shares of shell companies.

Similar sorts of tax advantages still apply in other countries, e.g. the United States. Firms with accumulated tax allowances will issue preferred stock to corporate investors rather than debt, on which their potential tax deductions are worth little. Under U.S. tax law the investing corporates can utilise the deductions on dividends received, and the issuing company derives the benefit in terms of a lower coupon on its preference issue. In the case of New Zealand, banks were big investing corporates, taking advantage of the dividend exemption.[11] However, the 1992 Amendment seems to have closed off the profitable loophole.

Notes

1.   The NZSE has recently released a discussion paper on the definition of units for its trading purposes, that would further blur the distinctions, were they to be adopted.

2.   A potentially more effective way of estimating the betas would be to back them out of options prices, where the option is a cross-option between the SPI and the stock in question. This is automatically of the character of an ex-ante beta. As yet we do not have such options in the New Zealand market. It would be useful to have them.

3.   For an excellent review of the issues, see Fitzsimons, P. (1994), 'The New Zealand Stock Exchange: Rights and Powers', in Walker, G. and Fisse, B. (eds), *Securities Regulation in Australia and New Zealand*, Auckland: Oxford University Press.

4.   Cheung, J., Vos, E. and Low, C.K. (1990), *IPO Underpricing in New Zealand*, School of Management Studies, University of Waikato, mimeo.

5.   These references to culture and the classics (in this case philosophy) are quite deliberate. We are building up your defenses against the social engineers. Try Bertrand Russell's *History of Western Philosophy* for a write-up on Heraclites.

6.   For a brief but informative review in the New Zealand context see Fitzgerald, G. and Tubb, G. (1995), 'Opportunity Knocks – Share Buy Backs Under the Companies Act 1993', in *Treasury Note*, September.

7.   The Telecom float took the form of an initial institutional tender in the U.S. and New Zealand, after which the price was set at $2.00 per share, to apply to both institutional and private investors. On the first day of listing, the shares traded in the $2.20–2.30 range.

8.   Amery, M.I. and Emanuel, D.M. (1988), 'Takeover Announcements and Shareholder Returns', *Pacific Accounting Review*, vol. 1.

9.   Fitzsimons, P. (1995), *The Reform of Takeovers Regulation in New Zealand: Unfinished Business?*, School of Law, University of Waikato, mimeo.

10. On such aspects, you could try a batch of papers by Emanuel, D.M., 'Capitalization Changes and Share Price Movements: New Zealand Evidence', *Australian Journal of Management*, vol. 4 (1979); 'A Note on Filter Rules and Stockmarket Trading in New Zealand', *Economic Record*, vol. 56 (1980); 'The Information Content of Sign and Size of Earnings Announcements: New Zealand Evidence', *Accounting and Finance* (1984).

11. See Gough, P. and Brown, K. (1995), 'The NZ Market for Preference Shares: The Impact of this Tax Regime', Department of Finance and Q.A., University of Otago, no. 9501, mimeo.

Chapter 6

Exchange-Traded Derivatives

6.1 Generalities

A derivative is an instrument whose payoff at some designated time in the future is tied by a specified formula to the price at that time (or 'exotically', before that time) of an underlying 'physical'. The physical (loosely, 'commodity') can be:

(a) A commodity in the true sense. Thus a wool future is an instrument where payoff is tied to the price of wool.
(b) A currency. FX futures and options are tied to the price of one currency in terms of another.
(c) A financial security, such as bills and bonds. A March bank bill future is technically tied to the price of a bank bill delivered in March.
(d) Company equities. Major companies often have options written and traded on their stock; the payoff is tied to the future price of the stock.
(e) The value of an index, such as the NZSE–40.
(f) The value of another derivative, e.g. options on bank bill futures.
(g) The outcome of future events, such as some All Black success index defined on the outcomes of a future Rugby World Cup.

For the last example, you might get the idea that derivatives are a form of gambling. In a sense, this is true; they represent a bet on the outcome of something and they are structured so that you can make or lose a great deal of money for just a small – or even zero – initial outlay. In somewhat imprecise terms, they are heavily levered, and therefore a great medium for speculation. However, derivatives also have a quite sober use in the management of portfolios of stocks or bonds. In this, they assume a hedging role. You can use them to offset the movement on an underlying physical to which you might be exposed. Often this is far cheaper and more convenient than hedging operations in the physical market itself. Dotted throughout this book you will find examples of this – hedging a swaps position with bond futures, for example. In this role, derivatives have become an essential portfolio adjunct in recent years.

The classic examples of derivatives are:

Forwards and Futures

These are (pretty well) pure bets on the spot price of the underlying physical at some point in time in the future (the 'expiry', 'maturity' or 'delivery' date). Perhaps the purest form of forward contracts are *hedge settlement* contracts. If the agreed (now) forward price for a six-month (hence) forward was F and the actual spot price of the commodity was S at the end of the six months, the payoff would be S-F if you were 'long' (had bought forward) or F-S if you were 'short' (had sold forward). The F is set now (at time zero, when the spot price is, say S_0). The S will only be known at expiry and you settle up on the difference. Contracts of this form are much used in FX hedging.

Variants of this sort of arrangement are:

(a) A deliverable forward.

This is simply a contract to buy or sell a quantity of some physical at expiry date, at a price F agreed on now, the contract date.

(b) A market futures contract.

For a given contract, the forward price F will typically change every day up to the point of expiry. The daily change is $F_t - F_{t-1}$ (the value at day t less that at day t-1). At the outset you establish an account with your broker, called the margin account, into which you make an initial deposit – 15 per cent or so of the contract value is typical. Every day your margin account is credited if $F_t > F_{t-1}$ or debited if $F_t < F_{t-1}$. Unlike other forms of forward contract, a futures contract therefore entails a day-to-day cash flow. The final value of F is just S, the expiry spot price.

Options

An option is a contract that pays off when the underlying price of the physical (S) passes a preassigned level, called the *strike price* (X). A call option will pay S-X if S exceeds X, nothing otherwise. A put will pay X-S, provided S<X. The payoff can be only at maturity (a 'European' option); or else the option can be 'exercised' at any intervening point (an 'American' option).

You can see that an option is essentially a one–way bet on the future physical price S, whereas forwards are two-way bets. With a forward you can lose a lot as well as win a lot, since the payoff is essentially the difference F-S and this can be negative as well as positive; whereas a call option has zero losses if S<X. Because of this one-way facility, options cost money at inception; they have a purchase price, often called the option 'premium' (π, say). Figure 6.1a is a simple schematic end of period payoff for a call option (because our valuations are end of period, we have adjusted the purchase price π by an interest factor ρ). Figure 6.1b is a similar sort of diagram for a (long) forward.

You can get fancy sorts of option contracts where an end of period payoff depends on everything that happened to the physical price over the whole contract period (such as the average price over the period); so-called 'exotics'. Or contracts where S is the value of some index (options on the S.P.I.); or options where S is in fact F, the futures price (options on futures).

Figure 6.1a: Call Option Payoff

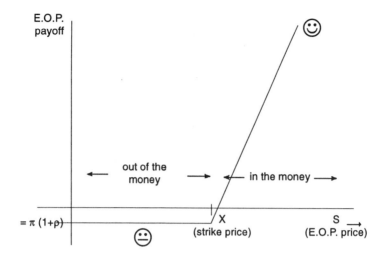

Figure 6.1b: (Long) Forward Payoff

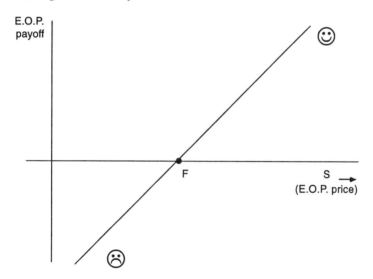

You can have options attached to bonds for conversion to common stock at some preassigned price (convertible bonds), or options attracted to stock issues to purchase further units at some preassigned price (warrants). On a different tack, you can get swaps (encountered in Chapter 2), where you exchange a fixed coupon flow for a variable (floating) interest rate flow. These can be interpreted as more generalised forwards.

The above are examples of derivatives and in this chapter we will look at the traded New Zealand derivatives most commonly encountered. We do not discuss in depth some important matters, *pricing* in particular. If you are prepared to specify or hypothesise about the underlying stochastic process that drives the physical price S, you can in principle calculate a price that the derivative should be worth. This is usually done by trying to recreate the day-to-day payoff on the derivatives by means of a portfolio of the underlying physical together with a long or short position in a bill or interest-bearing account. This leads to a pricing formula of the general form.[1]

(1)   *market price of derivative = f (current spot price of physical, current interest rate; other specific details (strike price, time to maturity, spot price volatility, etc. as appropriate).*

Formulae of type (1) are 'no-arbitrage formulas'; if their underlying assumptions are satisfied, then nobody can make sure money out of derivative securities priced in this way. The famous 'Black-Scholes' formula for the price of a European option is an example. However, such formulas often make quite specific assumptions about the way the physical, or spot, price is supposed to behave and about the trading possibilities on the underlying physical. Empirical studies show that the Black-Scholes, for instance, is good (i.e. describes actual prices quite well) except when the option is a long way out of the money.

Regardless of exactly how they are priced, you do need a very liquid market for your physical in order to write options on it. A liquid market is one where the commodity concerned is constantly being bought and sold, so that at any time you have a precise idea of exactly what its price is. Futures, on the other hand, are not quite so demanding (you can have wool futures where wool itself is not constantly traded). Provided the payoff is defined in terms of some universally accepted version of a defined price event, it is quite possible to base a market simply on perceptions of what that payoff will be. For this reason you will often find options written off the back of the *futures* market, rather than the underlying physical – it makes much more sense to have options on wool futures rather than options on wool spot. For each of the futures contracts quoted on the NZFOE (see §6.2) you will also find options contracts specified off the back of them. There is another reason for basing an options market on a futures contract. For no-arbitrage pricing purposes you need a facility whereby you can go short in the physical, as well as long. This is no trouble with a future, but it may be with the corresponding underlying physical.

By and large, this chapter is about standardised, exchange-traded derivatives, bought and sold on the New Zealand Futures and Options Exchange (NZFOE). However, another source of derivatives are the forwards (etc.) and options created privately, to order, by banks and investment banks. This is the OTC ('over the counter') market. An interest-rate swap is OTC – similarly, caps, collars, etc. OTC instruments are especially important in FX, so we will delay further consideration until the chapter on foreign exchange. In many cases, options are written and traded privately in the course of equity dealings such as takeovers, mergers, or management compensation plans. On another tack, derivatives analogues are also starting up in electricity supply and other long-term contractual commitments. It is an interesting question, but a little outside our present scope, as to the issue terms and implied pricing of such agreements.

It is important to reiterate that standard futures and options, exchange traded or otherwise, by no means exhaust the list and usage of derivative instruments. The swaps phenomenon is a classic case in point. We looked at interest rate swaps in Chapter 2 and FX swaps will be considered in the next chapter, on foreign exchange. Nonetheless, swaps are derivatives as are other 'products' like interest-rate caps, collars, etc. Their payoffs are more ongoing than terminal (though this, too, is not a watertight distinction), but they are tied to some underlying physical and they have a market value at any point in time. Indeed, in volume terms, interest rate swaps dwarf the formal exchange traded instruments for fixed interest futures. However, exchange-traded bond futures are used by swaps dealers to hedge their swaps until matching counterparties can be found.[2] So the formal exchange-traded instruments are really complementary to the swaps industry and much the same is true for other OTC products.

6.2 The NZFOE

Exchange-traded futures had a woolly beginning in New Zealand, starting in 1953 with the trading of wool futures via the London Exchange. However, the first local exchange was established only in 1985 with the New Zealand Futures and Options Exchange Ltd (actually its later title), a limited liability company working within regulations set by New Zealand Acts of Parliament and the Securities Commission. Head Office is in Auckland. Like many other good things, it is now owned abroad, by the Sydney Futures Exchange (from February 1994). However, the local exchange achieved much even before the takeover, in particular with the establishment of the world's first fully computerised automated trading system (ATS), more on which below. The company is the only futures exchange registered under the Securities Amendment Act 1988, which in effect also gives it monopoly power by requiring all dealers acting in the market on behalf of other persons to be members of an authorised futures exchange, or be otherwise authorised by the Commission. The NZFOE is also a registered stock exchange pursuant to the Shareholders Act 1908. Further legislation (the Futures Industry (Client Fund) Regulations 1990) reinforced the Exchange's requirement for the separation of client funds from a broker's house funds and require all client funds to be immediately paid into client bank accounts. Apart from this, the Exchange has established a number of house rules regulating the trading and other activities of dealers, some of which we will look at below. Self-regulation of this sort is consistent with the general stance of the Securities Commission in its current 'over the shoulder' monitoring role.

At present there are 24 New Zealand and 19 Australian dealers authorised to trade on the New Zealand market. The New Zealand dealers are listed as Appendix A to this chapter. There are three classes of dealers on the Exchange:

(a) *Public brokers* are authorised to deal on behalf of other persons, as well as principals (for themselves) and are authorised to accept and hold client money and property.
(b) *Introducing brokers*, can deal as above, but cannot hold client money or property and must direct all client transactions through a trading permit holder (q.v.).
(c) *Principal traders* generally trade only on their own account, although they may act from time to time as agents for other dealers.

A cross-classification of the above is the *trading permit holder* – these are able to deal directly on the Automated Trading System; dealers who are not permit holders must deal through others who are. Most of the banks and investment banks have organisational offshoots that are trading members, plus a few specialist futures commodity or brokers and several large corporates.

Contracts Traded

1. Futures Contracts

Below we summarise the futures contracts currently traded on the NZFOE. With each futures contract is associated a corresponding options contract. Full details of both futures and options contracts for the 90-day bank bill and three and 10-year NZGS, are given in the Appendix to the chapter. The name of the game in trading such contracts is standardisation, which is necessary to create volumes and therefore market liquidity, as well as to forestall costly or litigious imprecision. For example, if you are betting on the future price of something like a financial instrument you need a mutually agreed formula to compute the value of that instrument in terms of today's parameters; e.g. the value of a bill or a bond in terms of the yield as a current market variable. Thus you will find 'value formula' in the appendix, as well as things like expiration dates, settlement provisions, contract sizes and so forth. Full details of all the other contracts, including the equity options, are available from the NZFOE, together with much useful literature on their use.

Table 6.1 has four columns. Starting with the fourth, the initial margin is what you need to deposit with the broker to establish your margin account. The contract size is pretty well self-explanatory except possibly for the index items; you take the current value of the NZSE–10 capital index and multiply by $25 to get the face value of the NZSE–10 index contract; and the current wool indicator price, which is a weighted average of grades prepared by the Wool Board expressed as so many cents a kilo and multiply it by 2,500 to get the face value of the wool futures contract. The third column is the 'tick size'. A tick is the minimum price fluctuation in the contract; if a single tick movement occurs it would register as a change in your margin account, as well as the minimum quotable price change. You will notice that the settlement months are generally fixed at three-monthly intervals. The last column refers to the settlement arrangements. In the old days you could settle by taking delivery – there is an apocryphal story about Keynes asking if Kings College Chapel was available to store the wheat he was caught with. The physical delivery facility is increasingly a thing of the past and settlement is a cash payment reflecting the last day's trading with the terminal physical price as the settlement price.

In the past, the Exchange has offered other contracts: five-year government stock, New Zealand wheat, a NZD contract (against the USD), an overall share price index (the Barclay index) and an additional wool contract for crossbred wool. In August 1995 the physical underlying the stock price index changed from the NZSE top 40 to the NZSE top 10. Of the current contracts the last two on the list are only thinly, if at all, traded (see §6.3 below).

Table 6.1:   Futures on the NZFOE

Commodity	Size	Tick Size (point value)	Initial Margin	Settlement Months	Trading Hours	Spot Month Ceases (hours)	Delivery
90-Day Bank Bills (BBC)	$500,000	Approx $12	$500	Mar/Jun/ Sep/Dec	0800–1200 1300–1700	1700 (1)	cash
NZ 3-Year Government Stock (TYS)	$100,000	Approx $25	$800	Mar/June/ Sep/Dec	0800–1200 1300–1700	1700 (1)	cash
NZ 10-Year Government Stock (10)	$100,000	Approx $60	$2000	Mar/June/ Sep/Dec	0800–1200 1300–1700	1700 (1)	cash
NZSE–10 Share index (TOP)	$25 x index	$25	$850	Mar/June/ Sep/Dec	0800–1200 1300–1700	1700 (2)	cash
US Dollar (USD)	US$50,000	$5	$1500	Mar/June/ Sep/Dec	0800–1200 1300–1700	1700 (1)	cash
NZ Wool (WFC)	2.500 c/kg x Indicator	$25	$500	Feb/Apr/ June/Aug/ Oct/Dec	0800–1200 1300–1700	1700 (2)	cash

(1) Trading ceases on the first Wednesday after the ninth day of the settlement month
(2) Trading ceases on the second to last business day of the settlement month NZFOE 11/95 CO–01

Source: NZFOE.

2. Options

The three principal financial futures contracts, namely the 90-day bank bill, three, and 10-year government stock, have options traded off the back of them. In other words, the physical or commodity is a futures price. There is also an options contract written off the NZSE–10 index. Table 6.2a lists the details.

Currently (November 1995) there are also seven exchange-traded equity options, as illustrated in Table 6.2b.

Table 6.2a: Financial Options on the NZFOE

Commodity	Size	Tick Size (point value)	Settlement Months	Trading Hours	Spot Month Ceases	Delivery (hours)
90-Day Bank Bill Options (BBO)	1 BBC future	Approx $12	Mar/Jun/ Sep/Dec	0800–1200 1300–1700	1700 (1)	futures (A)
NZ 3-Year Government Stock Options (TYO)	1 TYS future	$25	Mar/Jun/ Sep/Dec	0800–1200 1300–1700	1700 (1)	futures (A)
NZ 10-Year Government Stock Options (TNO)	1 TEN future	Approx $60	Mar/Jun/ Sep/Dec	0800–1200 1300–1700	1700 (1)	futures (A)
NZSE–10 Share index options (TPO)	1 TOP future	$25	Mar/Jun/ Sep/Dec	0800–1200 1300–1700	1700 (2)	futures (A)

Source: NZFOE.

Table 6.2b: Equity Options on the NZFOE

Share Options						
Brierley Investments Ltd (BRY)	1000 shares	$1	Feb/May/ Aug/Nov	0800–1200 1300–1700	1700 (2)	shares (A)
Carter Holt Harvey Ltd (CAH)	1000 shares	$1	Mar/Jun/ Sep/Dec	0800–1200 1300–1700	1700 (2)	shares (A)
Fletcher Challenge Ltd – Ordinary (FLC)	1000 shares	$1	Feb/May/ Aug/Nov	0800–1200 1300–1700	1700 (2)	shares (A)
Fletcher Challenge Ltd – Forestry (FFS)	1000 shares	$1	Feb/May/ Aug/Nov	0800–1200 1300–1700	1700 (2)	shares (A)
Goodman Fielder Ltd (GMF)	1000 shares	$1	Jan/Apr/ Jul/Oct	0800–1200 1300–1700	1700 (2)	shares (A)
Lion Nathan Ltd (LNN)	1000 shares	$1	Jan/Apr/ Jul/Oct	0800–1200 1300–1700	1700 (2)	shares (A)
Telecom Corporation of New Zealand Ltd (TEL)	1000 shares	$1	Mar/Jun/ Sep/Dec	0800–1200 1300–1700	1700 (2)	shares (A)

(1) Trading ceases on the first Wednesday after the ninth day of the settlement month
(2) Trading ceases on the second to last business day of the settlement month
'A' denotes American-style options

Source: NZFOE.

Mention might also be made of EFP ('exchange for physical') contracts, which involve two parties agreeing to exchange the physical, e.g. three-year NZGS, with a simultaneous exchange of offsetting futures contracts at agreed on prices. Such contracts are often used in hedging the physical, especially in 'thin' markets, where it might otherwise be difficult to arrange futures hedges at the right prices. They save a lot of hassle and transactions expense, including bid-offer spreads.

Trading Mechanism

(a) The Automated Trading System (ATS)

The NZFOE market operates using the ATS 2,000 system developed by Sunguard Capital Markets Ltd. The ATS provides a forum for competitive trading and price discovery. Electronic screen-trading is ideal for the relatively small size and geographical spread of the New Zealand market, with screens based in dealers' offices in Auckland, Wellington, Christchurch and Sydney.

The ATS was selected for the New Zealand industry, in preference to the more traditional 'open outcry' or 'pit', because of the benefits it had to offer users of the market. Trades are executed by dealers entering buy and sell orders into terminals situated with each market principal. The ATS processes all orders in the sequence of entry and automatically seeks to match, by price, buyers and sellers. Any unmatched portion of an order is added to the queue of outstanding orders awaiting matching or is immediately cancelled, depending on the order type.

Screen-trading provides centralisation, transparency and offers timely execution of transactions for the market. The transparency comes from the ability of brokers to view any portion of the market they wish. Using windows technology the NZFOE allows cross referencing of information on screen and the opportunity to view the whole market. Dealers authorised to trade directly on the Exchange simply enter buy and sell orders into the system where they are matched by price and processed in chronological order.

In addition to the automated trade system trading permit holders also have a price reporting service which provides real time data for each contract listed on the Exchange. This price reporting service provides information on dealer identity, price and quantity for the open/high/low/last price, size of last order and a live ticker. This 'ticker' provides order by order information, stating who wished to buy/sell, what quantity and for which contract.

(b) Order Types

Each time an order to buy or sell is placed in the ATS, specific instructions are placed with it. This allows the trader to control how long the order stays within the system. The following are some of the more common order types.

(i)   *Good For Day (GFD)*: Remains in the system until executed, cancelled by the broker or automatically cancelled at the end of the day's trading. GFD is the most common order type.
(ii)   *Good Until Cancelled (GTC)*: Remains in the system until executed or cancelled by the broker.
(iii)   *Good Until Over (GTO)*: Remains in the system for as long as it remains the 'best' price. It is automatically cancelled at the end of the day.
(iv)   *Immediate Or Cancel (IOC)*: If not immediately executed, the order will be cancelled.

(v) *Straddle (STR)*: The broker selects two different delivery months and the order will be traded at a premium or discount differential between the two. To be effective both the buy and the sell executions must be successful and if the range set cannot be matched immediately the entire straddle will be cancelled.

(vi) *Immediate At Best (IAB)*: Will attempt to execute the selected volume at the single best available price at time of entry. Any unfilled balance will be cancelled immediately.

(vii) *Cross Order (CRO)*: Entered into the system to buy and sell an equal number of lots at the same price at the same time, the buy and sell sides will always involve the same principal. A prerequisite is the existence of at least one existing offer and bid in the system for that contract and delivery month. If the order price is between the best price and the best offer, a deal will be generated.

(c) Exceptional Events

Trading in futures is a rather fragile operation with all sorts of potential for things to go wrong, ranging from simple mistakes to attempts to manipulate the market. At all times there is a market manager in the NZFOE head office, aided by compliance and surveillance staff.

In the event of a mistake on the part of a dealer, the market manager will 'ring around' the market to find out if it accepts that it was a genuine mistake; if so, then the deal can be voided. The Exchange also has powers to deal with attempts to manipulate the market. This can take various forms: for example attempting to 'sway' the market by buying or selling much higher or lower than the market at present, or by large or sudden dealings in the physical market at or near to the maturity of one's futures position, hoping to influence the futures price at close-out. An extreme version is the 'short squeeze', where a dominant supplier of the physical either withholds or buys stock to force up the final spot price and therefore the settlement price on futures. In some cases, a ring around will help the trading managers to resolve such complaints; in other cases, more formal prosecutory action may be necessary, in terms of Exchange rules.

An interesting recent occasion for supervisory deliberation occurred in March 1994 when Telecom made a capital reconstruction, specifically a cancellation of one in five shares plus $1 paid to every holder of a cancelled share. The Exchange initially treated the $1 payment as a dividend, which had the effect of reducing the NZSE–40 capital index[3] by 24 points. However, brokers succeeded in convincing the Exchange that this was a capital distribution and the value of the index should not have changed.

6.3 Volume and Liquidity

The bulk of NZFOE trading is done in the 'near' settlement months. For instance, on 27 January 1995, 3,097 March bank bill contracts were traded; 954 June contracts and 90 September contracts, with no December contracts reported. Likewise the bulk of the 3/10 year government-stock and NZSE–40 contracts are in the very near settlement months. As between the various contracts, bank bill futures are easily the biggest business, comprising 70 per cent or so of the contracts traded, with government stock futures around 20 per cent and other futures and options making up the remainder. Table 6.3 presents volumes over 1993–1994 for all three classes of exchange traded instruments. Generally, it is a story of substantial growth over the two years in most contracts, with one or two exceptions. The USD futures contract was suspended in late 1995. The wool contract also remains moribund but will have better prospects once the ill-fated intervention wool stockpiles in Australia and New Zealand are eliminated (about two to three years hence). The problem with the stockpile was that it essentially amounted to a fixed cap on the spot market. As a wool processor or user, why bother to hedge your future purchases by various elastoplast patch-ups, the fixed exchange rate system gave rise in 1973 to a *floating exchange rate* system. The essence of such a system is that there are no official reserve currencies: the USD does retain a special status and is still a part of reserves held by various central banks, but the system could survive without it. The price of one currency in terms of another varies just like any other price. Sometimes the float can be 'dirty', which means that central banks do intervene to try and smooth out fluctuations, although the New Zealand Reserve Bank has not in fact done this in recent years.

Now to local idiosyncrasies. The NZD had a transitional period; from July 1973 to June 1979 it was pegged against a basket of currencies (call it a shifting peg). From then to 1982, the New Zealand exchange rate was adjusted to reflect inflation rate differences between New Zealand and its trading partners. This is referred to as a purchasing power parity system and we shall discuss such things below. It was fashionable at the time. However, by 1982 the PPP regime had been found wanting and New Zealand resorted briefly to the above-mentioned adjustable peg in the basket. The economic watershed of 1984–1985 resulted in the floating of the NZD in1985. This brings us to the present. So far the floating system has worked well and there are no prospects for anything much different in the years to come.

7.2   The Spot Market

The spot market is the international market for the buying and selling of one currency against another for immediate delivery. Well, more or less immediate; delivery is usually in one or two days. In former times, the Reserve Bank restricted the entry of dealers, but this is no longer really true. For economic reasons, however, the market is dominated by 11 banks, who collectively form the New Zealand inter-bank network, which is an informal communication system operating via Reuters and Telerate. In addition there are three New Zealand-based brokers who also have links with brokers in Australia and the U.S. As the name suggests, the brokers are middlemen charged with finding the best deal for their client rather than dealing themselves. The six major dealing banks are the ones who push around large sums of money in the interbank market. The much smaller foreign bank note/travellers cheques market is mediated via players such as travel agents, foreign exchange bureaus and smaller banks, as well as the majors.

Quotations

The way that the NZD is quoted against other countries' currencies can be quite hard to understand. The following numbers (as at 23 January 1995) will serve as a basis for discussion:

	bid	ask	
U.S. dollar (USD)	0.6376	0.6483	[=1 NZD]
Australia dollar (AUD)	0.8326	0.8438	[=1 NZD]
Portugal (ESC)	100.0926	103.3832	[=1 NZD]

The first and rather obvious thing is that all these prices refer to one NZD taken as the numeraire or 'commodity'. We could call this quotation 'Kiwi direct'. The word 'direct' just by itself would refer to a system of quotation in which the USD is numeraire (see below).

Now the 'bid-ask' terminology. This is a two-way price. For every New Zealand dollar you wish to sell, the bank will bid 0.6376 U.S. dollars; and the dealer will ask 0.6483 U.S. dollars for every New Zealand dollar that you wish to buy. The NZD is the commodity being bought or sold and the settlement is thought of as being in terms of USD. In the newspaper, you may find the bid-ask order reversed, e.g.

	'buy'	'sell'
U.S. dollar	0.6483	0.6376

In this version the 'buy' and 'sell' refers to you rather than to the bank (dealer). If you want to buy a New Zealand dollar with U.S. dollars, you will do so at the rate of 0.6483; or if you want to sell a New Zealand dollar you will get 0.6376 U.S. dollars.

So the two versions are equivalent – they just look at things from the point of view of different agents. The bid-ask terminology is more widely used internationally, so we shall stick with it. These are the figures that the dealer will post as his two-way prices.

To test your comprehension, suppose you wished to switch 500,000 Australian dollars from your Melbourne bank account to your New Zealand dollar bank account in Wellington. For a sum of this magnitude, the bank would offer you 'wholesale rates', which are characterised by a smaller bid-ask spread than for smaller amounts which would attract only 'retail rates'. Now, which rate do you use: 0.8326 or 0.8438? You can solve this in two ways:

1. The virtuous way. How will the dealer respond to your call? Remember you will be selling AUD, so the ask price for this will be 0.8438 AUD. Hence your conversion is:

    500,000 AUD @ 0.8438 AUD per NZD
    = *500,000*
    0.8438
    = NZD 592,557.48

2. The disgraceful way. If you cannot remember all the bid-ask-buy-sell stuff (and who can?) just think of it as the 'screw you' principle. Take the worst rate and that will be it. In the above example you are clearly going to be dividing, so take the worst number to divide by, namely 0.8438 rather than 0.8326. It always works.

To test your understanding further, you could do an inversion. Suppose the USD is now the commodity currency and the bid-ask is on this basis, with settlement being thought of as New Zealand currency.

	bid	ask	
NZ dollar	B	A	[= 1 USD]

B and A will both be in terms of NZD. To get B, for instance, the bank will be bidding so many New Zealand dollars for one U.S. dollar. Schematically,

$$\frac{USD}{NZD} = \frac{1}{\left(\dfrac{NZD}{USD}\right)} .$$

Remember that where bid-ask rates are involved, you cannot simply invert – you have to choose which of two numbers to invert and which to place where in the bid-ask slots. To do the latter, remember the format: the small number first, the big number second. To get the small number first you have obviously to use the larger of the two New Zealand-direct quotes, namely 0.6483. Hence:

Notes

1. Technical note: An alternative general formulation of the pricing problem is: market price = E* (payoff, discounted back to the present). Here the E* is a special kind of expectation: the mathematical expectation, but where your expected payoff is discounted for risk – you construct a 'risk neutral world' by penalising all stochastic returns for risk, then imagine everybody is neutral to risk once this is done. This is called 'equivalent martingale' pricing.

2. Suppose, for instance, that as a dealer you have just put into place a pay-fixed side of a three-year vanilla interest-rates swap. Naturally, you would like to find an offsetting receive. Before you can do so, you will hedge the interest rate exposure by * buying? * selling? three-year bond futures. Which, and why?

3. At that time, the basis for the SPI future, but now replaced by the top 10.

Chapter 7

Foreign Exchange

7.1 History Again

The post-war history of the New Zealand dollar is complicated – not to put too fine a point on it, a real dog's breakfast. It was, however, an international dog's breakfast. The full history of international exchange rate regimes is a matter for specialist courses in economic history or international finance. For our purposes we can partition all the changes into those that followed international developments and those, of a somewhat later date, that represented local idiosyncrasies. Starting with international changes, there are two main dates to remember: July 1944 (Bretton Woods) and March 1973 (the world floats).

The Bretton Woods agreement – which also established the IMF – established a system that operated in terms of two reserve currencies (USD, GBP), with the USD pegged against gold, initially with a price of $35. This basically meant that we were all on a gold standard. In this regime of *fixed exchange rates*, central banks committed themselves to a (more or less) fixed exchange rate against the reserve currencies. To achieve this, they had to hold large buffer reserves of the USD and GBP. If you sold foreign currency in New Zealand, the Reserve Bank credited your bank with high-powered money in exchange – hence balance of payments surpluses or deficits resulted in major changes in the New Zealand money supply. If there were crises of confidence in a currency, the official exchange rate could be changed, but such a bump and grind adjustment often proved extremely expensive for a beleaguered central bank charged with fighting a losing battle to support their currency's value. At any rate, a *fixed exchange rate* system and basically a *gold standard* emerged.

It all broke down in the seventies, for two basic reasons. First, countries such as Germany and Germany (joke) started to run massive balance of payments surpluses – their currencies became more and more undervalued. Second, the U.S. got embroiled in the Vietnam War and financed it by printing money (okay, borrowing from the Federal Reserve – see Chapter 2). There was no way they could maintain convertibility at a fixed rate against gold. So after years of upheaval and buying wool futures when the potential for price upsurges is so low? Recently there has been a proposal to set up a forward trading risk intermediary as a subsidiary of Wool International (the fomer Australian Wool Corporation) in Sydney. If this comes to pass, such an intermediary would have to hedge its operations with the futures market. So we might be right for a resurgence in wool futures volumes.

Equity options, in particular, have zoomed ahead. A longer term growth perspective is portrayed in Figures 6.1a and b, the former representing a number aggregation over all contracts traded on the Exchange and the latter representing aggregated equity options alone. As well as the general growth, notice the considerable fluctuations that have occurred. Trade in bank bill and bond futures is very responsive to periodic bouts of uncertainty about the future course of the respective interest rates.

Table 6.3:   NZFOE Volumes and Open Interest Summary for December 1994

Contract	Volume						Open Interest		
	Dec 1993	Dec 1994	% Incr/ % Decr	Jan-Dec 1993	Jan-Dec 1994	% Incr/ % Decr	End Dec 1993	End Dec 1994	% Incr/ % Decr
Futures									
90-Day Bank Accepted Bills (BBC)	25429	58374	130%	463141	608460	31%	14856	22608	52%
3-Year Government Stock (TYS)	11298	6511	-42%	74128	101229	37%	4390	1888	-57%
10-Year Government Stock (TEN)	2548	2346	-8%	20996	42541	103%	1271	1018	-20%
NZSE–40 Capital Share Price Index (FIF)	485	805	66%	3633	7397	104%	112	352	214%
US Dollar (USD)	2	0	-100%	9	21	133%	1	1	0%
NZ Wool Futures (WFC)	0	0	0%	0	0	0%	0	0	0%
5-Year Government Stock (GSC)*	–	–	N/A	50836	0	N/A	–	–	N/A
Total Futures	**39762**	**68036**	**71%**	**612743**	**759648**	**24%**	**20630**	**25867**	**50%**
Financial Options									
90-Day Bank Accepted Bills (BBC)	0	100	N/A	8193	6870	-16%	320	700	119%
3-Year Government Stock (TYS)	200	0	N/A	1000	80	-92%	200	0	N/A
10-Year Government Stock (TEN)	0	600	N/A	120	4200	3400%	0	600	N/A
NZSE–40 Capital Share Price Index (FIF)	235	700	198%	596	1985	233%	220	350	59%
5-Year Government Stock (GSC)*	–	–	N/A	1652	0	N/A	–	–	N/A
Total Financial Options	**435**	**1400**	**222%**	**11561**	**13135**	**14%**	**740**	**1650**	**123%**
Share Options									
Brierley Investments Ltd	1165	3125	168%	10812	38254	254%	1265	9410	644%
Carter Holt Harvey Ltd	856	1335	56%	8114	23673	192%	5724	7415	30%
Fletcher Challenge Ltd – Forestry	0	0	N/A	0	1780	N/A	–	40	N/A
Fletcher Challenge Ltd – Ordinary	839	2273	171%	9215	39797	332%	1576	6248	296%
Goodman Fielder	–	0	N/A	0	854	N/A	–	518	N/A
Lion Nathan Ltd	5	1720	N/A	10014	17616	76%	1885	1261	-33%
Telecom Corporation NZ Ltd	780	1125	44%	11832	24425	106%	413	3390	721%
Total Share Options	**3645**	**9578**	**163%**	**49987**	**146399**	**193%**	**10863**	**28282**	**160%**
Total	**43842**	**79014**	**80%**	**674291**	**919182**	**36%**	**32233**	**55799**	**73%**

* Delisted 16 June 1993

Source: NZFOE.

Figure 6.2a: Total Monthly Volume, NZFOE, 1985 to December 1994

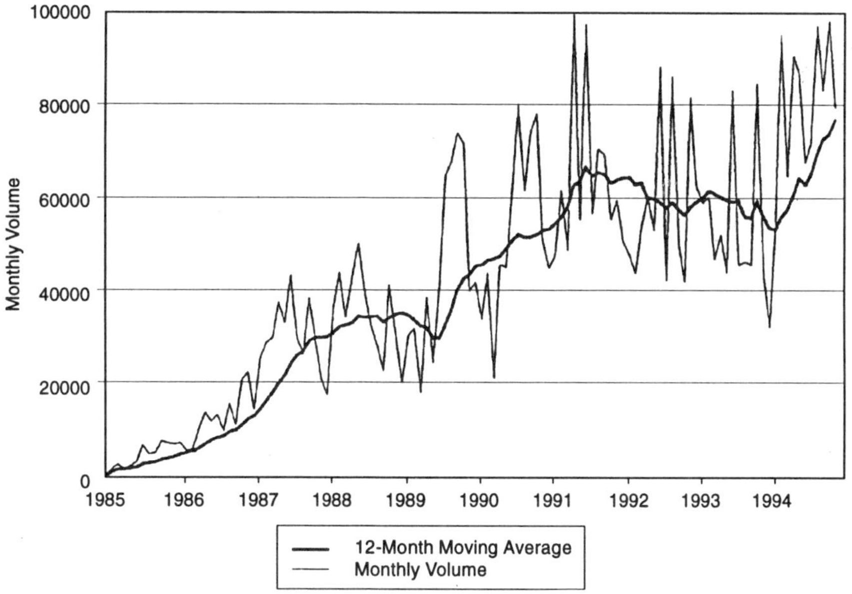

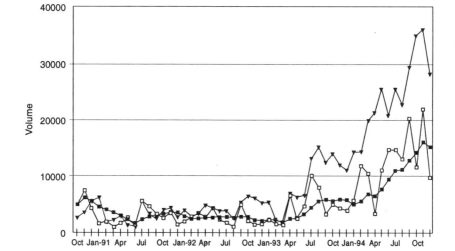

Source: NZFOE.

Figure 6.2b: Total NZFOE Share Option Volume

Source: NZFOE.

$$B = \frac{1}{0.6483} = 1.5425 \ .$$

Similarly, $A = \frac{1}{0.6376} = 1.5684 \ .$

So the quotation in these reversed terms is (1.5425, 1.5684).

Cross Rates

Suppose for some reason you wanted bid-ask rates for one Australian dollar against the Portuguese escudo:

	bid	ask	
ESC	B	A	[= 1 AUD]

By the convention, the little number comes first. How can you make the very littlest (sensible) number? You can see that the numbers are both going to be a little bit bigger than (103.3832, 100.0926), for these are quotations against the NZD and the AUD is 'stronger than the NZD' (words only). A good guess would be:

	bid		ask	
ESC	$\frac{100.0926}{0.8438} = 118.6212$		$\frac{103.3832}{0.8326} = 124.1691$	. [=1AUD]

These numbers satisfy the algebraic scheme:

$$\frac{AUD}{ESC} = \frac{AUD}{NZD} \times \frac{NZD}{ESC} \ .$$

but they do so in such a way that the implied bid-ask spreads in a transition such as $AUD \rightarrow NZD \rightarrow ESC$ and vice versa are satisfied.

In point of fact, the whole cross-rate chain goes via the USD as intermediary, so the above example is a bit misleading.[1] Thus the market would say:

$$\frac{AUD}{ESC} = \frac{AUD}{USD} \Big/ \frac{ESC}{USD} \ .$$

or in terms of bid and ask:

$$\text{bid} \left(\frac{AUD}{ESC} \right) = \text{bid} \frac{AUD}{USD} \Big/ \text{ask} \frac{ESC}{USD}$$

$$\text{ask} \left(\frac{AUD}{ESC} \right) = \text{ask} \frac{AUD}{USD} \Big/ \text{bid} \frac{ESC}{USD}$$

The Australian dollar should trade within these limits against the escudo. If not it can be subject to arbitrage attack, operating via one of the two implied conversion legs: between AUD and USD or between the USD and ESC (so-called 'triangular arbitrage'). Of course, one could expect the cross rate of the AUD against the ESC to have quite wide spreads, because of the infrequent trading problem; but there is an arbitrage implied limit given by the above equations for bid and ask.

Notice the role of the USD as the common denominator currency. This has the effect of reducing a potentially multilateral quotation system to a much simpler bilateral arrangement.

Dealing

The six banks mentioned above are the *price-makers* in the market. They stand ready to buy and sell currencies at their stated bid-ask rates. It is the bid-ask spread that provides the dealers with their bread and butter. A bid-ask of (0.6376, 0.6483) represents a spread of seven points, which is characteristic of the interbank market, where large sums ($5m upwards) and very competitive pricing are the rule. The spread is larger for wholesale corporate or individual transactions and larger still for smaller retail deals. On banknotes or travellers cheques the spreads are pretty gross, 100 points or more – look at them in the window next time you pass a bank, travel agency, etc.

The other component – the cake so to speak – of the spot dealer's income comes from speculative positions, i.e. outright gambles on which way the currency is moving. Each dealer will have personal limits, usually cast in terms of his specialist currency. The end of day limits are continually marked to market, i.e. valued at the current spot rate, to ensure that the effective value exposure does not exceed the dealer's limits. The general idea is to cut your losses and let your profits run.

So suppose you are a dealer and you have an order to buy AUD$5m. You will call up other dealers to find the market: 'G'day mate, what's your market in Aussie dollars', or such words. You won't let on whether you wish to buy or sell. The other dealer will quote you a bid-ask pair that reflects his own estimates of where the market is going – she may inflate the spread in one direction if she does not really want to transact in that direction (remember she *has* to make a market). Once she has quoted, you then have five seconds or so to consider whether to accept that quote (in this case, the other dealer's bid figure) or whether to try another dealer in the hope of getting a better price. Some dealers have told us a bit longer, but in the words of our Poet Laureate:

> Seconds five or seconds thirty,
> Fart around and she'll get shirty.

So far as your own price is concerned, both sides of the spread have to be constantly adjusted in line with where you perceive the market to be. If you get it wrong you will be bombarded with orders on one side of your spread and you will end up buying (say) more than you are selling. The consequence of this is an unintended speculative exposure that you have to get rid of pronto. From the economic point of view this is all part of the process by which the market as a whole mimics the hypothetical Walrasian auctioneer, charged with adjusting prices in line with excess demand.

Volumes

Table 7.1 gives a breakdown of the currency pairs traded daily in the New Zealand market during 1992.

Table 7.1: Popular Pairs in Currency Trading

Currency pair	Turnover U.S. $ billion	%
NZD / USD	0.439	22
NZD / other	0.059	3
USD / DM	0.721	36
USD / JY	0.320	16
USD / AUD	0.170	9
USD / GBP	0.156	8
USD / other	0.027	1
All other	0.090	5
	1.982	100

Source: *Reserve Bank Bulletin* (1993), vol. 56, no. 1.

You will notice that 92 per cent of the transactions involved the USD as one half. Of these, the greatest single item, namely USD against DM, did not even involve the NZD at all. This is generally attributed to the time zone advantage – recall from earlier chapters that the New Zealand markets wake up first to the new day. Much of it is regarded as speculative in nature. In spite of this putative advantage, however, the New Zealand market still accounts for only 0.4 per cent or so of global FX market turnover. Very little New Zealand dollar trading occurs in overseas centres – it would mainly be associated with trade and other financing such as debt transactions. In summary, we are small beer, but the peanuts are nevertheless worth having.

7.3   Constructed Exchange Rates

Several 'notional' or 'constructed' exchange rates are in widespread use by economists and policy-makers. While a full discussion of these belongs to courses in international finance, we will list them and give a brief explanation of their use.

Trade Weighted Exchange Rates (TWI)

Recording bilateral exchange rates between New Zealand and each of its trading partners misses the full story of how we are doing 'on the whole'. A strengthening of the NZD against the AUD may not represent an export disaster if the NZD simultaneously weakens against the Yen or USD, and a strengthening against the Escudo will not in itself mean very much at all. A measure that focuses on the overall trade implications is the trade weighted index (TWI). One assembles all the per cent changes in our major trading partners' currencies and weights these with the proportion of our trade values associated with those countries. The latter are measured as the sum of import and export volumes from the most recent finalised end-of-year merchandise trade results, using a country of origin/destination basis. A weighted average exchange rate movement is then derived. Using this to adjust an arbitrary starting value for the index (June 1979=100) yields a time series for the TWI. Below are the weights as at June 1995:

Australia	34.02%
Japan	25.38%
United States	24.81%
United Kingdom	10.11%
Germany	5.68%
	100.00%

The TWI has acquired market importance through its use by the Reserve Bank to monitor its exchange rate 'comfort zone'. The TWI is a.k.a. the 'nominal effective exchange rate'. Figure 7.1 plots the TWI over the last 15 years.

Figure 7.1: Our Sins Exposed – Trade Weighted Exchange Rate Index June 1979 to June 1995

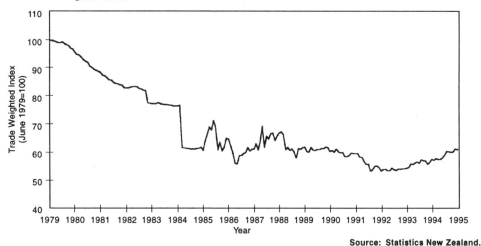

Source: Statistics New Zealand.

Real Exchange Rates

This is a somewhat difficult concept to grasp and linked intimately with the idea of *purchasing power parity* (PPP). Perhaps the best way to start is with an informative mnemonic:

$$R = \frac{purchasingpowerof1NZDabroad}{purchasingpowerof1NZDathome} \; .$$

Thus suppose R>1. It would be better to source your goods from abroad, so New Zealand would be at a competitive disadvantage – the current account of the Balance of Payments would be in the red light area. In symbolic terms, suppose we could define an aggregate price level index for NZD for all goods and services; suspend belief for the moment as to exactly what form this might take, or whether it is even possible in principle. Call it P. Then the purchasing power of 1 NZD at home would be $\frac{1}{P}$. Alternatively we could take our NZD and convert it to USD (say) at rate S: 1 NZD ® S.USD. Its purchasing power over there would be $\frac{S}{P}$ where P_* is the U.S. price level. So

$$R = \frac{\frac{S}{P_*}}{\frac{1}{P}}$$

(1) $$= \frac{SP}{P_*}$$

would be the real exchange rate against the USD.

Now go a step further and take per cent changes. Using equation (1), we obtain:

% changes in R = [% change in P – % change in P.]
+ % change in S.

A more informative way to express this is in terms of the inverse exchange rate: 1 USD = e.NZD. An increase in e from, say, 1.5425 to 1.6968 would represent a depreciation of 10 per cent in the NZD against the USD. In these terms:

(2)   % change in R = [% change in P – % change in P$_*$] – % change in e.

Now we go back to the meaning of P or P$_*$. Instead of actual prices, interpret them as price indexes: GDP (gross domestic product) deflators. Formula (1) has no meaning in these terms (can you think why?). But formula (2) does:

(3)   % change in R = [NZ inflation rate – U.S. inflation rate] – % change in exchange rate (e)].

In an ideal world, exchange rate changes should reflect changes in relative inflation rates. If New Zealand prices are roaring along at 10 per cent faster than U.S. prices, then the NZD should be depreciating at just 10 per cent relative to the USD.

If the exchange rate were not depreciating, then the NZD real exchange rate would be rising. If domestic prices are rising faster than overseas prices, with little change in the exchange rate to compensate, then it is better to source your goods from abroad; or alternatively New Zealand exporters face rising costs with smaller exchange rate rewards from a depreciating local currency. Thus a rising real exchange rate harms the export sector.

Expression (3) is a dynamic version of the real exchange rate, as it refers to changes. However, once you have the per cent changes, you can reconvert to a 'levels' index: simply take a base year as 100 and apply the annual per cent changes to this (to end up with a sequence like 100, 105.5, 109.6, etc.). You can then call this 'the' real exchange rate, although of course it is just an index.

Equation (3) has an analytical use. *Purchasing power parity* says that the best predictors of exchange rate changes are just anticipated inflation rate differentials. In other words you reinterpret the RHS terms in (3) to refer to expected inflation, rather than actual and the hypothesis then becomes that the per cent change in R is zero; the real exchange rate should not change. You can then predict what the exchange rate should be at one year hence, in terms of the expected inflation rate differentials.

There is some evidence that over the very long run the PPP theory of the exchange rate is true.[2] It patently is not true over shorter periods – exchange rates are affected by all sorts of other influences, such as interest rates (see later).

The version of PPP just given is called 'dynamic' PPP. The 'absolute' version of PPP is based on formula (1) above and the identification of P, P$_*$ either with specific prices or else with 'basket prices'. An example of the former is the so called *'law of one price'*, which says that if P, P$_*$ are the local and overseas prices of widgets then R=1 (otherwise you could ship widgets to take advantage of cheaper prices and do widgetrages).

An amusing example of absolute PPP is the *Hamburger theory of exchange rates*. Suppose that P, P$_*$ refer to the price of a McDonalds quarterpounder in Hamilton, New Zealand and in Hamilton, Ontario respectively. A hamburger (the theory goes) contains all sorts of priced inputs and represents a mixed price index for New Zealand and Canada respectively. Suppose you find the Canadian burger badly overpriced, once you convert to CD at the current NZD exchange rate, i.e. you find $eP^*_h \gg P_h$. Then the Canadian dollar is overpriced on the Hamburger exchange rate theory and holders of the CD risk being pickled in ketchup. In the author's experience this theory has worked well in one case (the Deutschmark) and not at all well in another (the Yen). It also suggests that the NZD is currently overvalued with respect to the USD and moving further that way! Still, if there is something to it, can we expect to see McDonalds posting all their international hamburger prices in your local store?

Figure 7.2 graphs the real effective exchange rate index. Quite a mouthful – can you figure out what it all means? How far do you think purchasing power parity has held over the past five years or so?

Figure 7.2:   PPP or not [to] PPP? Real Effective Exchange Rate Index June 1988 to December 1993

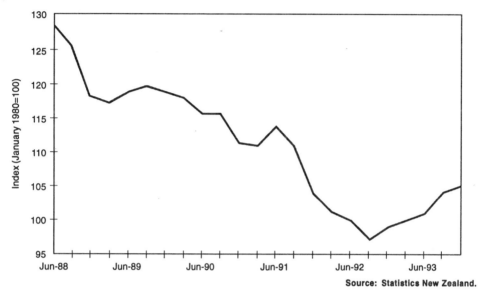

Source: Statistics New Zealand.

7.4   FX Derivatives

In this section we will look at the following kiwi-based foreign exchange derivatives:

(a) Forwards
(b) Futures
(c) Options
(d) Swaps of various kinds.

The bulk of turnover in NZD foreign exchange occurs via the spot market and the swaps markets: about 47 per cent and 48 per cent respectively in 1992. Forwards accounted for four to five per cent and futures and options for a fraction of one per cent. The data suggests that we ought to pay special attention to the swaps phenomenon, but for convenience we will start instead with the other instruments.

1. Forwards

An FX forward is simply an agreement to buy or sell foreign currency for delivery at some specified time in the future. No money changes hands now. How much money actually changes hands at delivery date depends on the precise nature of the agreement. Importers, exporters will usually want to take or make delivery of the foreign currency at due date. However, banks entering the forward market will normally do so on an offsetting basis, which means that they receive or pay up only the difference between the rate specified in the forward contract and the spot rate as it transpired on delivery day. In Australia this sort of arrangement is called a 'hedge settlement' contract and used to be quite widely available, although less used these days.

Forwards are OTC instruments; that is, they are created by banks on a customised basis for their clients and are not traded on any exchange. There are seven or so active pricemakers in the market; the four large local banks, BT, Citibank and Hongkong Bank. All price-makers quote up to six months. Average daily turnover is not large – about $191 million in 1992. However, volume has declined in very recent years; many dealers think that forwards have had their day and might be replaced by FX options.

The pricing of forwards is reasonably straightforward. Like many other derivatives, no-arbitrage pricing specifies the forward rate as some function of the spot rate and interest rates, specifically those of New Zealand and of the other country. The basic covered *interest parity* formula for FX forwards (e.g. against the USD) is:

$$(4) \qquad F = \frac{S(1+i_*)}{1+i}$$

where: S is the spot rate such that 1 NZD = S USD;
          i = NZD interest rates over the forward period;
          i_* = USD interest rates over the forward period;
          F = the forward rate for 1 NZD = F USD at maturity.

The easiest way to justify the above formula is to imagine yourself faced with two alternatives: (a) investing your NZD here and earning NZD $(1+i)$ at the end of the period, or (b) switching it to USD at rate S, investing at $1+i_*$, then switching back to Kiwi at rate $\frac{1}{F}$ at maturity. All elements of (a) and (b) are known at the outset, so the two must be equivalent, giving rise to formula (4).

In practice, bids and asks also apply to quoted forward rates, so formula (4) is no more than indicative. There are more precise spread bounds available. The interest rates would usually be taken as Bank Bill – remember to adjust the annual rates for the holding period concerned.

Below are some forward quotations on the NZD/USD for 23 January 1995.

	bid	ask
Spot	0.6376	0.6483
Forward		
- 1 month	0.0015	0.0016
- 3 months	0.0041	0.0043
- 6 months	0.0080	0.0082

Source: Hongkong Bank/*New Zealand Herald.*

Notice the way forwards are quoted here. Given that NZD interest rates were higher than the corresponding USD interest rates at the time, what are the actual forward rates? Was the Kiwi dollar trading at a forward premium or a forward discount?

Forward rates have a rather loose connection to *expectations* of future spot rates. The forward rate should theoretically be equal to the expected future spot rate plus or minus a risk premium, which could be of either sign. The risk premium is – in the simplest form – equal to a 'market price of risk' for the currency concerned times the volatility of the spot rate, measured by the standard derivative of its recent changes. So higher FX spot volatilities lead to higher premiums or discounts relative to expected future spot rates, provided the price of NZD risk remains constant.

Forwards are still widely used by exporters and importers. The attraction is that you know exactly what your foreign currency cash flow is going to be down the track; so that if you sold a machine for delivery six months ahead at a nominated price in USD, you would be able to sell the USD forward (buying NZD forward) at the present time point and know exactly what the NZD proceeds are going to be down the track. This protects against 'transactions exposure', in the jargon. Most FX forwards are written for short periods (≤ 1 year), but much longer-term cover is available at a rather poorer sort of pricing spread.

FX Futures

We recall the essential difference between a future and a forward. The former is an exchange traded contract which is marched to market each day and gains or losses credited to the margin account held with your broker. Most futures contracts are not physically delivered, but sold back to the exchange at maturity. The pricing is effectively the same as for a forward.

The only contract listed in New Zealand is a U.S. dollar contract on the NZFOE. Each contract is of USD50,000 and has a margin of $1,500. Tick size (the quantum charge in the contract's price) is $5; if the exchange rate moves by one point, then a $5 profit or loss is made. Unfortunately the market is still very thin – indeed the contract was suspended in late 1995 because of lack of interest and remains in limbo. FX futures are far more liquid for major currencies overseas. To the extent that the Australian and New Zealand dollars tend to move together, it is possible to utilise AUD futures [AUD/USD], which are far more liquid and traded on such exchanges as the Sydney Futures Exchange and Philadelphia Exchange.

FX Options

Recall the nature of an option. Such contracts give you the right to buy (call) or sell (put) foreign exchange at a prearranged exchange rate. To take up the earlier example of the exporter selling a machine – he could buy a put USD options contract whereby if the NZD rose against the USD he could exercise the option and receive the strike price, or sell back the option at an enhanced price. In this way he would protect himself against a decline in NZD export receipts when money for the machine finally changes hands. If, on the other hand, the NZD fell against the USD in the interim, the option would expire worthless but the exporter would have gained when he finally remitted the USD proceeds from the machine back to NZD. An FX option is thus a one-way bet on the relevant exchange rate. As a one-way bet, it costs – the price is the premium paid for the option. A forward or future has no upfront price, but it can entail considerable losses[3] as well as gains.

FX options are not currently exchange traded, but are priced and arranged on an OTC (over-the-counter) basis by the major banks. The four large local banks together with Citibank and B.T. are all considered to be market makers. The market is reasonably liquid for parcels of NZD5–10 million out to 12 months, with the NZD/USD and NZD/AUD as the principal contracts. Premiums are payable within two business days of the contract being written. There is anecdotal evidence of trading in NZD options once written, by brokers in Australia or by originating banks with branches or headquarters overseas. Against this, however, is the non-standardisation of the contracts, which are customised.

At this point we can draw together and summarise the key features and differences between the three types of instrument so far considered.

Table 7.2:   FX Instruments Compared

Characteristic	Forward contract	Currency futures	Currency options
Delivery discretion	None	None	Buyer's discretion. Seller must honour if buyer exercises
Maturity date	Any date	Set by exchange	Usually set, but customisable in NZ
Maximum length	Several years	12 months	Usually 12 months, although available for periods over 12 months in NZ
Contracted amount	Any value	USD50,000 only in NZ	Usually standardised but any amount in NZ
Secondary market	Must offset with bank	Can sell via exchange	Can sell through bank in NZ
Margin	Informal	Formal – USD1,500 in NZ	Usually, but not in NZ
Contract variety	Swap or outright	Outright	Outright
Guarantor	None	Exchange	Bank in NZ
Major users	Primarily hedgers	Speculators, but too thin in NZ for trend	Hedgers and speculators

Swaps

This term covers a variety of arrangements in the FX and related interest rate markets. Moreover, there is a fair bit of notational confusion: different authorities use the same name for quite different arrangements, so be sure you ascertain which is which. On the inter-bank market, two banks may agree to exchange two currencies at some time in the future at a preassigned forward rate and to make the reverse transaction now in spot. An elaboration of this arrangement is a 'straight currency swap', where the spot and forward transactions are both at the same current exchange rate, but one party pays the other interest to compensate for the forward rate premium or discount.

FX swaps in the interbank market are used to fund forward positions or rolling spot positions, typically on an 'overnight' basis or to cover the roll from New York close to New Zealand open for the new trading day. The bulk of the 48 per cent by FX volume referred to earlier will be of this general class. In addition, FX swaps are also used to swap USD commercial paper proceeds back to NZD. Longer-term swaps action centres around debt denominated in different currencies. Generally the idea is for the parties to exchange with each other coupon and principal repayment obligations and in doing so to achieve a preferred currency obligation. There are several distinct arrangements of this type (for which, see most international finance textbooks), but the one most relevant for New Zealand is the *cross-currency interest rate swap*.

A cross-currency interest rate swap is very similar to a common or generic interest rate swap – typically the exchange of a fixed coupon payment for a floating payment, every six months. However, the two interest payments are denominated in different currencies; you could also have floating against floating (interest rates) in the different currencies. And there is usually an actual exchange of principal amounts, both at settlement (uplift) of the loans and then again the reverse transaction at final maturity. Both the initial and final principal exchanges are made at the same exchange rate, namely the current spot rate.[4] In this way each party accesses the currencies it needs at the outset.

Example

This is a hypothetical swap deal underlying a Euro-Kiwi issue by a non-New Zealand issuer ('Kiwicorp'). A Euro-Kiwi issue is an issue of bonds or floating rate notes offshore but denominated in NZD. The floating rates are set with reference to an international benchmark six-month interest rate, LIBOR. The acronym stands for the 'London Inter-Bank Offer Rate', the market rates at which banks lend euro currencies of various kinds to each other in London. [Another benchmark is SIBOR, the Singapore version; and there are yet others. LIBOR is the main one.]

Kiwicorp (our local hero) requires NZD and can borrow domestically at the equivalent of 100 basis points above LIBOR. It has an AA credit rating, but cannot itself borrow in the Euromarkets because it has no 'name' there; rather like school leavers being unable to get a job because they have no work experience!

Ozcorp (a foreign corporation) requires USD funds. It has the same credit rating as Kiwicorp, but Ozcorp is well known in European markets. Hence it can borrow NZD in the Euromarkets at 50 basis points above LIBOR. Both Kiwicorp and Ozcorp can borrow USD at LIBOR flat.

The following swap deal is put together by a bank, who will sit in the middle, just as for domestic interest rate swaps. Kiwicorp borrows floating rate USD at LIBOR and passes the funds on to Ozcorp at the current exchange rate, with the reverse exchange at maturity as above. Ozcorp issues Kiwi Eurobonds at 50 above LIBOR, passing the issue proceeds through to Kiwicorp. (A word on conventions: Eurobonds have a fixed coupon, whereas the characterisation '50 above LIBOR' looks like and technically is, a description of a floating rate. A better bit of jargon would be 'swap plus 50', which means 50 basis points above the fixed coupon (side) on a swap between LIBOR floating and fixed, for instruments of the same maturity as the Eurobond.)

The terms of the fixed–floating interest rate interchange each six months are that Kiwicorp will pay a NZD coupon – the fixed side – at NZD Swap + 75 (or LIBOR + 75) to Ozcorp, while the latter will pay USD LIBOR flat to Kiwicorp on the floating side. These terms are equivalent (in terms of the current swap rates between fixed and floating) to Kiwicorp borrowing NZD at 75 basis points above LIBOR and Ozcorp borrowing USD at 25 basis points under LIBOR. Each party is happy. Kiwicorp's 75 basis points above LIBOR are better than what it could do in the New Zealand domestic market, while Ozcorp is chuffed at effectively paying 25 points under LIBOR for its USD obligations. The diagram below summarises.

Figure 7.3:   Swap Deal Underlying Euro-Kiwi Issue

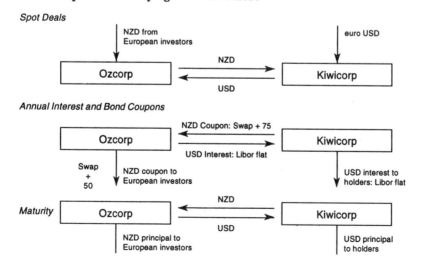

Notice the way comparative advantage drives this deal. One party is well known in the Euromarkets, the other is not. The Euromarket is (or was) a better place to borrow than the domestic markets. So they got together to solve the informational problem. Such swaps are also very useful when company articles or policies forbid certain sorts of borrowing (e.g. fixed, or in certain currencies). One simply arranges a swap with the counterparty doing the forbidden thing. Technically, swaps do not figure on company balance sheets – they are 'off-balance-sheet' items, in the jargon, although they should be reported as notes in the accounts.

As the above example shows, describing a cross-currency interest rate swap is most sensible when set in the context of a complete series of transactions, all operating off the back of debt raisings. At the conclusion of this chapter we present a case-study, kindly supplied by Neil Bradley, the ECNZ Treasurer, of a recent euro-Yen medium-term note issue by the Electricity Corporation of New Zealand. This particular transactions diagram is a bit more complicated than that described above, as there is an intermediate swap involved – the sequence is Yen → U.S. dollars → N.Z. dollars. However, the flow diagram is pretty clear and we suggest you take some time out to read the study and look at some of the accompanying documentation.

7.5   Sourcing Funds Abroad

Note on Euromarkets

Although not all New Zealand overseas borrowing is via the Euromarkets, it is impossible to understand either the practices or recent economic history of the fixed-interest markets without some prior understanding of what the Euromarkets are. Basically, the NZD Euromarket is the market for the investment of New Zealand dollar funds that are held offshore. There are lots and lots of them, a reflection of our past current account deficits. It may not be an unfortunate reflection, for were the facilities not to exist, foreigners would not have felt happy about holding New Zealand funds domestically and the value of the NZD would perhaps be much lower than it is now. At any rate, there they are now: a large pool of New Zealand dollars sloshing around out there quite beyond the control of the New Zealand Government.

The Euromarket originated as a result of the Suez Canal crisis of 1956, in which the British Government's sterling problems resulted in their prohibiting external sterling loans. However, British banks had made a good thing out of those and turned to U.S. dollars instead, funding them by offering to take in U.S. dollar deposits at competitive interest rates. The idea proved to be *awesome*, although not entirely original. Then in the early sixties the U.S. had balance of payments problems of its own and tried to impose taxes on American purchases of foreign securities issued in the U.S. – not something to appeal to the European investors at all. Likewise they tried to restrict lending by U.S. banks to U.S. multinationals. And in the meantime, the Cold War meant that the (then) Soviet Union, while wanting to hold U.S. dollars, was not too keen on holding them in the U.S. where they could be frozen. So the U.S. Eurodollar market, based initially in London but later in Europe and world-wide (not quite 'euro-'!), exploded through the sixties and seventies. The idea spread to other currencies, especially those that had historically run massive balance of payments deficits.

This is where New Zealand came in. However, at this point we are getting ahead of ourselves.

Sources and Types

There are two principal ways you can source funds from overseas:

(a) by borrowing in overseas currencies
(b) by borrowing in the Euro-Kiwi market, in New Zealand dollars.

To which we could possibly add:

(c) Borrowing in overseas currencies and swapping them back to New Zealand currency obligations (or perhaps other forms of hedging, where available).

Option (a) is the older. The classic way for the New Zealand Government to raise funds was to issue coupon debt denominated in U.S. dollars, originally in the U.S. markets, but later in the Euromarkets. This has to be done either in the form of longer-term coupon bonds, or more recently in the form of medium-term floating-rate notes. The trouble with option (a) is that you have to make up your mind about exchange rate risk. What happens if the NZD falls out of bed? You are stuck with more expensive coupon payments – when brought back to your NZD accounts. And the damage will also extend to your balance sheet from the principal liability. The New Zealand Government took a king hit in the seventies and eighties by electing to borrow unhedged U.S. funds.

On the other hand, borrowing in overseas currency can make a great deal of sense if there is a natural hedge available from your operations. In November 1994, Carter Holt Harvey issued USD500m of 10 and 30-year registered bonds in the U.S. market. In the jargon, these are 'Yankee' bonds, the name for debt issued in the U.S. market by a foreign body. The CCH bonds were in fact the first issued by a private New Zealand corporate. The company is a substantial exporter of forest products, most of which are priced in U.S. dollars; indeed their forests are valued in USD. Hence there was a natural 'transactions hedge' currency hedge available, certainly for the USD coupons; and arguably for the principal as well, since the NZD value of the company would rise or fall with the value of its future earnings, brought back to NZD.[5] A subsequent issue was made in April 1995. The following table gives the details. The two ratings given are for Moody's and Standard and Poor respectively.

	November 1994		April 1995	
Amount (USDm)	350	150	150	150
Maturity (years)	10	30	7	20
launch pricing (bps over				
U.S. Treasuries)	+92	+132	+67	+93
Coupon (per cent)	8.875	9.500	7.625	8.375
Rating		Baa2/BBB		Baa2/BBB

Source: Reid, Ted (CCH Treasurer) (1995), 'Raising Funds in the United States of America', *Treasury Note*, September.

The issue process for such bonds is similar in some respects to that for Eurobonds, described in detail below. To anticipate this discussion, there is a lead manager (CS First Boston, in the CCH case) and co-lead manager (JP Morgan and Salomon Brokers), plus a legal adviser. However, U.S. registration requires a more considerable due diligence process, monitored by the U.S. Securities and Exchange Commission; with a detailed prospectus containing information about the company and the issue and a reconciliation to U.S. accounting standards. Adequate credit ratings have to be established. Informational aspects – the establishment of a 'name' – also have to be considered. CCH mounted an extensive 'roadshow' for its first issue, which paid off when it followed up the bond issues with a USD commercial paper programme shortly after the bond issues. For a review of the CCH placements, see the excellent account by Reid (ibid.).

The CCH bonds were an example of a public offering. Other options in the Yankee market are private placements, or else a section 144A offering. The latter basically allows some institutions in the U.S. to hold bonds initially registered offshore.

Returning to the question of currency exposure, what happens if the loan raiser does not have a natural currency hedge? In this case option (c) above, i.e. a cross-currency interest rate swap, could be implemented. Historically, however, private New Zealand corporates have not followed such a path, preferring instead to issue in the Kiwi Eurobond market. It is to the latter that we now turn.

Option (b) is the Kiwi Euromarket. As remarked earlier, the Euro-Kiwi or Kiwi Eurodollar market refers to issues of bonds or notes, denominated in NZD but made offshore, principally in Europe. A variant is the Yankee-Kiwi market, which covers similar issues made in the U.S.; by extension, the term also refers to placing NZD bonds in, say, the Dutch markets. Initially the market was used by blue chip companies to gain access to long-term fixed rate NZD; more recently it has allowed lesser name corporate borrowers to achieve similar funding through the use of swap transactions.

In general, Euromarkets provide a number of advantages to issuers:

1. Access to a large market, largely free of regulatory controls. The size is important: a company considering a large issue may be deterred from the domestic market because it would attract a pricing penalty simply by virtue of the size of the issue. This is less of a problem in Europe.
2. Flexibility. Debt can be raised fixed or floating, in a range of maturities.
3. Sometimes rates can be substantially below those available in the domestic market, or through local banks. For example, in 1991 McDonalds (NZ) raised NZD50m in a 9¾ per cent, eight-year Euro-Kiwi issue, much better than it could get locally.

The Euro-Kiwi Market

The major form of borrowing is in the form of fixed coupon bonds, or 'Eurobonds'. They are bearer securities providing anonymity to the investors who buy them and they are issued tax free on the coupons. This is one reason that they are popular with issuers, because they will attract a higher issue price (or lower coupon) than equivalent domestic bonds and therefore constitute cheaper financing. Maturities range from 2–5 years. Below are some examples of issues for the March 1992 quarter.

Issuer	Maturity	Coupon	Issue Price	Yield	Amount (millions)
Euro-NZD Telecom	3/4/2000	9.50	101.4	9.633	NZD 60
Yankee-NZD Exportfinans	24/2/1995	8.125	100.5	7.934	NZD 125

Kiwi Eurobonds have had a damburst type of history: first a trickle, then a flood, finally back to a trickle. The first Euro-Kiwi placement took place in 1975 when a NZ$50m, six-year issue for the New Zealand Government was made. Following this government issue, the first Euro-Kiwi issue by a corporate was made in 1983 by New Zealand Forest Products for NZ$22.5m and a second for the same amount, by Woolworths in 1984. The early trickle of Euro-Kiwi issues turned into a flood in 1985, partly because of high domestic interest rates, because of the difficulties in obtaining long-term fixed rate funds domestically and because the lifting of exchange controls created a more open borrowing environment. The yearly volumes of issues in the Euro-Kiwi and Yankee-Kiwi markets are displayed in Figure 7.4.

Figure 7.4:   Yearly Volume of Euro-Kiwi and Yankee-Kiwi Bond Issues

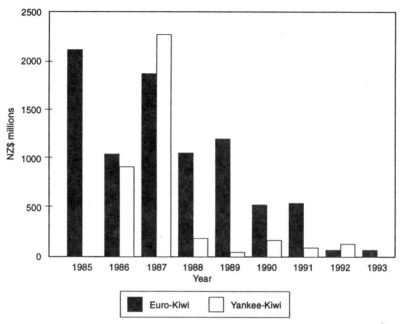

Source: RBNZ.

Various authors cite different reasons for the growth in the Euro-Kiwi market during the mid to late 1980s:

1. [Demand side]. Despite the fall in value of the NZD, European investors became increasingly willing to take the currency risk in exchange for the interest rate gain. For example, a Swiss investor early in 1985 comparing his own Swiss (SFR) bonds at 5.5 per cent and NZD bonds at approximately 14 per cent, could afford a large loss on the NZD currency before the Swiss investment began to look more attractive. With the NZD down so far, would it really fall much further? Likewise, during the late 1980s New Zealand interest rates remained high while U.S. rates fell. During this period currencies such as the Australian dollar (AUD) and NZD were the main benefactors of European retail, yield-conscious investors.
2. [Supply side]. Euromarkets offered both private and public sectors an alternative source of funding and offered fixed rate medium-term money at a lower cost than that that was available domestically and without the FX risks involved in borrowing in low coupon non-NZD currencies.

As a result of declines in domestic New Zealand interest rates relative to rates in Europe, volume in the Kiwi Euromarket has declined quite substantially in recent years. Of the NZ$750m of Euro-Kiwi bonds that matured in the quarter ended December 1991, only NZ$50m were rolled over. Likewise, the current reinvestment or roll over rate is approximately 10 per cent. Figure 7.5 displays the volume of maturing Euro-Kiwi bonds as at 1 January 1991.

The recent fall from favour of the Euro-Kiwi has seen the market decrease from its peak of NZ$3.3 billion as at February 1987 to its current level of approximately NZ$1.3 billion. Similarly, the Yankee-Kiwi market has shrunk from big ticket deals of NZ$50 and 100m to deals of between NZ$5 and 10m. As at 1 June 1994 only one Yankee-Kiwi deal was outstanding.

Figure 7.5:   Profile of Maturing Euro-Kiwi Bonds as at 1 January 1991

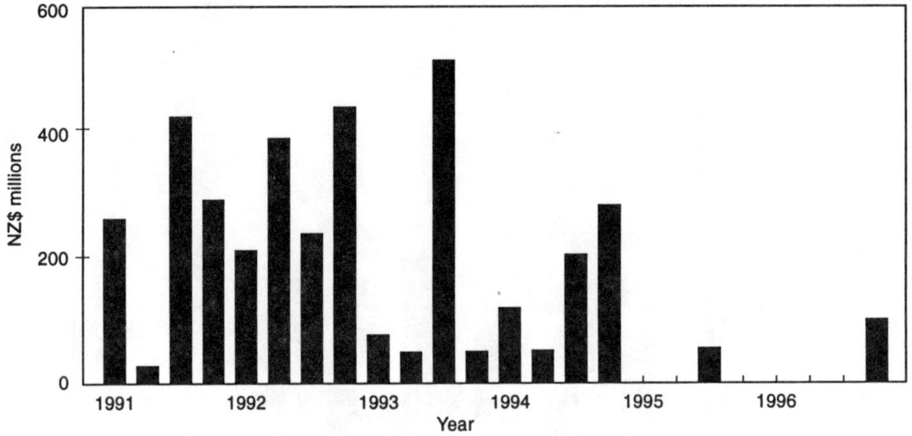

Source: RBNZ.

The Borrowers

An analysis of the names of Euro-Kiwi issuers points to the fact that the NZD market sees far more swap deals than in any other market. Indeed, as much as 98 per cent of the NZD bonds issued are tied to an underlying cross-currency interest rate swap to generate the preferred currency. This occurs for three reasons. First, many New Zealand organisations are not encouraged to come in their own name to the Euromarket by the strict withholding tax rules which are imposed on them – these rules do not apply to foreign borrowers. Second, the coupons were at such a level as to enable quasi-arbitrage opportunities between the euro's and floating rate USD, as the earlier SBNSW/Kiwicorp example showed. Finally, many New Zealand names are unknown on the continent and such anonymity can add significantly to borrowing costs. Thus, most issues are made by corporates or other borrowers with no natural connection with New Zealand at all.

Table 7.3 contains information on the maturing Yankee and Eurobond issues for the June 1992 quarter, an unusually busy one. A review of the names of the issuers affirms the earlier point that many issuers are not domiciled in, or have any direct connection with, New Zealand. Other recent Euro-Kiwi issuers include Nederlandse Gasunie, Swedish Export Credit Bank, BP, Compagnie Francaise de Petroles, Belgian Savings Bank, and Kriedietbank (Luxembourg).

Table 7.3:   Maturing Yankee and Euro-Kiwi Bonds in the June 1992 Quarter

Maturity Date (1992)	Name	Type	Coupon	Amount NZD (millions)
April 4	NZ Breweries Finance	Euro	15.875	25
May 4	US West Financial	Yankee	13.0	50
8	GMAC Australia Finance Ltd	Euro	14.0	50
15	State Bank of South Australia	Euro	14.0	50
19	Societe Generale	Euro	13.5	50
23	Finance Company of South Australia	Euro	14.125	50
27	Toronto Dominion Australia	Euro	13.5	60
June 9	ANZ Banking Group	Euro	14.0	60
12	Societe Generale	Euro	13.75	50
17	Okobank	Euro	9.5	25

Some New Zealand corporates do turn to offshore markets and raise funds directly through Euro-Kiwi issues. The most deals in the Euro-Kiwi market for any one issuer have been for Telecom Corporation New Zealand Ltd. The success of the Telecom issues reflects the stature of the issuer as the most familiar and creditworthy name in the New Zealand market. Figure 7.6 shows what kind of borrowers have raised funds in Euro-Kiwi.

Figure 7.6:   Distribution of Euro-Kiwi Issuers in 1990

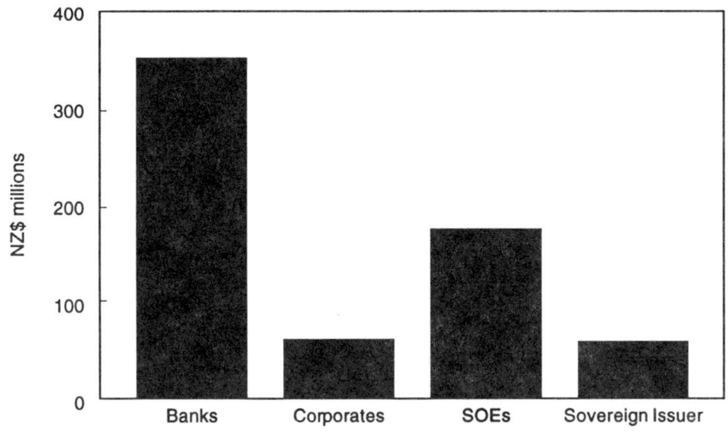

Source: RBNZ.

The Investors

Eurobonds typically offer a yield advantage over comparable domestic issues in the designated country or countries, so a major part of every issue is aimed at local investors. These investors may have an interest in the NZD, but this is often limited to those times when the currency has a particular, speculative interest. The issues of New Zealand bonds in 1987 were aimed directly at Swiss and German private investors who considered that the high coupon compensated for the currency risk. Institutional investors soon followed and this resulted in record new issue volumes at the time.

Tax efficiency (or avoidance), even tax evasion, are attractive to the professional classes in Europe. This is a widely attributed reason for the popularity of Euro-Kiwi bonds and the like. The typical investor is often stereotyped in jest as a Belgian dentist, looking to invest his savings in instruments which, unlike his domestic bonds, do not have tax deducted at source. If he redeems his coupons in Antwerp, resident withholding tax will be deducted from the proceeds. However, the Eurobond coupons can be cashed anywhere in Europe. So this can be his après-ski while on holiday in Switzerland.

Although the Kiwi Euromarket is a small market that cannot take too many issues, there does exist a solid investor base for Euro-Kiwi issues. Buying is spread throughout the continent, with the German, Swiss and Austrian institutions driving the market. Likewise in the Low countries, the weight of demand for the NZD paper matches that for AUD. The Dutch have shown particular appetite for the paper. There has also traditionally been a good uptake in South-east Asia, in a quite different geographic area, with many individual holders.

As mentioned earlier, support for the New Zealand paper historically came from the yield difference that European investors are able to pick up over comparable domestic bonds. Although the coupons on Kiwi bonds were high in the late 80s/early 90s, the Euro-Kiwi market faced competition from other high yielding currencies like the AUD and the Canadian dollar. As of late, it has been very difficult to place Kiwi bonds as retail clients are less interested in the coupon levels currently being offered. There does, however, exist some small amount of institutional buying. Market participants report that borrowers are still in abundance, but the investors are not terribly interested.

A wide bid-ask spread in the secondary market for Euro-Kiwi indicates that investors in Euro-Kiwis are mainly private individuals (the proverbial Belgian dentists) who hold the investment over a length of time – to maturity, perhaps. The August 1993 NZ$75m Telecom issue[6] was primarily aimed at private clients preferring to reinvest in Euro-Kiwis rather than to take currency losses. In general, European investors face an appreciable exchange rate risk as the NZD has been such a volatile currency. Other risks experienced by investors in the Euromarkets include economic, political, credit and market risks.

Issuance

The Euro-Kiwi market has relatively standardised issuing procedures. The first step in the creation of a new Eurobond issue is the appointment of a lead manager to underwrite the issue. Fay, Richwhite and Co. pioneered the Euro-NZD market for New Zealand issuers in 1984 as lead manager. Fay Richwhite and Hambros bank (U.K.) have lead the majority of issues in the Euro-Kiwi market; others to lead issues have been Westpac and Kriedietbank. Below are the Euro-Kiwi lead managers for the first six months of 1990.

Lead Manager	NZ$ millions	Number of Issues
Fay, Richwhite and Co.	150.0	3
Hambros bank	50.0	1

The amount, issue price, coupon, maturity, repayment schedule, covenants, security – if any – and commissions have to be agreed to before the issue can be announced. The lead manager, usually with the agreement of the borrower, invites a group of European banks and securities houses to form a selling group and to jointly underwrite the issue; those that accept become co-lead managers and co-managers (depending on the amount of the issue underwritten). The amounts underwritten by the co-lead managers and co-managers are referred to as the ticket sizes. The group is selected on the basis of their relationship with the lead manager and based on their distribution capabilities. The borrower pays the lead manager a fee which is usually split into two parts: a management and underwriting fee to be shared by the managers and underwriters and a selling concession, computed as a percentage of the value of the security.

The selling group lists the Euro-Kiwi bonds alongside other foreign currency denominated bonds (e.g. BMW – DEM) to provide alternatives for retail investors. The borrower does not receive the NZD funds until six months after the lead manager is appointed. During this six months the prospectus and other legal documents are drawn up. Figure 7.7 opposite displays the issuance process.

7.6   New Zealand's Overseas Debt

The Overseas Public Debt

Whether by value or volume, government debt has historically been the largest block of New Zealand's overseas debt. The rapid increase in the early seventies stemmed from two factors: a perceived need to support economic activity in the wake of the 1973 oil shock, and an expanded borrowing programme resulting from several large-scale energy related projects – the famous

Figure 7.7:   Getting the Euro-Kiwi to Fly

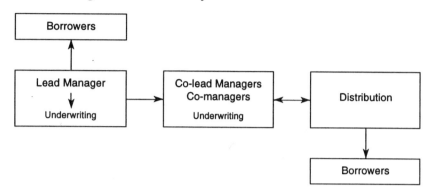

Think Big episode, later revised to 'Sink Big'. During the eighties, most of the New Zealand overseas public debt was denominated in USD and amounted to about half of the total public debt. Correspondingly, there was a pretty substantial servicing burden: about eight per cent in relation to, say, New Zealand exports of goods and services.

In the last two years or so, the government has been in the happy situation of not strictly needing to borrow at all, although it will continue to do so for other reasons, such as making a market or keeping its name in the market. Indeed since 1991 it has concentrated on refinancing its debt through a successful euro-MTN (medium-term note) programme, a form of private placement. It has placed more than USD2 billion since the inception of the programme, at below LIBOR. The general intention was to shorten the duration of New Zealand's overall debt composition, and floating rate notes are a way to do this. The MTN's were placed in a variety of currencies (on occasion mixed, with principal in one currency and coupons in another), but mostly swapped back into floating rate USD obligations. Note, however, that the NZDMO does not generally (there is one exception) either issue in euro-Kiwi or swap back into NZD.

Following the sale of Forestry Corporation in September 1996, the net FX component of New Zealand debt was reduced to zero. The word *net* is the operative one here. If you did swap back into NZD, you could always achieve net FX debt of zero, no matter how large the *gross* exposure. However, the PR is a bit more virtuous than that. In recent years the government has built up a portfolio of FX assets in the form of cash deposits and marketable securities, plus some contributions from favourable swap revaluations. So both liabilities and assets now have the same NZD value, around $9b. The net effect of this has been to cancel out a large chunk of the FX exposure. Liabilities in USD slightly exceeded USD assets in the June 1996 financial statements, but this may well have been reduced to zero since.

Which brings us on to the topic of hedging, against either or both interest rate and FX exposures. More recently the NZDMO has been actively hedging the interest rate exposure, attempting to maintain a net zero duration of the book in each currency. The reader may like to refer back to Chapter 2 for this concept – it essentially means that the book does not change in value if there are uniform rises or falls across the term structure.

Hedging against the FX exposure appears to have been a different matter. Historically, apart possibly from natural hedges, the government did not hedge against foreign exchange risk by indulging in cross currency interest rate swaps back to Kiwi, or other derivatives. By not doing so, it suffered massive losses over the period 1987–1989 and again in 1992, although it will by the same token be a winner since late 1993. The exchange rate gains of NZ1.2b in the December 1993 quarter helped assuage the pains of the earlier period, such as the $1.4 billion slug in the

September 1991 quarter. Since 1993, the overall hedging philosophy has obviously been to match currency exposures on liabilities with those of the growing assets book. The NZDMO does use CCIRS to switch its primary raisings in other currencies back into USD floating, but swapping back into NZD is not favoured.

Should the New Zealand Government have formally hedged its currency exposures against NZD in the past, and should it do so now? To answer this entails all sorts of enquiries:

1. Were there derivative hedge facilities available, say from 1987 onwards, in sufficient volume? Apart from the liquidity question, the NZDMO was not empowered by legislation to use derivatives, though this has recently changed.
2. Are there natural hedges available – in other words are there counterbalancing currency gains and losses from other economic activities? For instance might the tax base actually be augmented following a devaluation? Likewise building up FX assets has independent value for operational purposes, or to help with a run on the NZD if support was ever needed. To the extent that such assets are needed, they also constitute a natural hedge.
3. And the sovereign aspect: the government is a major player in the determination of the NZ dollar. In conjunction with the Reserve Bank, it can take corrective action on this score, and thereby fix the exposure problem as a principal agent, so to speak. Indeed, suppose it did decide to hedge against FX exposures by operating in the markets. What sort of signal about the future of the currency would the FX market thereby receive?

Evidently, the whole question of hedging interest rate and FX exposure – if you happen to be a sovereign government – is by no means trivial. In some circumstances, operational rules are fairly clear. For instance, if you expect interest rates to fall in your liability countries, then you should repay debt (why?), which is just what the government has been doing in recent times. If you expect interest rates to rise, then better to build up a matching assets portfolio until the right moment for repurchase, if you can pick it.

Lots of interesting questions. At the moment they are rather academic. Cynically, one can expect fiscal rectitude to wear a bit thin following an MMP election. So the questions might re-emerge: whether to borrow locally or offshore; euro-Kiwi versus FX; whether to hedge, and so forth.

Total Overseas Debt

Finally, a few remarks on the total overseas debt, including private as well as public sources. Overseas debt is defined as the outstanding total gross liabilities, excluding equity capital, of New Zealand located organisations to all overseas organisations and persons. New Zealand's gross overseas debt has grown rapidly since the early 1970s,[7] one both in absolute terms and relative to the size of the economy. There has not only been a rapid increase in reported overseas debt, but also a marked shift in the composition of that debt, with the government (gross) component falling from almost 100 per cent to the current level of around 20 per cent in this time.

Overseas debt statistics are prepared for three specific sectors of the New Zealand economy – the New Zealand Government sector, the local government and other semi-official sector, and the private sector. Figure 7.8 shows borrowing balances for each of these sectors for the last decade, expressed in NZ dollars. It is clear from the above figure that the growth in external debt over the past five years has occurred as a result of borrowing by the private sector as opposed to borrowing by the official government sector.

Figure 7.8:   New Zealand Overseas Debt by Sector, September 1989 to March 1995

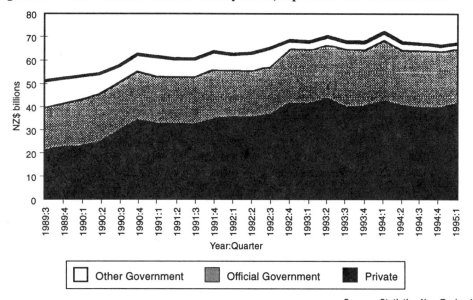

Source: Statistics New Zealand.

The removal of exchange controls has allowed portfolio diversification to extend into external liabilities. The make-up of New Zealand's overseas debt by currency of denomination is contained in Table 7.4. The NZD continues to be New Zealand's primary offshore borrowing currency, illustrating the importance of Euromarkets and domestically issued securities (taken up by non-residents) as a medium for raising funds.

New Zealand's current overseas debt has mostly been raised in the form of loans, bank bills and bonds. Table 7.5 gives the breakdown as at 31 December 1994. Figure 7.9 portrays the maturity profile of New Zealand's outstanding debt as at 31 December 1994. The major components are 90-day bank bills and long-dated bonds – the dreaded[8] barbell structure for a debt portfolio.

Table 7.4:   New Zealand Overseas Borrowing, by Currency as at 31 December 1994

Currency	Debt Outstanding NZ$ millions	%
New Zealand dollar	29,107	43.1%
United States dollar	23,230	34.4%
Japanese Yen	6,117	9.1%
Australian dollar	3,335	4.9%
British Pound	1,338	2.0%
German Deustchmarks	591	0.9%
Swiss Francs	496	0.7%
Other Currencies	1,580	2.3%
Unallocated estimate	1,738	2.6%

Source: Statistics New Zealand.

Table 7.5:   Breakdown of New Zealand's Overseas Debt as at 31 December 1994

Type of Instrument	Debt Outstanding NZ$ millions	%
Loans	22,547	39.7%
Bills and Bonds	16,478	29.0%
Deposits	14,659	25.8%
Accounts payable	1,374	2.4%
Unallocated estimate	1,738	3.1%

Source: Statistics New Zealand.

Figure 7.9:   New Zealand's Overseas Debt: Type of Instrument

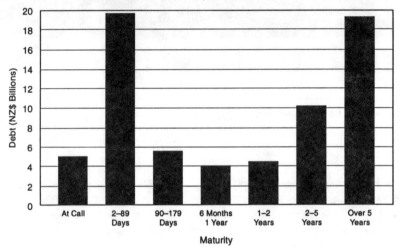

Source: Statistics New Zealand.

7.7   So What Drives Exchange Rates?

The short answer is what everybody thinks everyone else thinks about the future of the NZD. Keynes put it well with a much quoted passage (indeed, I used it in a previous book – beats rolling your own).

> Or, to change the metaphor slightly, professional investment may be likened to those newspaper competitions in which the competitors have to pick out the six prettiest faces from a hundred photographs, the prize being awarded to the competitor whose choice most nearly corresponds to the average preferences of the competitors as a whole; so that each competitor has to pick, not those faces which he himself finds prettiest, but those which he thinks likeliest to catch the fancy of the other competitors, all of whom are looking at the problem from the same point of view. It is not a case of choosing those which, to the best of one's judgement, are really the prettiest, nor even those which average opinion genuinely thinks the prettiest. We have reached the third degree where we devote our intelligences to anticipating what average opinion expects the average opinion to be. And there are some, I believe, who practise the fourth, fifth and higher degrees.
>
> (Keynes, J.M. (1936), *General Theory of Employment, Interest and Money*, London: Macmillan)

All this – applied to the FX market – means that the market can be hopelessly wrong in economic terms. The market is undoubtedly affected from time to time by bubbles, sunspots and other economic cancers. Someone with the best understanding in the world of economic fundamentals could nonetheless end up as a nicely casseroled woodduck. In the longer run, however, macroeconomics does probably prevail. The only trick is to know just when this will be the case. If I knew the answer to that, would I have to write this book?

At any rate, back to the fundamentals. Start by recalling these truths, which we hold to be self-evident, about balance of payments tables. (a) The top half of a BOP table is the current account. Things like trade flows, netting to the trade balance. Or freight, insurance payments, royalties and other 'invisibles'; interest and dividends and other investment flows. Collectively, they all net out to the current account balance. N.Z. and Oz have traditionally run a smallish trade surplus but largish current account deficits. (b) The bottom half of the BOP table is the capital account. This represents the flow of investments or divestments associated with debt, equities, direct investment in subsidiaries, etc. purchase of real estate and so on.

The capital account is often regarded as the balancing side for the current account. It is certainly true that if you run a current account deficit you must be also running a capital account surplus, i.e. going further in hock to the rest of the world, purely as a matter of financing. However, this is getting carried away with accounting. Suppose I said instead: 'The capital account is very strong – foreigners are just bursting to get their hands on prime New Zealand assets, so the current account has fallen into deficit'. This is not by any means far-fetched. The reason that the U.S. continues to maintain a reasonably strong currency while it runs massive current account deficits, is that foreigners like the quasi reserve status of the USD. A more complete story is that the current and capital accounts are jointly determined, although with independent influences on each.

It is the capital account that has the most immediate effect on the exchange rate. Given the expectations and apprehensions – good or bad – about the future course of the NZD, foreigners and locals will form an idea of their required rate of return on NZD assets. Remember that to a U.S. or Japanese investor the rate of return on a New Zealand equity consists of two parts, the normal return in NZD and the exchange rate return, if, say, the NZD appreciates, or on the other hand falls out of bed. So if the future of the NZD is a worry, foreigners will require a higher NZD return on the asset, to compensate them for the risk involved, not to mention the worry.

For example, consider the NZD return (a) on bank bills or overnight cash, major repositories of hot money. Rewrite equation (4) of §7.4 above as:[9]

(5) $\qquad i = i_* - \dfrac{F - S}{S}$; 1 NZD = S USD spot = F USD forward.

To a first approximation, the forward rate F can be regarded as a market prediction of the end of period spot rate: $F = S_1^e$, the rate after period 1. So we can replace the forward rate premium $(F–S)/S$ by the expectational premium, to end up with:

(6) $\qquad i = i_* - \dfrac{S_1^e - S}{S}$.

Equation (6) is the famous 'uncovered interest parity' relationship. For given foreign interest rates and expectations S_1^e about end of period or future exchange rates, it is an instantaneous equilibrium relationship[10] connecting local interest rate i and the current exchange rate S. You will notice that equation (6) is incomplete as an explanation of i and S; two variables but only one equation. However, it suffices to establish the flavour of some of the arguments.

Suppose, for instance, that people get an attack of the willies about the future of the NZD (S_1^e ↓). On the basis of equation (6), two polar scenarios are possible, plus, of course, others in between:

Scenario A: If current exchange rates S are to remain unaffected, local interest rates i must rise, to compensate for the possible exchange rate loss.

Scenario B: If local interest rates were held constant for some reason, the exchange rate must weaken (S ↓).

Which of the two scenarios do you think the Reserve Bank would go for?

We could go on and add risk to the story, i.e. augment equation (6), but that would take us too far afield. For a treatment of risk and volatility for New Zealand FX, see Note 10. However, a final word is in order on the time frame involved. How, for instance, does purchasing power parity fit into all this?

If a country permits a rate of inflation above that of its trading partners, it will run a persistent current account deficit. Eventually investors will become unwilling to absorb the volume of New Zealand capital on their hands. At the same time, they will start to get worried about the future of the NZD. Either:

A: Required returns on NZD assets must rise; or
B: The NZD falls out of bed.

Either way, ppp will hold. Under scenario A, rising interest rates choke off the inflation. Under scenario B, changes in exchange rates occur and follow the differences in inflation rates, preserving the real exchange rate. All this happens (according to the theory) in the long term. In the shorter run, however, substantial divergencies can occur from ppp.

This is all we can say here about exchange rates. It is a fascinating and, needless to say, important topic, one on which much misunderstanding exists. Constructing a decent FX model for New Zealand, both short and long term, would materially help us to understand the ways in which the various forces – market, economic and policy – interact to drive exchange rates and interest rates.

Indeed, it is appropriate to end the book on such a note. It has been (almost) as much to describe what we do not know as what we do know, that has motivated the writing of this book. To date little really creative research has been accomplished in New Zealand financial economics. Much of what has appeared represents routine adaptations to New Zealand data of overseas studies, or is constrained by the special needs of large-scale econometric model building. Neither genre significantly augments our understanding either of economic processes in general or as they apply to New Zealand. Truly original research benefits us all: market players, media commentators, academics, policy-makers and the general public. It is therefore worthy of financial and moral support, neither of which will be noticeably forthcoming under the constraints facing the New Zealand academic world. The results hitherto have been all too apparent. Somehow, we have to do better.

Notes

1.   The actual rate will lie somewhere between the two bounds given (i.e. 118.6212, 124.1691), but these may not be the 'tightest' bounds. These will usually be given in terms of the USD-denominated cross-rate calculations, below.

2.   Though even here there are theoretical reasons why it might not be true. For example, 'biased technical progress' is the idea that technical progress is greater in motorcars than haircuts. The former are traded, the

latter not, but the internal price index includes both. PPP should apply to traded goods prices, but not necessarily the entire C.P.I.

3. Actually this is not quite fair. You lose on the future or forward, but of course you have gained on your product sale; the next effect is for a zero gain or loss in either direction. In other words, you have immunised your position. On the other hand, with an option you stand to lose only the premium, but could win on both the option and your product sale.

4. More technically the 'official' spot rate, as the current settlement rate for forward hedge contracts.

5. Since the time of issue, CCH has also acquired a majority US-based shareholder (International Paper).

6. Maturity: 29/10/2000, coupon: 6.50%.

7. In 1974/75 the total of New Zealand's external debt was approximately NZD1 billion. Compare with Figure 7.8!

8. At this point it may be useful to cast our minds back to Chapter 2.1. Barbell portfolios (big cash flows fore and aft, skinny in the middle) have high convexity. Good if you are a holder (long). Terrible if you are a borrower (short).

9. Yes I know, it is not exactly the same as (4). But it is a close approximation. Don't write.

10. There is a similar relationship connecting forward interest rates with forward exchange rate expectations. This enables us to relate the entire term structure of one country with another. For further discussion see: Bowden, R.J. and O'Donovan, B., 'Financial Volatility and Economic Policy', in the Bollard, Lattimore and Silverstone book quoted in §1.4.

Questions for Discussion

Chapter 1

1. The following quote is taken from Ian Wishart's book *The Paradise Conspiracy* (1995), Howling at the Moon Productions.

> As part and parcel of jettisoning the baggage of the Muldoon years, the Labour administration moved swiftly to deregulate the economy – left, right ad centre. Farmers – traditional supporters of the blue ribbon National Party – lost their taxpayer-funded production subsidies, financial markets were thrown open with no restrictions, overseas investors were invited to browse and shop in 'supermarket New Zealand', where anything, even citizenship, was up for sale.
>
> Such no-holds-barred tariff reduction and openness were brave/foolhardy, considering that no other Western nations had taken such drastic steps. Not to worry, said the Labour government, we'll be an example to the rest of the world and lead the way in new right economics. Pretty soon everyone will be doing it.
>
> As a whole, the New Zealand population fell for it, although a small group, notably people like Peters, cynically compared it to a rather obese, middle-aged individual striding down a beach towards a group of tanned and slim beauties, whilst throwing off every item of clothing in the expectation that the other sexy young things on the beach will do likewise.
>
> In the international game of truth-or-dare, New Zealand was exposing its bloomers to the rest of the world. Unfortunately, other countries misinterpreted this act of magnanimous generosity as a hostile act, and instead, we took an economic hiding in the decade that followed.
>
> Among the few winners in New Zealand: some of the major corporates who took advantage of financial deregulation to act, in some cases almost simultaneously, as advisors to the government on which state corporations should be sold, and also as purchasers of those same state assets.
>
> New Zealand in the 1980s was regarded by many as the 'Dodge City' of the entire Western world. Nowhere, not even Wall Street at its worst, came close to the unregulated corporate gunslinging that took place downunder.

Mr Wishart seems to think (a) that unilateral deregulation was a bad idea; and (b) that deregulated financial markets inevitably become mired in ethically unacceptable behaviour. Do you agree? And if so, what sort of regulatory processes would you put in place to ensure more socially acceptable outcomes?

2. Is ownership concentration (of financial assets) a good thing?

3. Could we solve market liquidity problems by having a common currency with Australia, or any other specified commonalities? What are the economic and/or political feasibilities entailed in such a proposal?

4. Do you think it is possible for markets to be driven by vacuous information, and could the latter thereby become valuable information? Consider, for instance, the effects of investment *gurus*.

Chapter 2

1. New Zealand interest rate term structures seem to stay inverted for some time. Over what years since about 1985 has this been the case? Historically, have the forward expectations implied by the term structure been good forecasts of the actual spot (short-term) rates that transpired?

2. Suppose that a five-year floating rate note Euro-Kiwi loan goes off and is swapped back into fixed rate (NZD) obligations. What effect do you think this would have on the level and/or shape of the New Zealand term structure? Does our smallness predispose to term structure instability?

3. Swap rates are good things to use to compile zero couple rates. Why? But what would be the problem in using market swap rates to estimate zeros on NZGS?

4. Using your knowledge of interest rates and capital gains or losses, analyse the credit risks attached to a swap, especially in times when interest rates are changing markedly.

Chapter 3

1. How much leverage do you think the Reserve Bank really has over interest rates? Could circumstances ever arise in which Bank action was ineffective?

2. To what sort of economic conditions do you think bank margins would be sensitive? Would they tend to follow external interest rates; if so, which ones, and what would be the timing involved?

3. Analyse interest rate conditions and dynamics in a world where the cash target had been reduced to zero.

4. How might capital adequacy requirements influence (or bias) a bank's investment (assets) policy? Do you think that there is a case for investment banks to be required to follow similar rules?

Chapter 4

1. What are the economic functions (apart from making their owners rich) of investment banks?

2. Should other deposit-taking institutions be brought into line with banks in respect of capital adequacy requirements?

3. Of all the DTIs surveyed in this chapter, which do you think undertake significant maturity transformation?

4. What caused the historical changes portrayed in Figure 4.1?

Chapter 5

1. The cost of equity is the required rate of return for cash flows accruing to the shareholders from company projects. How might this be estimated from market return data, and what problems would arise in using it?

2. (Regulation)

   (a) Should insider trading be freely allowed?
   (b) What takeover rules would you like to see in a company of which you are a shareholder? If you like you could consider two cases; in one you are a major, the other a minority, shareholder. Do you think leaving it up to individual company articles is the way to go, or do you think that there should be a common takeover code?

3. Do you think the NZSE should be regulated by statutory or administrative law, rather than contract law?

4. (a) Should firms require employees to belong to a superannuation fund?
   (b) Do you think there should be special tax breaks for superannuation type funds?
   (c) Some 'pollies have suggested a compulsory 'national superannuation fund'. Do you think this is a good idea?

Chapter 6

1. Design a futures contract based in some manner upon either:

   - the outcome of New Zealand's first MMP election; or
   - the outcome of the next Rugby Union World Cup.

   Remember the overriding requirement that people have to be interested enough, or involved enough, to actually want to bet on your contract.
   Your answer should cover:

   (a) Definition of the underlying index or magnitude on which people are betting.
   (b) Typing a monetary payoff to that magnitude, including contact standardisation.
   (c) Administrative details such as settlement, tick size, margins.

2. Why do some market-traded derivatives contracts 'take off' in terms of public acceptance, while others do not? Give examples of each category.

3. What are the largest regular categories of user, or user purpose, for bond futures and bill futures respectively?

4. How might futures markets be subject to 'large player' or 'undue manipulation' effects. Do you know of any actual or reputed examples in recent years?

Chapter 7

1. Pollies and the general public worry that 'the exchange rate is too high'. Should they mean the nominal rate or the real rate? Historically, is the real rate unusually high at the current time?

2. Criticise the 'hamburger theory of exchange rates'.

3. (More difficult.) Try to generalise forward-spot parity (formula (4) of §7.4) in terms of bid-ask spreads F_b, F_a. You should end up with arbitrage-driven inequalities of the form $x < F_b < F_a < y$, where the outer limits x, y are determined in terms of:

   (a) bid-ask quotes, S_b, S_a for the spot rate;
   (b) bid-ask (or lend, borrow) rates for i and i_* ; i_b , i_a and i_{*b} , i_{*a} .

4. Historically, the New Zealand Government decided not to hedge the FX exposure on its foreign currency denominated debt. The decision was expensive in the eighties but came back the other way in the nineties.

   (a) Suppose that it had so decided, and that all the instruments surveyed in this chapter were then available and liquid (some think they were). What would have been the best way of protecting coupons and principal against changes in the value of the NZD?
   (b) But was the Treasury right anyway, in deciding not to hedge? What are the economic arguments for and against?
   (c) The government has recently prioritised the retirement of foreign currency denominated debt as a matter of budgetary provision. Do you agree?

Appendices

Chapter 2

Appendix 1

Example – Generic Vanilla Interest Rate Swap

Party A requires five-year debt financing. Party A has access to comparatively cheap floating-rate finance but wants a fixed-rate obligation.

Party A can borrow at the following rates of interest:

floating-rate financing (50 bps)	annual New Zealand Bank Bill Rate + 0.5 per cent
fixed-rate financing	annual 10.00 per cent

Party B requires five-year financing. Party B has access to comparatively cheap fixed-rate financing but wants a floating-rate obligation.

Party B can borrow at the following rates of interest:

floating-rate financing	annual New Zealand Bank Bill Rate flat
fixed-rate financing	annual 9.00 per cent

Table A2.1: Interest Rate Swap – Initial Borrowing Costs for the Two Parties

	Fixed-rate (five years)	Floating-rate
Party A	10.00%	NZBBR + 0.5%
Party B	9.00%	*NZBBR* flat
Advantage	1.00%	0.50%
'Comparative advantage'	0.50%	

As can be seen in Table A2.1, Party B has an absolute advantage in both fixed- and floating-rate markets. Party A has a comparative advantage in the floating-rate market and Party B has a comparative advantage in the fixed-rate market. This comparative advantage of 0.50 per cent can be shared by both parties if they enter the swaps market and undertake a swap with a swaps dealer.

The swap dealer comes into the swaps transaction between the two parties. The swap dealer has the following interest rate profile:

floating-rate financing: annual New Zealand Bank Bill Rate flat
paying fixed rate: annual 9.20 per cent
receiving fixed rate: annual 9.25 per cent

The difference between what a swap dealer pays and receives in the fixed rate is the margin that the swap dealer earns for acting as a market maker. In this case it is 0.05 per cent or five bps.

In the swap transaction Party A borrows in the floating-rate cash market and enters a fixed for floating swap with the swap dealer to obtain the fixed-rate obligation it desires. Party B on the other hand borrows in the fixed-rate cash market and enters a floating-for-fixed swap with the swap dealer to obtain the floating-rate obligation it desires.

The cash flows arising from this swap transaction are presented in three figures. Figure A2.1 shows the initial borrowing of the two counterparties in the cash markets.

Figure A2.1: Interest Rate Swap – Initial Drawdown of Debt

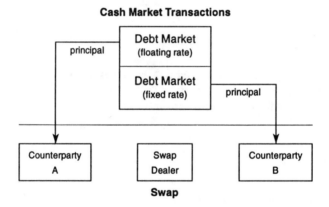

Figure A2.2 shows the counterparties servicing their debts in the cash markets and the cash flows with the swap dealer.

Figure A2.2: Interest Rate Swap – Debt Service Payments with Swap Services Payments

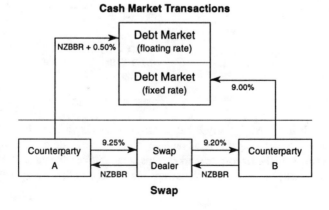

Counterparty A who wanted the fixed-rate obligation pays a fixed rate of 9.25 per cent to the swaps dealer. This counterparty also pays NZBBR + 0.50 per cent to the cash markets but receives NZBBR flat from the swaps dealer. The NZBBR components offset one another therefore eliminating the flexible-rate component of Party A's obligations.

The final financing cost for Party A is calculated (ignoring day-count conventions) in Table A2.2.

Table A2.2:   Interest Rate Swap – Party A's Financing Costs

	Cash market floating-rate obligation:	NZBBR + 0.50%
Less	Floating rate received in swap:	NZBBR flat
Equals	Net cost differential:	0.50% pa
Plus	Fixed-rate swap obligation:	9.25% pa
Equals	**Final financing cost:**	**9.75% pa**
Less	Cash market fixed-rate obligation:	10.00% pa
Equals	**Saving from employing swap**	**0.25% pa**

Counterparty B who wanted the floating-rate obligation pays a floating rate of NZBBR flat to the swaps dealer. The counterparty also pays a fixed rate of 10.00 per cent to the cash markets but receives 10.20 per cent from the swaps dealer. The fixed-rate components offset one another eliminating the fixed-rate component from Party B's obligations. The final financing cost for Party B is calculated (ignoring day-count conventions) in Table A2.3.

Table A2.3:   Interest Rate Swap – Party B's Financing Costs

	Cash market floating-rate obligation:	9.00% pa
Less	Fixed-rate received in swap:	9.20% pa
Equals	Net cost differential:	-0.20% pa
Plus	Floating-rate swap obligation:	NZBBR flat
Equals	**Final financing cost:**	**NZBBR -0.20%**
Less	Cash market floating-rate obligation:	NZBBR flat
Equals	**Saving from employing swap**	**0.20% pa**

Table A2.4 shows the distribution of the 0.50 per cent comparative advantage arising from the swap transaction.

Table A2.4:   Interest Rate Swap – Distribution of the Comparative Advantage

Savings made by Party A	0.25% pa
Savings made by Party B	0.20% pa
Swap Dealers margin on swap transaction	0.05% pa
Total Comparative Advantage	0.50% pa

Figure A2.3 shows the counterparties repaying the principals in the cash markets.

Figure A2.3: Interest Rate Swap – Repayment of Principals

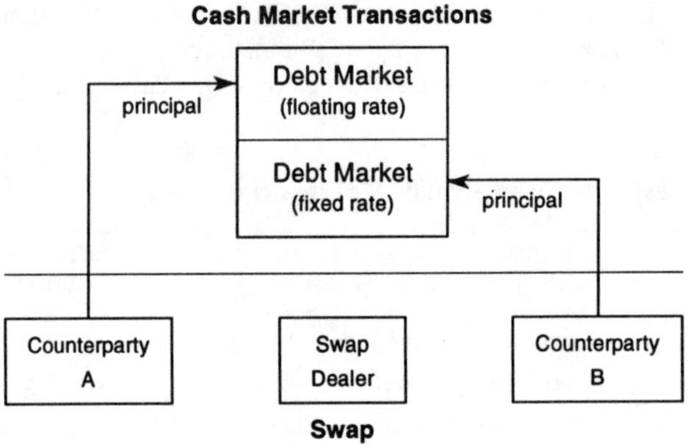

Cash Market Transactions

Appendix II

Seven Long Years: Economic History 1987–1993 as Priced into Five-year Government Stock

The ensuing graphs have been kindly supplied by the National Bank of New Zealand. Note that after (about) 1993, five-year stock lost its status as a 'hot' stock and liquidity problems might therefore distort the series unnecessarily.

Figure A2.4: Five-year Government Stock: January–December 1993

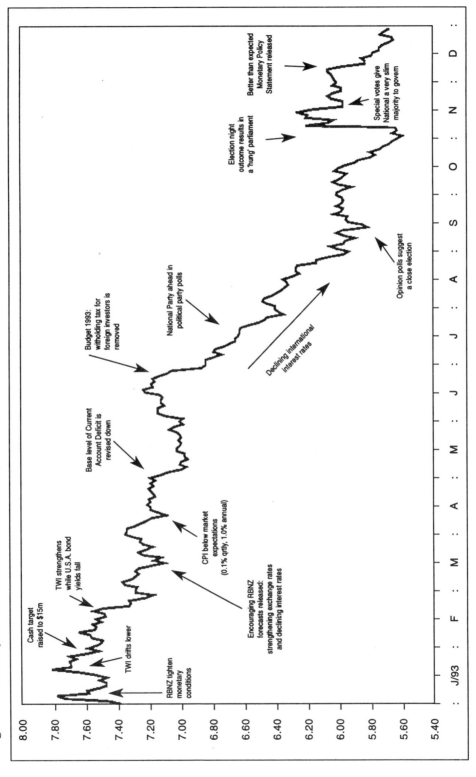

Figure A2.5: Five-year Government Stock: January–December 1992

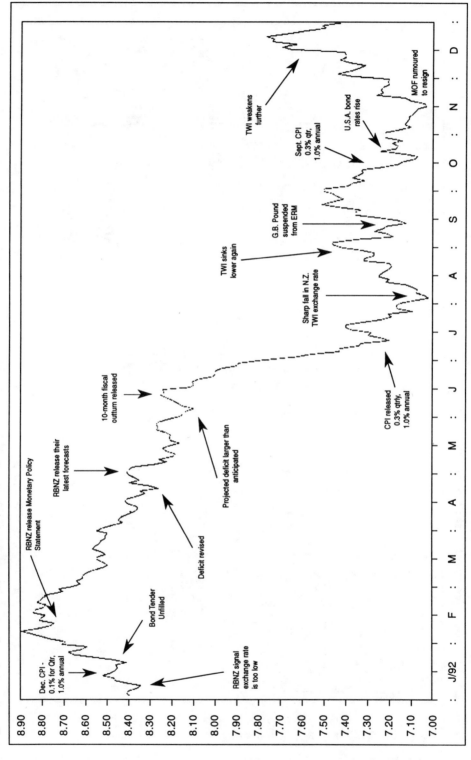

Figure A2.6: Five-year Government Stock: January–December 1991

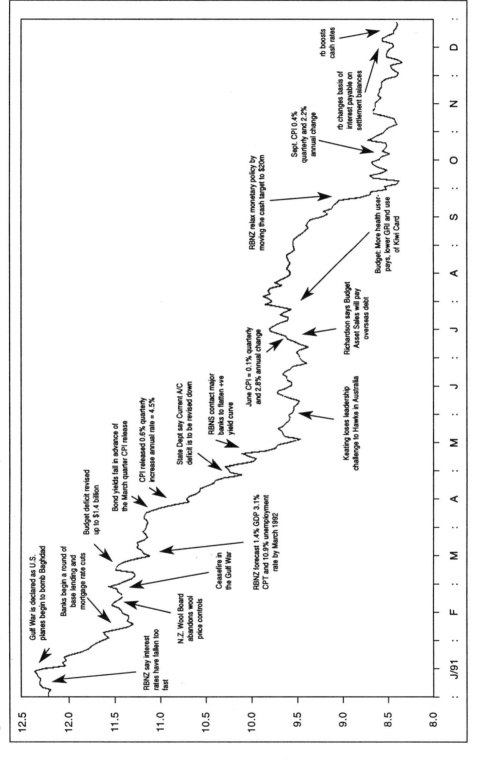

Figure A2.7: Five-year Government Stock: January–December 1990

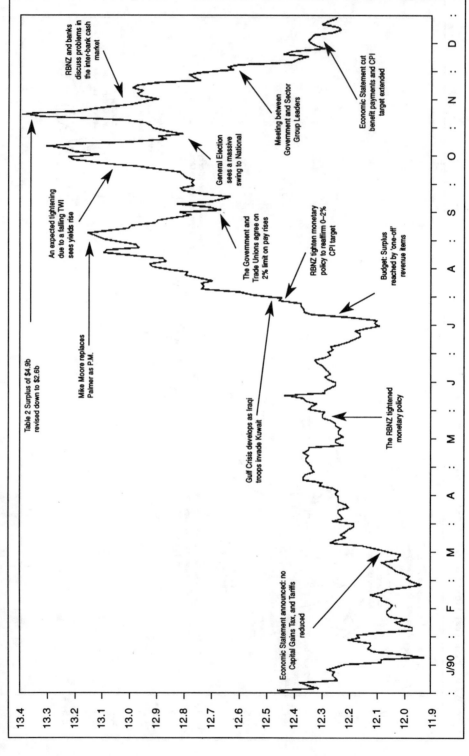

Figure A2.8: Five-year Government Stock: January–December 1989

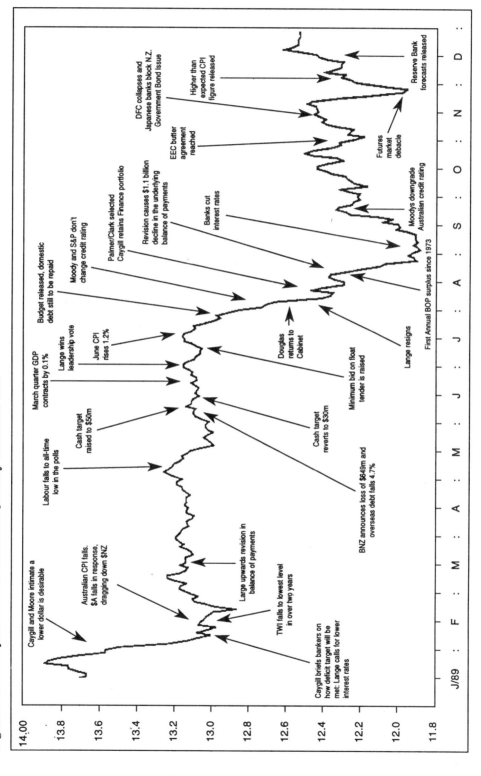

Figure A2.9: Five-year Government Stock: January–December 1988

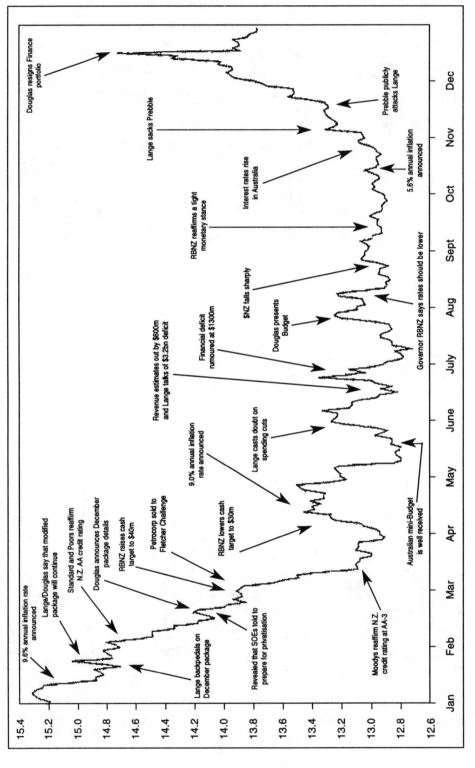

Figure A2.10: Five-year Government Stock: January–December 1987

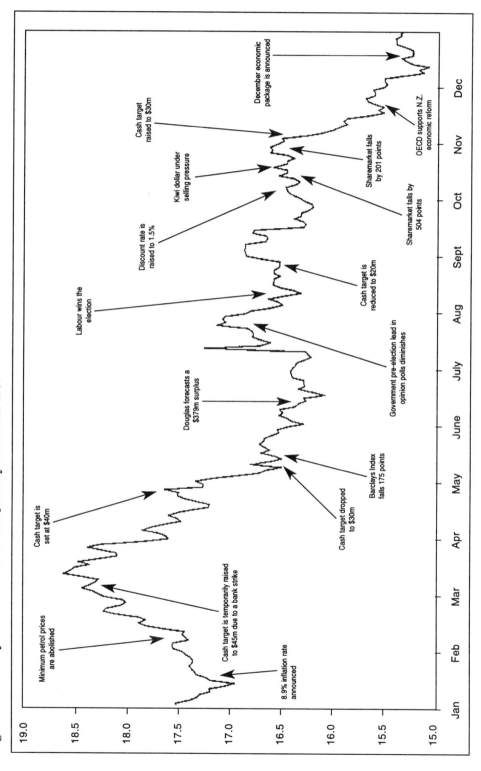

Chapter 3

Reserve Bank of New Zealand Policy Targets Agreement

This agreement replaces that signed under section 9(4) of the Reserve Bank of New Zealand Act 1989 (the Act) between the Minister of Finance (the Minister) and the Governor of the Reserve Bank of New Zealand (the Governor) on 19 December 1990.

It is made under section 9(4) of the Act and also under section 9(1) of the Act, so that it shall also apply during the Governor's next term of office.

In terms of section 9 of the Act, the Minister and the Governor agree as follows:

1. **Price Stability Target**

   Consistent with section 8 of the Act and with the provisions of this agreement, the Reserve Bank shall formulate and implement monetary policy with the intention of maintaining a stable general level of prices.

2. **Measurement of Price Stability**

   (a) In pursuing the objective of a stable general level of prices, the Bank will monitor prices as measured by a range of price indices. The formal price stability target will be defined in terms of the All Groups Consumers Price Index (CPI), being the measure that is monitored most closely by the public.

   (b) For the purposes of this agreement, 12-monthly increases in the CPI of between 0 and 2 per cent will be considered consistent with price stability.

3. **Deviations from the Targets**

   (a) There is a range of possible price shocks arising from external sources, certain government policy changes, or a natural crisis which are quite outside the direct influence of monetary policy. The Bank shall generally react to such shifts in relative prices in a manner which prevents general inflationary pressures emerging.

   (b) This approach means that the CPI inflation rate can be expected to move outside the 0–2 per cent range in response to particular shocks. The principal shocks are considered to be:
   - significant changes in the terms of trade arising from an increase or decrease in either import or export prices;
   - an increase or decrease in the rate of GST, or a significant change in other indirect tax rates;
   - a crisis such as a natural disaster or a major disease–induced fall in livestock numbers which is expected to have a significant impact on the price level;
   - a significant price level impact arising from changes to government or local authority levies; and
   - a movement in interest rates that causes a significant divergence between the change in the CPI and the change in the CPI excluding the interest costs component.

(c) In the event of such shocks, the Reserve Bank shall be fully accountable for its handling of the price effects and, in particular, for any movements outside the 0–2 per cent band. In each Policy Statement made under section 15 of the Act, the Bank shall detail fully its estimate of the direct price impact of any such shock and the impact on the Bank's achievement of the price stability target. The Bank shall also detail what measures it has taken, or proposes to take, to ensure that the effects of such shocks on the inflation rate are transitory.

4. Renegotiation of the Targets

The policy targets are established on the understanding that the monetary policy instruments available to the Bank are adequate to achieve the objective. The Governor shall inform the Minister if he considers that any changes in the availability or effectiveness of these policy instruments impair the conduct of monetary policy. The Minister and the Governor may then set new policy targets.

5. Implementation

(a) The Bank shall implement monetary policy in a sustainable, consistent and transparent manner.

(b) Each Policy Statement released by the Bank under section 15 of the Act shall contain a statement of how the Bank proposes to formulate and implement monetary policy to ensure that price stability is maintained over the succeeding five years.

Ruth Richardson	Donald T. Brash
Minister of Finance	Governor
	Reserve Bank of New Zealand

16 December 1992

Chapter 5

Overseas Securities Listed on the NZSE

(Source: NZSE)

Overseas Listed Equity Securities Settled Through FASTER

Code	Sector	Share Registry	Security Description
ABH	21	CPST	AUSTRALIAN BREWING & HOSPITALITY GROUP PTY LIMITED
ANZ	09	CPST	AUSTRALIAN & NEW ZEALAND BANKING GROUP LIMITED
CMC	25	CPST	COMALCO LIMITED
CPU	18	CPST	COMPUTERSHARE LIMITED
CLS	25	RGLT	CULTUS PETROLEUM NO LABILITY
FAL	10	RGLT	FOODLAND ASSOCIATED LIMITED
GPY	20	RGLT	GLOBAL PROPERTY FUND
GMF	10	GMFT	GOODMAN FIELDER LIMITED
GPG	13	RGLT	GUINNESS PEAT GROUP PLC
JFA	13	DBST	JARDINE FLEMING ASIA PACIFIC LIMITED
JFAOB	13	DBST	JARDINE FLEMING ASIA PACIFIC LIMITED OPTIONS 12/95
JFC	13	DBST	JARDINE FLEMING CHINA REGION LIMITED
JFCOA	13	DBST	JARDINE FLEMING CHINA REGION LIMITED OPTIONS 01/95
MDL	05	BKPT	McCONNELL DOWELL CORPORATION LIMITED
NMF	13	CPST	NMFM ASIA INVESTMENTS LIMITED
NMFOA	13	CPST	NMFM ASIA INVESTMENTS LIMITED OPTIONS 03/98
TPC	13	BKPT	TAG PACIFIC LIMITED
TIG	13	BKPT	TIGER INVESTMENT COMPANY LIMITED
TIGOA	13	BKPT	TIGER INVESTMENT COMPANY LIMITED OPTIONS 01/99

Overseas Listed Equity Securities Not Settled Through FASTER (NF)

Code	Sector	Security Description
ABN	13	ABTRUST NEW DAWN INVESTMENT TRUST PLC
ABT	05	ADELAIDE BRIGHTON LIMITED
AMC	11	AMCOR LIMITED
ARA	13	ARIADNE AUSTRALIA LIMITED
BOR	05	BORAL LIMITED
BHP	05	THE BROKEN HILL PROPRIETARY COMPANY LIMITED
BIT	13	BANKERS INVESTMENT TRUST PLC
BTR	18	BTR NYLEX LIMITED
BPH	08	BURNS PHILP & COMPANY LIMITED
CAA	08	CAPRAL ALUMINIUM LIMITED
CML	21	COLES MYER LIMITED
CRA	25	CRA LIMITED
CSR	05	CSR LIMITED
CSRGA	05	CSR LIMITED 8% CONVERTIBLE NOTES
DTM	18	DATAMATIC HOLDINGS LIMITED
DML	10	DEFIANCE MILLS LIMITED
EML	18	EMAIL LIMITED
EMA	13	EMERGING MARKETS COMPANY LIMITED
FAI	12	FAI INSURANCES LIMITED
FOI	13	THE FLEMING OVERSEAS INVESTMENT TRUST PLC

	13	FOREIGN & COLONIAL EMERGING MARKETS INVESTMENT TRUST PLC
FCT	13	FOREIGN & COLONIAL INVESTMENT TRUST PLC
FCS	13	FOREIGN & COLONIAL SMALLER COMPANIES PLC
GPT	20	GENERAL PROPERTY TRUST
GPTOA	20	GENERAL PROPERTY TRUST OPTIONS 06/96
ICI	04	ICI AUSTRALIA LIMITED
ICIPA	04	ICI AUSTRALIA LIMITED 5% CUMULATIVE PREFERENCE SHARES
LLC	13	LEND LEASE CORPORATION LIMITED
LLD	09	LLOYDS BANK PLC
MIM	25	MIM HOLDINGS LIMITED
NAB	09	NATIONAL AUSTRALIA BANK LIMITED
NZT	13	NEW ZEALAND INVESTMENT TRUST PLC
NCP	16	THE NEWS CORPORATION LIMITED
NCPSA	16	THE NEWS CORPORATION LIMITED PREFERRED SHARES
NBA	25	NORTH LIMITED
PDP	22	PACIFIC DUNLOP LIMITED
PBY	18	PARBURY LIMITED
PLP	25	PLACER PACIFIC LIMITED
STO	25	SANTOS LIMITED
SCH	20	SCHRODERS PROPERTY FUND
TEM	13	TEMPLETON EMERGING MARKETS INVESTMENT TRUST PUBLIC LTD COMPANY
TEMWA	13	TEMPLETON EMERGING MARKETS INVESTMENT TRUST PUBLIC LTD COMPANY WARRANTS
TGG	13	TEMPLETON GLOBAL GROWTH FUND LIMITED
TNT	24	TNT LIMITED
TRF	13	TR FAR EAST INCOME PLC
TRP	13	TR PACIFIC INVESTMENT TRUST PLC
TYA	13	TYNDALL AUSTRALIA LIMITED
VKI	18	VIKING INDUSTRIES LIMITED
WFT	20	WESTFIELD TRUST
WBC	09	WESTPAC BANKING CORPORATION

Key

NS	NON-STANDARD LISTING

CHAPTER 6

Appendix I

Interest Rate

Contract Specifications

90-Day Bank Bill Futures – BBC
90-Day Bank Bill Options – BBO

Three-Year Government Stock Futures – TYS
Three-Year Government Stock Options – TYO

Ten-Year Government Stock Futures – TEN
Ten-Year Government Stock Options – TNO

CONTRACT SPECIFICATIONS

Contract:	**90-Day Bank Accepted Bill Futures Contract**
Reference Code:	BBC
Ticker Code:	BB
Underlying Security:	90-day bank accepted bill of exchange complying with the Bills of Exchange Act 1908
Unit Size:	face value of $500,000
Price Quotes:	yield percent per annum quoted as 100 percent minus price
Minimum Fluctuations:	0.01 percent per annum

Contract Value and Mandatory
Settlement Value Calculations:

$$Value = \frac{500,000 \times 365}{365 + \frac{(Px90)}{100}}$$

the calculation within the brackets will be carried out to 8 decimal places

the values will be rounded to the nearest cents

0.5 of 1 cent will be rounded up

Contract Value:	in the above formula:
	P – price expressed as a yield percent per annum
Mandatory settlement Value:	in the above formula:
	P = Mandatory Settlement Price expressed as a yield percentum per annum
Final Trading Day:	the first Wednesday after the ninth day of the relevant Settlement Month
	trading will cease at the close of trading on the Final Trading Day
Settlement:	cash settlement with the parties making payment to or receiving from the Clearing House (whichever is applicable) the amount of the difference between the Contract Value and the Mandatory Settlement Value by no later than 1400 hours on the Mandatory Settlement Day
Mandatory Settlement Day:	the business day following the Final Trading Day
Mandatory Settlement Price:	(i) the 3 month FRA settlement rate as published at approximately 1045 hours on the Final Trading Day by Reuters New Zealand Limited on page BKBM of the Reuters Monitor Screen (or its successor page)
	the FRA settlement rate will be rounded to 2 decimal places and deducted from 100
	where the third decimal place is 5 the average will be rounded to the next highest second decimal place
	(ii) if the Mandatory Settlement Price is not able to be declared in accordance with the above procedures, Approved Settlement List Procedures will apply

Approved Settlement List Procedures:

- time of announcement:	the Mandatory Settlement Price will be announced by the Clearing House by no later that 1330 hours on the Final Trading Day
- minimum no. of parties:	8
- underlying security for which buying and selling yields shall be quoted:	bank accepted bill with a face value of $500,000 and a 90-day term to maturity from the Final Trading Day

if no market exists for these securities, notional yields will be quoted as if such market did exist having regard to prevailing market quotes for other maturities and other securities, and such other factors as may be deemed relevant

- format of quotes: quotes shall be expressed to 2 decimal places

- time for obtaining quotes: quotes will be obtained between 1100 hours and 1130 hours for quotes as at 1030 hours on the Final Trading Day

- calculation procedures: the Company will randomly select 8 quotes

quotes with a spread of greater than 0.1 percent per annum will be discarded

midrates will be calculated and the 3 highest and 3 lowest midrates will be discarded

the average of the remaining midrates will be calculated to 3 decimal places and rounded to 2 decimal places

0.005 will be rounded up

the average so calculated and deducted from 100 will be the Mandatory Settlement Price

---

CONTRACT SPECIFICATIONS

Contract: **90-Day Bank Accepted Bill Futures Option Contract**

Reference Code: BBO

Ticker Code: BB

Underlying Security: a 90-Day Bank Accepted Bill Futures Contract at specified in BBC

Unit Size: 1 unit of the Underlying Security

Premium Quotes: yield percent per annum multiplied by 100

Minimum Fluctuations: 0.01 percent per annum

Premium Value

$$\left[\left[\frac{500,000x365}{365+\dfrac{ex90}{100}}\right]-\left[\frac{500,000x365}{365+\left(\dfrac{(e+0.01)x90}{100}\right)}\right]\right]xP$$

where:

$e =$ 100 – Exercise Price

$P =$ premium expressed as a yield percent per annum multiplied by 100

the calculation within the square brackets will be carried out to 2 decimal places

all other calculations will be carried out to 8 decimal places

the premium value will be rounded to the nearest cent

0.5 of 1 cent will be rounded up

Expiration Date: the first Wednesday after the ninth day of the relevant Settlement Month

trading will cease at the close of trading on the Expiration Date

Mandatory Settlement Day: the business day following the Expiration Date

Exercise or Abandonment: notice may be given to the Clearing House on any business day on which the Contract is traded

notice must be received by the Clearing House prior to 1730 hours

Assignment: for options exercised prior to expiry, the seller will be notified by the Clearing House no later than 45 minutes prior to commencement of the next business day's trading

for options exercised at expiry, the seller will be notified by the Clearing House no later than 0900 hours on the business day following the Expiration Date

---

CONTRACT SPECIFICATIONS

Contract: **Three-Year Government Stock Futures Contract**

Reference Code: TYS

Ticker Code: TY

Underlying Security:	New Zealand Government Stock with a coupon rate of 8 percent and a 3-year term to maturity
Unit Size:	face value of $100,000
Prices Quotes:	yield percent per annum quoted as 100 percent minus price
Minimum Fluctuations:	0.01 percent per annum

Contract Value and Mandatory Settlement Value Calculations:

$$Value = 1{,}000 \left[\frac{100}{(1+i)^6} + 4.0 \frac{1 - \frac{1}{(1+i)^6}}{i} \right]$$

the calculation within the brackets will be carried out to 8 decimal places

the values will be rounded to the nearest cent

0.5 of 1 cent will be rounded up

Contract Value:

in the above formula:

$$i = \frac{Price}{200}$$

expressed as a yield percent per annum

Mandatory Settlement Value:

in the above formula:

$$i = \frac{MandatorySettlement\,Price}{200}$$

expressed as a yield percent per annum

Final Trading Day:

the first Wednesday after the ninth day of the relevant Settlement Month

trading will cease at the close of trading on the Final Trading Day

Settlement:

cash settlement with the parties making payment to or receiving from the Clearing House (whichever is applicable) the amount of the difference between the Contract Value and the Mandatory Settlement Value by no later than 1400 hours on the Mandatory Settlement Day

Mandatory Settlement Day:

the business day following the Final Trading Day

Mandatory Settlement Price:

the Mandatory Settlement Price will be determined in accordance with Approved Settlement List Procedures

Approved Settlement List Procedures

- time of announcement: the Mandatory Settlement Price will be announced by the Company no later than 1500 hours on the Final Trading Day

- minimum no. of parties: 8

- underlying securities for which yields shall be quoted: 2 New Zealand Government Stocks with maturities as determined by the Company prior to the listing of the cash settlement month

- quotation time and requirements: the yields expressed to two decimal places at which the party would buy and sell each underlying security as at 9.30a.m., 10.00a.m. and 10.30a.m. (the quotation times) on the Final Trading Day

- time for obtaining quotes: quotes will be obtained within 15 minutes of the quotation time:

- calculation procedures: (a) for each quotation time;

the Company will randomly select 8 quotes

quotes with a spread of greater than 0.05 percent per annum will be discarded

midrates will be calculated from all remaining quotes and the 2 highest and 2 lowest midrates will be discarded for each stock

the average of the remaining midrates for each stock will be calculated

a yield will be calculated from the 2 averages so calculated by straight line interpolation or straight line extrapolation as the case may require using the following formula:

$$yield = i^1 + (i^2 - i^1) x \frac{n^1}{n^2}$$

where:

$i1$ = the average midrate of shorter dated stock

$i2$ = the average midrate of shorter dated stock

$n1$ = the number of days between the maturity of the shorted dated stock and the theoretical futures maturity

$n2$ = the number of days between the maturity of the shorter dated stock and the maturity of the longer dated stock

the yield will be expressed to the nearest second decimal place

0.005 will be rounded up

(b) the average of the 3 yields determined in accordance with (a) above will be calculated to the nearest second decimal place

0.005 will be rounded up

the average yield so calculated and deducted from 100 will be the mandatory settlement price

---

CONTRACT SPECIFICATIONS

Contract: **Three-Year Government Stock Futures Option Contract**

Reference Code: TYO

Ticker Code: TY

Underlying Security: a Three-Year Government Stock Futures Contract as specified in TYS

Unit Size: 1 unit of the Underlying Security

Premium Quotes: yield percent per annum multiplied by 100

Minimum Fluctuations   0.01 percent per annum

Premium Value:

$$1{,}000\,px\left[\left[\frac{100}{(1+i)^6}+4.0\frac{1-\frac{1}{(1+i)^6}}{i}\right]-\left[\frac{100}{(1+j)^6}+4.0\frac{1-\frac{1}{(1+j)^6}}{j}\right]\right]$$

where:

p = premium in yield percent per annum x 100

$$i=\left(\frac{100-Exercise\,Price}{200}\right)$$

$$j=\left(\frac{200i+0.01}{200}\right)$$

the calculation within the brackets will be carried out to 8 decimal places

the values will be rounded to the nearest cent

0.5 of 1 cent will be rounded up

Expiration Date: the first Wednesday after the ninth day of the relevant Settlement Month

trading will cease at the close of trading on the Expiration Date

Mandatory Settlement Day: the business day following the Expiration Date

Exercise or Abandonment: notice may be given to the Clearing House on any business date on which the Contract is traded

notice must be received by the Clearing House prior to 1730 hours

Assignment: for options exercised prior to expiry, the seller will be notified by the Clearing House no later than 45 minutes prior to commencement of the next business day's trading

for options exercised at expiry, the seller will be notified by the Clearing House no later than 0900 hours on the business day following the Expiration Date

---

CONTRACT SPECIFICATIONS

Contract: **Ten-Year Government Stock Futures Contract**

Reference Code: TEN

Ticker Code: TN

Underlying Security: New Zealand Government Stock with a coupon rate of 8 percent and a 10-year term to maturity

Unit Size: face value of $100,000

Price Quotes: yield percent per annum quoted as 100 percent minus price

Minimum Fluctuations: 0.01 percent per annum

Contract Value and Mandatory
Settlement Value Calculations:

$$Value = 1,000 \left[\frac{100}{(lxi)^{20}} + 4.0 \frac{1 - \frac{1}{(l+i)^{20}}}{i} \right]$$

the calculation within the brackets will be carried out to 8 decimal places

the values will be rounded to the nearest cent

0.5 of 1 cent will be rounded up

Contract Value: in the above formula

$$i = \frac{Price}{200}$$

expressed as a yield percent per annum

Mandatory Settlement Value: in the above formula

$$i = \frac{Mandatory\ Settlement\ Price}{200}$$

expressed as a yield percent per annum

Final Trading Day: the first Wednesday after the ninth day of the relevant Settlement Month

trading will cease at the close of trading on the Final Trading Day

Settlement: cash settlement with the parties making payment to or receiving from the Clearing House (whichever is applicable) the amount of the difference between the Contract Value and the Mandatory Settlement Value by no later than 1400 hours on the Mandatory Settlement Day

Mandatory Settlement Day: the business day following the Final Trading Day

Mandatory Settlement Price: the Mandatory Settlement Price will be determined in accordance with Approved Settlement List Procedures

Approved Settlement List Procedures:

-   time of announcement: the Mandatory Settlement Price will be announced by the company by no later than 1500 hours on the Final Trading Day

-   minimum no. of parties: 8

- underlying securities for which   2 New Zealand Government Stocks with maturities as
  yields shall be quoted: determined by the Company prior to the listing of the cash
                                    settlement month

- quotation time and requirements: the yields expressed to two decimal places at which the
                                    party would buy and sell each underlying security as at
                                    9.30am, 10.00am and 10.30am (the quotation times) on the
                                    Final Trading Day

- time for obtaining quotes: quotes will be obtained within 15 minutes of the quotation
                                    time

- calculation procedures: (a) for each quotation time

                                    the Company will randomly select 8 quotes

                                    quotes with a spread of greater than 0.05 percent per
                                    annum will be discarded

                                    midrates will be calculated from all remaining quotes
                                    and the 2 highest and 2 lowest midrates will be
                                    discarded for each stock

                                    the average of the remaining midrates for each stock
                                    will be calculated

                                    a yield will be calculated from the 2 averages so
                                    calculated by straight line interpolation or straight line
                                    extrapolation as the case may require using the following
                                    formula:

$$yield = i + (i^2 - i^1) x \frac{n^1}{n^2}$$

where:

$i1$ = the average midrate of shorter dated stock

$i2$ = the average midrate of longer dated stock

$n1$ = the number of days between the maturity of the
shorted dated stock and the theoretical futures maturity

$n2$ = the number of days between the maturity of the
shorter dated stock and the maturity of the longer dated
stock

the yield will be expressed to the nearest second decimal
place

0.005 will be rounded up

(b) the average of the 3 yields determined in accordance with (a) above will be calculated to the nearest second decimal place

0.005 will be rounded up

the average yield so calculated and deducted from 100 will be the mandatory settlement price

CONTRACT SPECIFICATIONS

Contract:	**Ten-Year Government Stock Futures Option Contract**
Reference Code:	TNO
Ticker Code:	TN
Underlying Security:	a Ten-Year Government Stock Futures Contract as specified in TEN
Unit Size:	1 unit of the Underlying Security
Premium Quotes:	yield percent per annum multiplied by 100
Minimum Fluctuations:	0.01 percent per annum

Premium Value:

$$1,000px\left[\left[\frac{100}{(l+i)^{20}}+4.0\frac{1-\frac{1}{(l+i)^{20}}}{i}\right]-\left[\frac{100}{(l+j)^{20}}+4.0\frac{1-\frac{1}{(l+j)^{20}}}{j}\right]\right]$$

where:

$p = premium\ in\ yield\ percent\ per\ annum\ x\ 100$

$$i = \frac{(100 - Exercise\,Price)}{100}$$

$$j = \frac{(200i + 0.01)}{200}$$

the calculation within the brackets will be carried out to 8 decimal places

the values will be rounded to the nearest cent

0.5 of 1 cent will be rounded up

Expiration Date: the first Wednesday after the ninth day of the relevant Settlement Month

                                    trading will cease at the close of trading on the Expiration Date

Mandatory Settlement Day: the business day following the Expiration Date

Exercise or abandonment: notice may be given to the Clearing House on any business day on which the Contract is traded

                                    notice must be received by the Clearing House prior to 1730 hours

Assignment: for options exercised prior to expiry, the seller will be notified by the Clearing House no later than 45 minutes prior to commencement of the next business day's trading

                                    for options exercised at expiry, the seller will be notified by the Clearing House no later than 0900 hours on the business day following the Expiration Date

Appendix II

New Zealand Futures & Options Exchange Limited (NZFOE)

There are the following classes of Dealers

1. Public Brokers (PB)
These Dealers are authorised to deal in contracts on behalf of other persons or on their own behalf.
They are also authorised to accept and hold client money and property

2. Introducing Brokers (IB)
These Dealers may deal in contracts on behalf of other persons or on their own behalf but may not hold client money or property. Introducing Brokers must direct all client transactions through a Trading Permit Holder.

3. Principal Traders (PT)
These Dealers generally trade only on their own account. They may deal on behalf of other Dealers but only on a give-up basis and are not authorised to hold client money or property.

Trading Permit Holders (TPH)
Where a Dealer also holds a Trading Permit they may deal directly on the Automated Trading System of the New Zealand Futures & Operations Exchange.
Those Dealers that are not Trading Permit Holders must deal through a Dealer who is a Trading Permit Holder.

Directory of New Zealand Dealers
As at 20 November 1995

AMP Investments (NZ) Ltd (PT)
PO Box 3764, Wellington
Level 4, City Tower, 95 Customhouse Quay
Wellington
Fax: 04 498 8821 Phone: 04 498 8000 (reception)
04 498 8174 (direct)
Contact: Mr Chris Holmes, Manager – Investment Operations

ANZ Banking Group (NZ) Ltd (PB & TPH)
PO Box 1492, Wellington
New Zealand Treasury
215–229 Lambton Quay, Wellington
Fax: 04 406 8639 Phone: 04 473 1960
Contact: Mr Jim Reardon, Manager – Domestic Trading
Mr Michael Stockley, Senior Manager – Domestic Markets

ASB Bank Limited (PT & TPH)
PO Box 35, Auckland 1015
Level 9, ASB Bank Centre
Cnr Albert & Wellesley Streets, Auckland
Fax: 09 307 8010 Phone: 09 377 8930
Contact: Mr Kerry Francis, Treasurer

Bank of New Zealand (PB & TPH)
PO Box 2392, Wellington
Head Office, Group Treasury
Level 21, BNZ Centre, 1 Willis Street
Wellington
Fax: 04 474 6446 Phone: 04 474 6999 (reception) 04 474 6469 (direct)
Contact: Mr Tony Cakebread, Group Treasury, Head of NZ Region

BT Futures New Zealand Ltd (PB & TPH)
(authorised as Clearing Member of the Sydney
Futures Exchange Clearing House Ltd)
PO Box 6900, Wellesley Street, Auckland
Level 8, Stock Exchange Centre
191 Queen Street, Auckland
Fax: 09 303 1851 Phone: 09 309 3226
Contact: Mr Conal Parr, Futures Dealer
            Ms Lindsay Wright, Vice President

Citibank NZ (New Zealand Branch)
(PT & TPH)
(PO Box 3429, Auckland
Citibank Centre, 23 Custom Street East,
Auckland
Fax: 09 308 9929 (direct) 302 1688 (via Dealing
Room) Phone: 09 302 3128
Contact: Mr Andrew Ayling

Clarke Wycherley Investments Ltd (IB)
PO Box 5595, Wellesley Street, Auckland Level
7, Tower 2, The Shortland Centre
55-65 Shortland Street, Auckland
Fax: 09 366 4692 Phone: 09 366 4689
Contact: Mr Jonathan Clarke

CS First Boston NZ Equity Futures Limited
(IB)
PO Box 3394, Wellington
10th Floor, Caltex Tower, 282-292 Lambton
Quay
Wellington
Fax: 04 474 4060 Phone: 04 474 4400
Contact: Mr Tony Broad
            Mr David Price

CS First Boston NZ Futures Limited
(PB & TPH)
PO Box 3394, Wellington
10th Floor, Caltex Tower, 282-292 Lambton
Quay
Wellington
Fax: 04 474 4432 Phone: 04 474 4400
Contact: Mr Alister Moss
            Mr Chris West

Egden Wignall & Co Futures Ltd
(PB & TPH)
PO Box 2335, Christchurch
Exchange House, 112 Hereford Street
Christchurch
Fax: 03 379 1196 Phone: 03 379 2600
(reception) 03 366 3804 (direct)
Contact: Mr Grant Williamson

Electricity Corporation of New Zealand Ltd
(PT)
PO Box 930, Wellington
Treasury Division, Level 10, Rutherford House
23 Lambton Quay, Wellington
Fax: 04 473 3189 Phone: 04 474 2314
(reception) 471 2662 (direct)
Contact: Mr Neil Bradley, Treasurer

Fixed Interest Brokers (NZ) (PB & TPH)
PO Box 11-274, Wellington
6th Floor, 107 Customhouse Quay
Wellington
Fax: 04 499 0074 Phone: 04 499 0009
Contact: Mr Tom Harris, Managing Director

Holroyd Capital Management Ltd (IB)
PO Box 3256, Auckland
6/90 Remuera Road, Remuera
Auckland
Fax: 09 523 3361 Phone: 09 524 4461
Contact: Mr Robert Holroyd, Director

J B Were Futures Pty Limited
(PB, TPH & CM)
(New Zealand Branch)
PO Box 887, Auckland
Level 21, Coopers & Lybrand Tower
23-29 Albert Street, Auckland
Fax: 09 309 9861 Phone: 09 309 9800
Contact: Mr Humphrey Sherratt
            Client Advisor

McIntosh Futures Limited
(PB, TPH & CM)
(New Zealand Branch)
PO Box 817, Auckland
Level 17, Westpac Tower, 120 Albert Street
Auckland
Fax: 09 356 2933 Phone: 09 356 2929
Contact: Mr Stuart Christie
             Derivatives Client Advisor

Ord Minnett Jardine Fleming
Futures-NZ- Limited (PB & TPH)
PO Box 5830, Auckland
Head Office, Level 8, Arthur Anderson Tower
205 Queen Street Auckland
Fax: 09 356 1323 Phone: 09 356 1300
Contact: Mr Colin Churchouse, Director

Ord Minnett Jardine Fleming Futures –NZ-
Limited (Wellington)
PO Box 290, Wellington
Levels 13 & 14, City Tower
95 Customhouse Quay, Wellington
Fax: 04 495 0373 Phone: 04 495 0333
(reception)
04 499 0027 (direct)
Contact: Mr Nigel Brunel, Dealer
             Ms Vanessa Porter, Dealer

Ord Minnett Jardine Fleming Futures –NZ-
Limited (Christchurch)
PO Box 13-186, Armagh, Christchurch
Level 17, 764 Colombo Street
Christchurch
Fax: 03 366 8852 Phone: 03 366 8851
Contact: Mr Mark Thiele, Dealer

SBC Warbug New Zealand Futures Ltd
PO Box 45, Auckland
Level 23, Stock Exchange Centre
191 Queen Street, Auckland
Fax: 09 307 4888 Phone: 09 307 4800
Contact: Mr David Halligan
             Manager – Futures Department
             Mr Hugh Caughley, General Manager

Strategic Futures & Options Limited (IB)
35 Lynfield Avenue, Christchurch 4
Phone: 03 358 2491
Contact: Mr Roderick Webb
             Governing Director

The Hongkong and Shanghai Banking
Corporation Limited (PT & TPH)
PO Box 5947, Wellesley Street, Auckland
8th Floor, Hongkong Bank House
290 Queen Street, Auckland
Fax: 09 302 0116 Phone: 09 309 3800
Contact: Simon Palfreyman
             Manager, Treasury and Capital
             Markets

The National Bank of New Zealand Ltd
(PB & TPH)
Wholesale Audit Services, PO Box 1791,
Wellington
Level 9, National Bank House
170-186 Featherston Street, Wellington
Fax: 04 802 2021 Phone: 04 494 4058
Contact: Mr Paul Chandler, Manager,
             Wholesale Audit Services

Trust Bank New Zealand Ltd (PB & TPH)
PO Box 2260, Wellington
Levels 14 & 15, Trust Bank Centre, 125 The
Terrace
Wellington
Fax: 04 471 1981 Phone: 04 473 2807
Contact: Mr Bob Morrison, Group Treasurer

Westpac Banking Corporation (PT & TPH)
PO Box 691, Wellington
Level 4, Westpac House, 318-324 Lambton
Quay
Wellington
Fax: 04 473 7879 Phone: 04 498 1275
Contact: Mr Richard Wilks, General Manager
             Institutional Banking Group NZ

Chapter 7

Case Study

Electricity Corporation of New Zealand
Euro MTN Issue No 2 (Nov 1994)

by Neil Bradley
Treasurer, ECNZ.

The Electricity Corporation of New Zealand (ECNZ) has a euro medium-term note programme (Euro MTN) which enables it to borrow on the international capital markets in any currency. The general object is to provide working capital for the Corporation and its subsidiaries.

During the last quarter of 1994 and the first quarter of 1995, there was a considerable funding advantage by borrowing in the Yen market and swapping that back into New Zealand dollars, thus allowing ECNZ to lower its debt raising costs by a considerable margin. The triangular arrangement described below is a fairly typical example of the type of financing that ECNZ has entered into over the past year in relation to its financing activities. The counterparties were Citibank International plc and the ANZ Banking Group.

As the basis for the transactions, ECNZ issued a five-year fixed-rate Euro medium-term note bearing a coupon of 4.45 per cent to Citibank International plc who then sold this MTN to Japanese Yen investors. This process required an offering circular – actually produced as a supplement to that for the standing programme – containing information about the issue and about the Corporation and its activities. Appended to the present study are selected financial data of the Corporation as it appeared in the supplemental circular.

Investors were very keen on receiving Yen obligations but were looking for offshore counterparties with a high credit quality. New Zealand at the time and New Zealand counterparties, were particularly attractive, as New Zealand had received a lot of positive media coverage with regard to its economic reforms, ahead of the Asian Development Bank Conference held in Auckland in May 1995. Therefore, New Zealand carried a high name recognition. Investors were happy to take ECNZ credit risk as long as it was denominated in Yen.

On the other hand, ECNZ wants all of its liabilities to be denominated in New Zealand dollars. Therefore a series of interest rate and currency swaps had to be undertaken to convert the Yen to N.Z. dollars. This was done by using a U.S. dollar swap as an intermediation swap. In other words, the yen obligations were first swapped into U.S. dollars; a second swap then took the U.S. dollar payments into NZD obligations.

The principal flows are as follows:

- ECNZ receives Yen 3 billion from the debt issue through Citibank International plc, ECNZ then transfers the Yen 3 billion to Citibank Tokyo (via the swap) and receives in exchange USD30 million.
- ECNZ redirects the USD30 million to ANZ Bank and in exchange receives NZD49 million – the amount they wish to raise.
- The same process is undertaken for the servicing of this principal flow. ECNZ has an annual Yen fixed-rate coupon of 4.45 per cent. On the USD–NZD swap, ECNZ pays ANZ Bank bank bill FRA rate – in exchange, it receives USD libor.
- ECNZ then pays USD libor to Citibank Tokyo. In exchange it receives annual 4.45 per cent Yen.
- ECNZ then in turn uses the 4.45 per cent annual Yen to service the MTN issue.

The various flows of principal and servicing payments are illustrated in the diagram.

Euro Medium-Term Note Issue No. 2: Citibank International as Agent

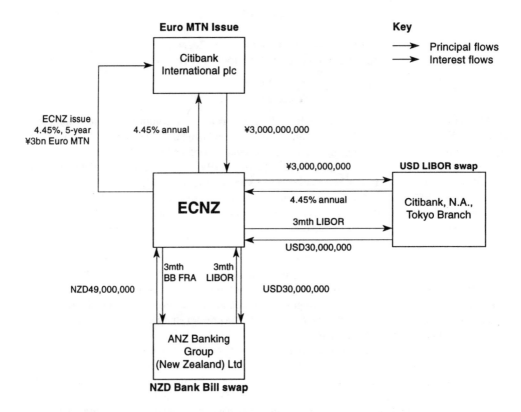

ECNZ has two principal borrowing programmes: the above-mentioned Euro MTN Programme and a domestic N.Z. dollar bond programme. Before ECNZ undertakes a borrowing, it assesses investor demand offshore versus onshore, on an all-in N.Z. dollar bank bill basis; i.e. the process we have gone through above, versus issuing N.Z. fixed-rate bonds and swapping them through the interest rate swap market back to floating-rate bank bills. ECNZ will then issue in either market, depending on which one is more competitive.

Most large creditworthy issuers within New Zealand adopt a similar approach, using one market to counterbalance any inefficiences in the other market. However, it is expected that in the near to medium term, more funding will be centred onshore rather than offshore, as there is a diminishing supply of government bonds due to the government running large fiscal surpluses. This reduces the need for government borrowing, placing a scarcity factor on long-term debt issues in New Zealand. We can therefore expect increased activity in the corporate bond market, with some margin contraction. This has been evidenced recently by the introduction of a corporate bond index developed by the Bank of New Zealand, which allows domestic investors to benchmark their corporate holdings in relation to an index (similar to the government stock index formulated by N.Z. First Capital).

S&C Draft of November 14, 1994

PRICING SUPPLEMENT No. 5 dated November 11, 1994
(to Offering Circular dated May 27, 1994 and the Supplemental
Offering Circular dated November 10, 1994)

ECNZ
Electricity Corporation of
New Zealand Limited

Yen 3,000,000,000
4.45 per cent Euro Medium-Term Notes, Series III
Due 11 October 1999

The description of the Yen Notes set forth in this Pricing Supplement supplements the description
of general terms and provisions of ECNZ's Global Medium-Term Notes, Series III set forth in the
accompanying Offering Circular and Supplemental Offering Circular. To the extent any statement
herewith differs from a statement made in such accompanying Offering Circular or Supplemental
Offering Circular, such statement shall modify or supersede the statement made in such Offering
Circular or Supplemental Offering Circular. Any such statement so modified or superseded shall
not be deemed, except as so modified or superseded, to constitute a part of the accompanying
Offering Circular or Supplemental Offering Circular.

Date of Issue/Settlement Date: 29 November   Currency or Currency Units: Japanese Yen
1994

Maturity Date: 11 October 1999   Issue Price (as a percentage of principal amount):
                                                  100%

  x Fixed Rate Note   Interest Rate Formula: Fixed
  __ Commercial Paper Rate Note
  __ Prime Rate Note
  __ CD Rate Note
  __ Federal Funds Rate Note
  __ LIBOR Note
  __ Treasury Rate Note
  __ N.Z. Bank Bill Rate Note
  __ Other:

Interest Rate: 4.45% per annum calculated on   Denominations: Yen 1,000,000
the basis of a 360-day year consisting of 12
30-day months

Interest Payment Dates: October 11, 1995 with a   Interest Reset Dates: N/A
short interest coupon, October 11, 1996, October
11, 1997, October 11, 1998 and October 11, 1999;
provided that if an Interest Payment Date falls on
a date which is not a Business Day (as defined

below), it shall be postponed to the next day which is a Business Day (as defined below) and payment shall be made on such day with the same force and effect as if made on the Interest Payment Date and no interest shall accrue for the period from and after such Interest Payment Date; and provided further that the last Interest Payment Date shall be the Maturity Date.

Interest Payment Period: Annually

Interest Reset Period: N/A

Interest Determination Dates: N/A

Index Maturity: N/A

Minimum Interest Rate: N/A

Maximum Interest Rate: N/A

Calculation Agent: N/A

Exchange Listing: The Yen Notes will not be listed on the Luxembourg Stock Exchange.
Call Option: None

Governing Law: New York Law

Business Day: Tokyo, New York, London, Wellington

Redemption: The Yen Notes may not be redeemed at the option of ECNZ prior to their stated maturity, except as set forth under the heading 'Description of Notes' in the accompanying Offering Circular.

The Notes may not be offered or sold except under circumstances that will result in compliance with the Securities and Exchange Law of Japan and other applicable laws and regulations of Japan. See 'Paragraph (14)' of the Supplemental Offering Circular.

Citibank International plc

Citibank International plc	*PO Box 242* *336 Strand* *London* *WC2R 1HB*	*071 438 1000 (Switchboard)* *071 438 (Direct)* *Fax 071 438 ....* *Telex 299831 CITIUK G*

To: Mahes Hettige / Brett Tulloch
Manager, Capital Markets
Electricity Corporation of New Zealand Limited
Tel 644 474 2314 / 471 2662
Fax 644 473 3189

cc.   Kenro Arimoto / Manabu Horiguchi
                         Citicorp International Securities Limited. Tokyo
                         Tel 813 5462 6203 / 5462 9221
                         Fax 813 5462 6267

cc.   Madarn Martiale Lockman / Claude Fapranzi
                         Kredietbank S.A. Luxembourgeoise
                         Tel 352 4797 5215 / 4797 3931
                         Fax 352 4797 5270

From: Colin Withers / Peter Ang
                         Citibank International plc
                         Tel 4471 438 0218
                         Fax 4471 438 1219

Date: November 14, 1994

**Confirmation of Terms and Conditions for Electricity Corporation of New Zealand Limited
USD 1,000,000,000 Euro Medium-Term Notes, Series II and Series III
Yen 3,000,000,000 Euro Medium-Term Notes due October 11, 1999**

Dear Mahes,

On behalf of Citibank International plc, we are pleased to confirm the terms as outlined below.

1. Notes

Issuer:	Electricity Corporation of New Zealand Limited
Purchaser:	Citibank International plc.
Principal Amount:	Yen 3,000,000,000.
Trade Date:	November 11, 1994.
Settlement Date:	November 29, 1994.
Maturity Date:	October 11, 1999.
Issue Price:	100 per cent.
Type of Instrument:	Euro Medium-Term Note.
Coupon:	4.45 per cent per annum payable annually in arrears on a 30/360 day basis with short first coupon on October 11, 1995.
Redemption Price:	100 per cent.
Listing:	None.
Denomination:	Yen 1,000,000.
Call/Put:	None.
Settlement:	Delivery against payment to our Cedel Account No. 11908.

2. Currency Swap

Counterparties:	Electricity Corporation of New Zealand Limited ('ECNZ').
	Citibank. N.A., Tokyo branch ('Citibank').
Yen Amount:	Yen 3,000,000,000.
USD Amount:	USD 30,721,966.21
Trade Date:	November 11, 1994.
Settlement Date:	November 29, 1994.
Maturity Date:	October 11, 1999.
Initial Principal Exchange:	On Settlement Date, ECNZ pays to Citibank the Yen amount and receives from Citibank the USD Amount.
Citibank Pays ECNZ:	4.45 per cent per annum on the Yen amount payable annually in arrears on a 30/360-day basis with short first coupon on October 11, 1995.
ECNZ pays Citibank:	3 month USD LIBOR – * b.p. on the USD Amount payable quarterly in arrears on an A/360 basis. Payment dates are January 10, April 10, July 10 and October 11 of each year with short first interest period from November 29, 1994 to

January 10, 1995 where LIBOR is interpolated between 1 month and 2 month USD LIBOR.

Final Principal Exchange: On Maturity Date. ECNZ receives from Citibank the Yen Amount and pays to Citibank the USD Amount.

The Notes will be issued in accordance with and subject to, the terms and conditions of the Notes described in USD 1,000,000,000 Euro Medium-Term Notes, Series II and Series III offering circular dated May 27, 1994.

Thank you for your mandate on this transaction and we look forward to working with you again.

Best regards.

Colin Withers   Peter Ang
Vice President   Vice President

CAPITALIZATION OF THE CORPORATION

The following table sets out the short-term debt and capitalization of the Corporation and its subsidiaries as at June 30, 1994. The following data should be read in conjunction with the financial statements of the Corporation for the period ended June 30, 1994 and the notes thereto.

	30 June 1994 (N.Z. $ in thousands)
Short-term debt(1)	1,923,630
Long-term debt:	
NZ dollar borrowings:	
10 per cent Bonds due 2001	577, 104
8 per cent Bonds due 2009	10, 155
Cable finance loan	55,075
Total term N.Z. dollar borrowings(2)	
	642,334
Foreign currency borrowings:	
Medium Term Notes	170,940
Total foreign currency borrowings	
	170,940
Total long-term debt	
	813,274
Shareholder's funds(3):	
Issued and paid-up capital	
1,000,000,000 ordinary shares of $1 each	1,000,000
800,000 redeemable cumulative preference shares of $ 1 each	
	800
Total issued and paid-up capital	1,000,800

Share premium reserve

Ordinary shares	1,500,000
Preference shares	
	799,200
Total share premium reserve	
	2,299,200
Total paid-up capital and share premium reserve	3,300,000
Hydrology reserve (previously called fuel burn reserve)	34,426
Capital redemption reserve	22
Retained earnings	
	520,636
Total shareholder's funds	
	3,855,084
Total capitalization(4)	
	6,591,988

(1)   The figure for short-term debt as of June 30, 1994 is made up as follows:

Call loans	10,000
U.S. commercial paper (converted to N.Z. dollars at the rate of NZ$ 1 = US$.5947)	74, 153
Medium-term Notes	273,829
Short-term Notes	16,880
10 per cent Bonds due 1996(5)	876,700
U.S.$ 9 3/8 per cent Notes due 1996(5)	326,645
U.S.$ Syndicated loan (5)	345,423
Total short-term debt at June 30, 1994	1,923,630

(2)   Since March 31, 1993, the Corporation has issued Medium-term Notes amounting to U.S.$250 million. Of this figure, U.S.$150 million matured within 12 months of balance date and is included under 'Short-term debt'. The remaining U.S.$100 million is included under 'Foreign Currency Borrowings'. The proceeds from the MTN were utilized to repay some of the NZ$ domestic bonds that matured in November 1993. A U.S.$225 million standby facility has been renegotiated for a 5-year period to November 1999.

(3)   As at June 30, 1994, the authorized share capital of the Corporation consists of 1,999,200,000 ordinary shares of $1 each and 800,000 preference shares of $1 each.

(4)   Preference shares of NZ$800 million with preference dividends of NZ$437 million were repaid on July 1, 1994 out of proceeds of the sale of Trans Power New Zealand Limited to the Crown.

(5)   Save as set forth below, there has been no material change to the short-term debt and capitalization of the Corporation and its subsidiaries since June 30, 1994:

On July 1, 1994 the Corporation extinguished N.Z.$1.588 billion of debt through an insubstance defeasance with the Crown, in relation to the sale of Trans Power New Zealand Limited comprising of:

10 per cent Bonds due 1996	876,700
U.S.$9 3/8 per cent Notes due 1996	326,645
U.S.$ Syndicated loan	345,423
	1,548,768

Accrued interest 39,232

1,588,000

Capitalization of the Corporation changed to the extent identified in Note 4, as a result of the sale of Trans Power New Zealand Limited. Also refer to Sale of Trans Power New Zealand Limited under 'Recent Developments'.

As of November 10, 1994 U.S. Commercial Paper outstanding was N.Z.$ equivalent of 258 million.

SELECTED FINANCIAL DATA OF THE CORPORATION

The selected financial information with respect to the Corporation for the years ended March 31, 1992 and 1993 set forth below is derived from the financial statements of the Corporation that have been audited by the New Zealand Audit Office and for the 15 month period ended June 30, 1994 by Coopers and Lybrand on their behalf. The Corporation's financial statements are prepared in accordance with accounting principles generally accepted in New Zealand. The following data should be read in conjunction with the financial statements of the Corporation for the period ended June 30, 1994 and the notes thereto.

	12 Months ended March 31		15 Months ended June 30
	1992	1993	1994
		(in thousands)	
Revenue	$1,631,484	$1,643,449	$2, 158, 179
Operating expenses including abnormal costs(a)	795,504	892,955	1,038,620
Net finance costs	214,074	345,326	405,029
Profit before taxation	621,906	405, 168	714,530
Taxation(b)	118,943	75,567	218,427
Extraordinary expense (net of taxation)	53,796	===	===
Profit after taxation and extraordinary expense	449, 167	329,601	496, 103
Share of losses of associate entity	–	–	382
Dividends(1)	335,034	280,436	506,362
Transfers to reserves	(16,237)	(21,313)	4,371
Retained earnings for the period	$130,370	$ 70,478	($15,012)

	1992	1993	1994
	---	---	---
Current assets	$1, 108,615	$544, 138	$473,644
Term assets(2)	385,097	34,218	2,862
Fixed assets	6,950,407	7,206,306	7, 127,875
Total assets	8,444, 119	7,784,662	7,604,381
Current liabilities	1,912,234	1,567, 160	2,739,987
Term liabilities(3)	2,534,972	2, 158,512	817,674
Deferred taxation (b)	180,353	193,265	191,636
Total liabilities	4,627,559	3,918,937	3,749,297
Shareholder's funds	3,816,560	3,865,725	3,855,084

(a) The operating expenses in the year ended March 31, 1993 include abnormal costs of $125,817 million associated with the water shortage in the hydro catchments from June to August 1992. There were no abnormal costs in 1993 or 1994.

(b) Accounting policy relating to deferred tax was changed in the year ended March 31, 1993. Trans Power New Zealand Limited, then a wholly owned subsidiary of the Corporation, changed from the comprehensive to partial basis of the liability method. The change reduced the year ended March 31, 1993 tax charge by $32 million and deferred tax balance by $155 million. Comparative figures for 1992 have been adjusted for consistency.

(1) See Note 8 of the Notes to the Individual Statements included in the annual accounts in the Annual Report for the period ended June 30, 1994.

(2) Includes various assets of the Corporation such as equipment leases.

(3) Liabilities not repayable within one year. On July 1, 1994 the Corporation extinguished N.Z. $1.588 billion through an insubstance defeasance with the Crown, in relation to the sale of Trans Power New Zealand Limited.

Glossary

Accumulation index:	An index of wealth originating from a given security, wherein dividends, coupons, etc. are imagined to be reinvested into security at its prevailing price. Percentage changes in the market value of the fund so created are the true rates of return on the security.
Arbitrage:	An operation wherein you can self-fund a position and make money for sure, a financial free lunch. Hence no-arbitrage, a set of prices preventing this.
Arbitrager:	(i) A person who is able to create a financial free lunch. (ii) [U.S.] A specialist in taking up positions in forthcoming takeover propositions, sometimes with the aid of inside information.
ATS:	(Automated trading system): Electronic screen trading system used by the N.Z. Futures and Options Exchange.
Austraclear:	Settlement system for money market securities run by the Reserve Bank. Members include banks, dealers and other financial institutions.
BBA:	Broker to broker accounts. Initiate settlement in NZSE operations by sending a broker to broker transfer to the relevant company's share registry.
Bank bill:	IOU issued by firm or individual but accepted or guaranteed by a bank, in the form of a pure discount (zero coupon) security with maturities of 30, 60, 90 and 180 days.
Basis point:	Last decimal place in quotation of price, exchange rate or interest rate.
Basle (Basel) Accord:	1987 agreement sponsored by the Bank for International Settlements (BIS) and the Basle Supervisors Group, concerning solvency requirements for banks. Specifies prudential limits in the form of minimal capital against different components of bank assets.
BBR, BBSW:	Bank bill swap reference rate for floating side of swaps, notified on Reuters and other screens each morning. Also used for forward rate agreements (FRA's) and bank bill futures settlements. BBSW is Strine.
Beta:	Theoretical regression coefficient of an individual security, e.g. share, on the rate of return of the market as a whole. Used correctly (rare) should refer to the predictive residuals.

Bill: IOU taking the form of a zero coupon (pure discount) security. Can be bank bills (q.v.) or commercial bills (q.v.).

Bond: Technically a debt instrument secured by a mortgage on corporate property, but nowadays used indiscriminately to refer to any long-term debt instrument whose yield is known at the time of purchase.

Broker: Middleman, who brings together buyers and sellers, extracting a commission. Extended to incorporate a trader in equities (NZSE) or derivatives (NZFOE) – hence *screen broker*, one who can trade off a screen.

Business rules: Set of rules governing the operations and procedures of the NZ Stock Exchange.

Buybacks: Purchase by a company of its own shares, legal in NZ since 1992. Used to capitalise a company more tightly, e.g. as potential takeover defence.

Call: (i) In options, the right to purchase an underlying security, exercised only if its price exceeds a preassigned strike price.

(ii) A debt instrument, where the issuer can buy it back before maturity at a preassigned price.

Capital adequacy: Necessary amount or otherwise of risk-adjusted bank capital under the Basle Accord (q.v.).

CAPM: Capital asset pricing model, a model of capital market equilibrium wherein the risk penalty attached to each security is related to that for the market as a whole by a beta coefficient (q.v.).

Caps: Short for capped loan, where the interest rate cannot rise above a preassigned limit.

Cash settlement accounts: Operating accounts for inter-bank clearance held at the Reserve Bank, used by the latter for monetary control purposes.

Cash target: Targeted sum of bank balances in cash settlement accounts, as desired by the Reserve Bank in the course of its monetary and interest rate control.

Closed end funds: Equity or other trusts in which initial subscriptions are closed, and the shares therein traded with no further subscriptions of capital necessary.

Collar: Loan where interest rate cannot fall outside upper and lower limits.

Commercial bills: IOUs in the form of short-dated zero coupon (pure discount) securities issued by corporates, but with no bank guarantee attached.

Commodity swap: Exchange of fixed for floating periodic payments, the latter representing or tied to the price of some commodity.

Convertible debt: Usually refers to debt convertible after a qualifying period to equity in the company, at a preassigned price or conversion ratio.

Convexity: Curvature of bond price with respects to its yield, equal to slope of the duration function when plotted against yield.

Coupon: Nominal interest rate on a bond with periodic payments.

Cross currency interest rate swaps: Exchange of periodic interest payments denominated in different currencies, with a similar exchange of principal amounts at termination, all made at the spot exchange rate ruling at initiation.

Cross rate: Exchange rate between two countries, neither of which is the U.S.

Currency swap: Exchange of two currencies at some time in the future at a preassigned forward rate, with the reverse transaction in spot at the time of initiation.

Alternatively all exchanges at the same exchange rate, but compensating interest payments are made.

Dealer: One who buys and sells financial instruments. See also pricemaker.

Debentures: Debt instrument, usually long term and fixed coupon, secured against the general but not specific assets of a company.

Derivative: A security whose payoff is tied in some way to the price or yield of another (the underlying 'physical').

Disintermediation: Issuing of debt and other instruments directly to the public instead of via banks as bank loans, etc.

Duration: Weighted average of the times to receipt of a set of future cash flows; the weights are proportional to the present values of the amounts to be received at each maturity 'bucket'.

Efficiency: Usually seen as *informational efficiency*, which refers to a market where prices quickly impound new information so that no super-normal returns are to be made.

Efficient frontier: In mean-variance analysis, locus of all points or portfolios that maximise expected return for a given level of risk, as the latter varies.

Euro: Generic prefix referring to securities issued in offshore markets (often Europe) whose currency of denomination is not that of the issue or trading locality. Hence eurobonds or euronotes may be NZD denominated but traded in Europe.

Exchange rate: The price of one country's money in terms of that of another. But see *real* exchange rate.

FASTER: Blanket name for the automated settlement process used by the NZSE.

Fixed: (i) Any periodic payment that is known at initiation of the relevant agreement or security, as in fixed side of a swap, or fixed bond coupon.
(ii) Of exchange rates, arrangement where central banks do not permit the exchange rate to vary, undertaking to buy or sell in the FX market to preserve a set parity.

Float: Process of originating and selling new securities.

Floating interest rate: Arrangement whereby long-term periodic payments are tied by some formula to a short-term interest rate such as the yield on bank bills.

Float tender: Way in which the RBNZ neutralises government-originated flows in and out of bank cash settlement accounts (q.v.).

Forward: In FX or commodity markets, a contract to buy or sell the subject item at a preassigned price (the forward price) on a designated day in the future.

Forward rate: (i) In interest rate theory, the rate agreed on, or implicitly priced now to apply to a single period of time (year, month) starting at some future date.
(ii) In exchange rates, the forward price of a unit of foreign exchange in terms of the domestic currency

FRA: Forward rate agreement. Locks you into a bank bill rate agreed on now to apply to some specified future date, usually six months or less away. Settlement based on the difference between the agreed rate and the actual rate.

Future: An exchange-traded contract of the nature of a forward contract but whose price is marked to market every day and the movement credited to or debited from the holders margin account with his broker.

Gold standard:	System of exchange rates wherein a country's exchange rate *vis-à-vis* other countries is fixed by being expressed directly or indirectly in terms of its price in terms of gold.
Group investment funds (GIFs):	Pooling of smaller estates or funds in the form of an investment trust established under the Trustee Companies Act. Comes in two flavours (A and B), subject to different taxation regimes.
GSBR:	government sector borrowing requirement. Additions each year to the public debt, the funding requirement of government after revenue.
Inflation indexed	Most recent variety has its principal sum indexed against inflation, with bonds: a fixed percentage coupon.
Initial public offering (IPO):	First offering of stock when a private company goes public (an 'unseasoned' issue).
Interest rate swap:	Arrangement where one type of coupon payment stream (e.g. fixed coupon) is exchanged for another (e.g. floating). Comes in many varieties. Always costless at initiation.
ISDA:	International Swap Dealers Association, set of rules governing all aspects of interest rate swaps.
Inverted term structure:	Where short-term interest rates are higher than longer-term.
Investment Bank:	Blanket name for a financial institution engaged in fee generating advisory work, underwriting securities, and raising and lending money on its own account. Virtually synonymous with Merchant Bank.
Kiwi bonds:	N.Z. Government bonds issued in small denominations for small investors.
Kiwi:	Market name for the N.Z. dollar. At least it's better than the 'loony', the market name for the Canadian dollar, after the Loon on one of its banknotes, a large diving bird with a strange cry or 'looning'.
Liquidity:	(i) The tradeability of a security or by extension, a market. (ii) Holdings of cash or near-cash assets.
Liquidity preference:	Motive for holding well traded short-dated securities, whose price does not rise or fall much when interest rates change.
Listing rules:	Requirements imposed by the NZSE on companies that wish to list on the Exchange.
Maturity:	The time left to run of a debt instrument, applied in particular to the length at the time of origination.
Maturity transformation:	Part of the financial intermediation function, whereby an institution funds itself using liabilities of one maturity class and creates assets of a different set of maturities.
Mergers	Takeover of one company by another, by mutual agreement of Boards, ratified by shareholder vote. Can also be symmetric (pooling).
Merchant bank:	Originally, a financial institution specialising in accepting bills for trade finance, these days virtually synonymous with Investment Bank.
MICR:	Magnetic ink character recognition. The cyberspace numbers at the bottom of your cheques which enable them to be machine read.
Mortgage-backed securities:	Particular reference is often to different mortgages bundled and managed together, the titles to the cash flow being sold off to third parties.
Netting:	Practice of offsetting positions or payments for credit risk purposes. Used *inter alia* in swap markets.

Normal:	Of a term structure, where long-term interest rates are higher than short-term (opposite to 'inverted').
Note:	Form of debt that is unsecured or low seniority, often floating rate and shorter maturity.
NZDMO:	New Zealand Debt Management Office, the branch of Treasury that manages the public debt.
NZFOE:	New Zealand Futures and Options Exchange, Ltd.
NZSE:	New Zealand Stock Exchange, Ltd.
NZSE-40, NZSE-10:	Indices of the top 40 and top 10 companies by market capitalization, published by the NZSE.
OMOs:	Open market operations, buying and selling of short-dated securities by the Reserve Bank with the objective of altering the amount of cash in the system and interest rates.
Open-ended funds:	Continue to take further subscriptions indefinitely. See closed-end funds.
Option:	An instrument that gives you the right but not the obligation to purchase or sell another security (the 'physical') at a designated price (the 'strike price'). The right may be exercised at any time up to maturity – an American option, or only at maturity – a European option.
OTC:	Over the counter, derivatives created to order by a bank or other institution.
Par:	Of a security, issued or trading at its face value, i.e. no discount or premium.
Policy Targets Agreement:	Periodic agreement between Minister of Finance and the Governor of the Reserve Bank, specifying the target zone for the inflation rate.
Preference shares:	Form of (quasi) equity in companies that carries a fixed coupon but rank ahead of ordinary equity in distribution.
Pricemaker:	Dealer who is committed to making a market in a particular security, standing ready to buy or sell up to a designated maximum amount at the quoted two way prices.
PVBP:	Price value of a basis point. Of a yield or interest rate, the effect on the price of the instrument of a one point (q.v.) movement in the quoted rate.
Promissory note:	A debt instrument relying on only the name of the issuer, a.k.a. commercial paper.
Purchasing power parity:	Hypothesis that exchange rates should fully reflect inflation rate differentials.
Real exchange rate:	An index whose percentage change is equal to the difference in inflation rates minus the depreciation of the home country relative to the partner. Measures a country's trade competitiveness.
Real interest rate:	Nominal interest rates less, or discounted by, the rate of inflation; an indication of the real reward from holding a debt instrument.
Reinvestment rate:	Implied yield on reinvestment of coupons in measurement of bond returns.
RTGS:	Real time gross settlement. New system of settling up interbank cash transfers as they are occurred.
Screen trading:	Automated process of entering and matching buy-sell orders with screen monitoring.

Sellback:	Short-dated loan from Reserve Bank to trading banks, using Reserve Bank bills as security.
Semis:	Semi-government institutions in the debt market, strictly used for the state-owned enterprises, but sometimes also used for local authorities, Crown Health Enterprises and other public organisations.
Spot:	Any transaction for value now or very quick settlement, by extension to the corresponding market. The spot FX market is for value the following day, and refers to the ordinary buying and selling of foreign exchange.
Spread:	Difference between designated comparator prices or rates, for example bid-ask which is the difference between the buying and selling price.
Swap:	Generic name given to any costless transaction involving future cash flows – may acquire value after initiation, but not at the time thereof.
Swap rate:	Fixed rate or coupon on a fixed/floating swap.
Swaption:	Option on an interest rate swap. The holder can elect to enter into a swap with a designated fixed side or coupon corresponding to the 'strike'.
Term structure:	Plot of interest rates against maturity for the designated class of debt instrument.
Treasury bills (T-bills):	Short-dated zero coupon securities issued by the government, used also in monetary control.
Trade weighted index (TWI):	Composite exchange rate index, weights percentage changes of our exchange rates with five major partners according to their importance in our trade flows.
Volatility:	Predictive variance of the price of a security or commodity, used to price option-type derivatives written off the security.
Yankee bonds:	Debt issued in a market – often U.S., but could be Japan or European countries, by a foreign-based body. Distinguished from Eurobonds because subject to the registration requirements for the country in which issued.
Zero coupon rate:	Yield on a pure discount (or 'zero coupon') security, one that repays nominal principal in one lump sum at maturity, and therefore issued at a discount to compensate the holder.